THE REALPOLITIK OF THE UNLISTED COMPANY BOARD

"Realpolitik" represents an immense body of work. Mike Baliman has approached the subject with the detailed analysis typical of probably the first Global Head of Risk in the City - for Kleinwort Benson then the City's pre-eminent investment bank. He has combined that with the precision of thought which emanates from his original trade as a software engineer, tempered by his experience of fund management which has given him great insight into what the 'market' wants from companies. Finally he has drawn upon the tremendous breadth of knowledge he has mined from interviewing major City and commercial figures for his hugely successful Fintech podcast. These include luminaries such as Lord Turner, the former Head of the FSA, Sir Paul Tucker, Deputy Governor of the Bank of England, the leading economist Professor John Kay as well as many others.

Brian Basham, *Chairman, Director, Angel and serial entrepreneur for over fifty years including founding and floating the Broad Street Group.*

THE REALPOLITIK OF THE UNLISTED COMPANY BOARD

MAKING YOUR BOARD AN ENGINE OF GROWTH

Content and Context

MIKE BALIMAN

First published in 2020 by Mike Baliman

Copyright © Mike Baliman 2020

ISBN 9798602167986

Also available as an ebook on Kindle.

Cover illustration: the East India Company, formed in 1600, was England's greatest ever Startup. Although not England's first Company it was the first one to survive with a seminal place in global history as well as that of the Company Board. Chartered Companies had a two-tier Board structure which, contrary to popular understanding, was an English invention exported to the Continent. This engraving, made in the year of its dissolution, shows their Court of Directors, East India House, London; from *The Illustrated News of the World*, 15 May 1858.

Dedication

—

To Leo for the journeying.

—

This report is also dedicated to the kind folks who gave freely of their time and experience and shared often difficult experiences, despite knowing that, as my interviews were entirely off the record, they would never personally get the credit they richly deserve.

In a world where all too often the narrative focuses on an allegedly self-obsessed and atomised society it is genuinely touching that so many extremely busy people donated their most precious commodities – time and hard-earned wisdom – so that others can learn from their successes and failures and so that the Startup and wider SmallCo community can be strengthened as a result.

May their meritorious acts bear fruit in consequent upgrades in SmallCo Boards to the benefit of all who work in those companies and society as a whole.

Contents

Foreword

'Realpolitik' represents an immense body of work. Mike Baliman has approached the subject with the detailed analysis typical of probably the first Global Head of Risk in the City – for Kleinwort Benson then the City's pre-eminent investment bank. He has combined that with the precision of thought which emanates from his original trade as a software engineer, tempered by his experience of fund management which has given him great insight into what the "market" wants from companies. Finally he has drawn upon the tremendous breadth of knowledge he has mined from interviewing major City and commercial figures for his hugely successful Fintech podcast. These include luminaries such as Lord Turner, the former Head of the FSA, Sir Paul Tucker, Deputy Governor of the Bank of England, the leading economist Professor John Kay as well as many others.

It has all provided a fertile grounding for Realpolitik. As it stands, the book will become required reading for entrepreneurs, professionals, regulators (horrible thought!) and politicians who wish to understand the dynamics of running a company.

Over the decades I have seen the Company and its Board from all angles. Having begun my career in the 1970s as a financial journalist working on the Daily Mail, The Telegraph and The Times, I then spent some time as a fund manager. I joined the seminal John Addey Associates – John has been called the founding father of modern financial public relations which he created in the 1960s and became so key to the modern stockmarket.

I founded the Broad Street Group in corporate communications in 1976 with £100 which I borrowed and listed on the London Stock Exchange in 1986 for £36 million.

I focused on M&A and we cornered the market. As a seminal player in "the deal decade" I was deeply involved in every single deal we worked with and thus the Realpolitik of the listed market.

I then co-founded a number of businesses, Primrose Care, a business caring for elderly people in their own homes which was sold to BUPA for a 29 times RoI, Equity Development, which I still own, and ArchOver, where I sold my stake for a 20 times RoI in thirty months. Along the way I instigated and guided the 1998 Treasury Report into the Smaller Quoted Company Market, was one of three founders of the Quoted Companies Alliance and ditto of the Centre for Investigative Journalism.

I remain Chairman of Equity Development which provides investors of all types with freely available equity research and, often, direct access to quoted companies' management. I have been Chairman, Angel and NED in many SmallCos.

All of which has left me with two passions – the rather different worlds of SmallCos and BigCos. Let me take the latter first.

The issues, opportunities, drivers and perils Mike describes relate beyond the "unlisted" companies to which the title restricts the book through to every company I've ever founded or advised except for, perhaps, the very largest. In such companies, by necessity, bureaucracy and process replace the vigour of the early founders and many become indistinguishable from large government departments in the way in which they operate.

The major change over my lifetime in Corporate Governance is the introduction of countless rules – mainly for listed companies, but, worryingly, with the introduction of the Wates Principles in 2019 these are creeping into unlisted companies. Corporate Governance has evolved into a mechanism for defusing blame. It too often moves difficult decision making out of the hands of the executives and into the hands of the lawyers.

It is all too easy for this to become an academic topic for a rarefied few, however the impact is anything but. The effect is most visible in the aftermath of the banking crisis where tens of thousands of small company owners have been ground into penury and quite literally suicide by lawyers who have used entirely legal but thoroughly immoral tactics in the unequal contest which is civil litigation between mighty corporations and private individuals.

Directors who should have stood up to recognise evidence of wrongdoing presented to them on a plate have brushed it under the carpet on the advice of their lawyers and ignored their moral responsibilities.

They have dragged out negotiation and eventually litigation with often elderly, small company victims of bank wrongdoing with the cruel objective of pushing them outside the six year time bar for civil matters. However, the battle is not over yet; increasing evidence is emerging of banker concealment and fraud both of which reset the civil clock and it looks as though a tidal wave of litigation is slowly advancing on the banks, which, combined with the banks' high gearing, implies a strong threat of yet another banking crisis. It's a perfect scenario for NEDs to take the reins but no actions as of yet.

Mike points out that corporate governance was better several centuries ago. He is almost certainly right about that but, I speculate, it wasn't so because of corporate governance rules and legal box ticking. Corporate governance was better because individuals suffered personal jeopardy either to their freedom or their capital. The development of the joint stock company has meant that personal jeopardy has almost entirely disappeared from the commercial world. That's why bankers have been able to escape deserved imprisonment (it is an astonishing thing that no main board banker has gone to prison in either the US or UK despite the fact that they caused a bigger financial disaster than 1929). The self-policing fear of personal jeopardy has been replaced with regulation which is not only ineffectual but which severely stultifies competition.

The whole Corporate Governance industry in the UK was in part set in train by concerns in the early 1990s over excessive inflation in senior executive salaries. Its ineffective impotence is best demonstrated by looking at this socially-divisive issue. One of the most dangerous roles of the NED is as a member of the Remuneration Committee. Often these committees are made up of CEOs of other companies earning a little extra cash and some experience as NEDs. Although great effort is made to ensure that they are not actively conflicted, they all suffer from what might be described as "passive conflict" because they all know that as remuneration is driven ever higher, new benchmarks are set for their remuneration, which are referred to by remuneration consultants when setting package levels.

The great investor, Warren Buffett, has referred to that "well known firm of Remuneration Consultants Ratchet, Ratchet and Bingo". Like the lawyers these consultants provide another fox hole in which directors can take shelter from morality; when questioned they smugly point to the fact that they have taken "independent advice".

As a result the pay of FTSE 100 chief executives soared by 23% in 2017, with the mean package worth £5.7m a year. It would take a UK worker on a mean salary of £29,000 a total of 195 years to earn that package. Even at the FTSE 250 level, CEOs are earning £1.18m a year on average. This at a time when zero hours contracts are driving people to using the demeaning charity of food banks. Interviewing Prime Minister Cameron in 2015, Jeremy Paxman pointed out that since 2010 the number of food banks had risen from 66 to 421, while around 900,000 people had received free food parcels in 2014. Since then the Trussell Trust network of food banks has reported that it handed out 1.6m food parcels in 2019.

For most listed companies the realpolitik is that corporate governance has one function – that is to provide a wall of defence for the directors when things go wrong. It also provides highly remunerated work for those drones of the corporate world, the non-executive director.

As Mike points out non-executive directors can be hugely influential in a business to help it succeed. But as companies get larger, the NEDs become more supine. They rise without trace through the backscratching world of recruitment agencies and achieve both wealth and position by being the person that most people least object to.

Many are good people trying to do the right thing in difficult circumstances whilst being given a zillion paralysing rules to follow.

Let me give you an example of how even the best listed Directors can, over time, get squeezed into conformity. In the 1990s a good friend of mine, Professor Sir Roland Smith (now deceased) read the Cadbury report which advocated new standards of strong Corporate Governance. He called me in some excitement and I realised that he saw it as a meal ticket for life. At the time, he was a Director and Chairman of a huge number of small companies where he had performed extremely useful roles using his great flair for marketing and communication. Eventually he rose through the ranks to the giddy heights of a member of the Court of the Bank of England, Chairman of British Aerospace, Chancellor of the University of Manchester Institute of Science and Technology (UMIST) and, most enjoyably, chairman of Manchester United Football Club.

He had fought an inspired battle against the great crook and African potentate, Tiny Rowland, of Lonhro. Roland was inspired, articulate and his statement at the AGM "get your tanks off my lawn" has gone down in history. He also drove UMIST forward, he controversially expanded BAe with the acquisition of the car maker Rover and pushed through a diversification of the group into property and construction. Sadly, however, like so many others that followed him he discovered that the route to success in the world of corporate governance was to not rock the boat and slowly, inch by inch, he was ground down until he became that model of the NED "the man that most people least object to". He learned his lessons well and, although cowed, he died a wealthy man.

There have been some 15 major corporate failures IN THE UK since 2010, many of them entirely predictable and some macro-economically disastrous. HBOS was perhaps the most macro-economically disastrous, given that it also brought down Lloyds, one of Britain's biggest banks. It was certainly predictable to Paul Moore, the hugely well-qualified HBOS Head of Risk.

As is well documented, Moore reported his concerns to the CEO Andy Hornby but was ignored. He was so concerned he went over Hornby's head to the main board, headed by Lord Stevenson former head of the Lords Appointment Committee.

Moore subsequently gave impeccable and penetrating evidence to the Commons Treasury Committee, which not only discussed his actions but also gave excellent advice that financial sector employees should undergo mandatory ethics training, advice of which Stevenson and his board might well have taken note. What happened? Under Stevenson's guidance the board united to vilify Moore. He was branded a "whistleblower", he was persecuted, denied his rights and eventually driven to a nervous breakdown. He has poignantly described his ordeal in a must-read book for anyone interested in corporate governance, "Crash, Bang, Wallop".

Moving on from the world of listed companies there has been an explosion in the formation of new businesses in the past twenty years. Like Mike, I'm more excited than ever about the potential for innovation.

The biggest driving force today is the tremendous trillion-fold increase in computing power since the end of the Second World War.

A friend who was running the online marketing for a major insurance company was paying £1 million for computing power up until he sold his business in 2009, today he is renting the same computing power for €40 a month from a supremely expert group of engineers and computer scientists in Cyprus.

As we all know small companies employ approaching 70% of all employees if you exclude the State and local government; last time I looked they accounted for 60% of all innovation by patents registered and, of course, unlike large companies, when they get into difficulties or go broke they create localised difficulty rather than a national or global disaster and, of course, unlike large companies they pay their taxes. As Sir Martin Sorrell, a truly great entrepreneur, is reported as having once said: "Paying or not paying tax is a corporate decision."

The great entrepreneurs are people who have driven their companies forward with brilliance and sheer force of personality – Jeff Bezos, Mark Zuckerberg, Bill Gates, Jack Ma and many others. Corporate Governance has had no part to play in their success. If they have stumbled, investors have sometimes insisted on change but they remove the driving force of the presiding geniuses at their peril.

In all this we have to ask why is the board important? To my mind, there's one answer to that; it can help small companies develop and they are the mainstay of the economy. People who can bring relevant, experienced and constructive ideas to small companies are worth their weight in stock options and remuneration. As Mike puts it, done well the board can turbocharge success, done badly it can be a ball and chain (or even hang you at the end).

The focus of SmallCo on added-value must extend to the NEDs. It's a long way from the description of a non-executive director in common usage when I was a young journalist on The Times and the Telegraph. Then a non-executive director was described as someone who "doesn't like to come in on Wednesdays because it buggers up two weekends". That seems still to be true of many BigCo "people that most people least object to" NEDs but there's no room for such people in small companies. There, they have to pull their weight.

The first rule of small company boards is "no wallflowers". Everybody on the board must have a clear function. People who don't are supernumerary – they know it and that is dangerous not only because they are useless to the company but much more damagingly because they will try to be useful. Their personal dignity will drive them to assert themselves and that can be disastrous.

Boards are like all committees from parish councils to ministerial cabinet, they break down when people who join them are there simply for show – to make investors happy, to make the board look more respectable or simply to exercise ego. Egos clash and all too quickly the company can find itself losing focus.

For many years I made my living fighting takeover bids. Protagonists too often made the mistake of thinking it was company A fighting company B but that wasn't the most helpful way to analyse the issue. There are always tensions within boards and I made it my task to find those tensions within boards and to exploit the fact that the likelihood is that company A board members will hate each other more than they hate company B. By fomenting the dissent within boards my clients benefited from the consequent lack of focus on the task in hand.

The second rule of small company boards is a far greater emphasis on creativity rather than control. When a large company gets into trouble it has a huge national, sometimes even global, impact. When a small company fails, it has a localised impact on relatively few people. Control is important in any business but the reality for a SmallCo is that without growth it will likely die. When faced with increased regulation, big companies just hire more lawyers and fill another floor with compliance people.

With small companies, like the secured and insured lending business I started called ArchOver, the chief executive finds himself spending a third of his time on compliance until the company grows large enough to employ a compliance professional. The same is true of my research business, Equity Development. The diligent chief executive spends again up to a third of his time on compliance. It's not only energy and capital sapping, it fails to recognise the relative risk to society.

Boards in SmallCos must focus primarily on business and growth. When they are comprised of people serving specific functions they can turbocharge the success of the company.

I have recently invested a significant sum in a beauty products business called Skin & Tonic. It's an unlikely investment for me because I know nothing about the beauty sector but the vast increase in processing power means that we can so mitigate the cost of marketing that we can compete with the biggest companies in the sector.

The board consists of two founders who are partners, Josh and Sarah; as Chairman, I try to give guidance on focus and fundraising; we have a brilliant non-executive marketing director who has advised L'Oréal and we have recently recruited the model Jodie Kidd as an ambassador for the brand and as someone who really believes in the organic and ethical qualities of the product. I have never worked with a more cohesive or complementary board and it is showing in the results of the company which is doubling its turnover every year.

A third rule of SmallCo boards is that companies can establish their own "inner morality" without having corporate governance thrust upon them. One company I particularly admire is Hunters Plc. It is an estate agency business which is growing through franchising what is effectively its core morality. In a sector which is a byword for chicanery and bad practice it has a 96% approval rating from all its customers.

Its chief executive is a woman, Glynis Frew, who is no pushover but who simply radiates kindness and decency. It will benefit from the curse of box ticking compliance because smaller agencies are simply overwhelmed, so as a larger business it can take on the compliance task within a larger capital base and in so doing buy a ten to fifteen year income stream whilst embracing the new companies within the Hunters family and culture. I'm sure that it adheres generally to good corporate governance, the Chairman, the Conservative MP Kevin Hollingrake, is the Chairman of the All Party Parliamentary Group on Fair Business Banking, and a thoroughly decent man himself. He is also Glynis Frew's brother and the company is all the more successful because of it.

In the course of every day of our lives we utilise countless products and services created by countless companies. Companies are essential to our lives.

The first challenge for society, however, is how to control BigCos, where clearly far too many are failing with often disastrous consequences. This is a challenge for those rule-makers of the future to reform the approach to Corporate Governance of the past few decades. It clearly has not solved the problem, and indeed, however well-intentioned, may have made it worse. Although included in 'Realpolitik' as context the history of how companies were governed in the past enables us all to take a much broader view of these challenges and to help us think out of the "box" that we find ourselves in. Over recent decades air travel, building sites or Formula One have become far safer yet still fulfil their purpose. We need a similar change in BigCo corporate governance.

The second challenge for society is also how to create fertile conditions for the growth of new SmallCos especially as we change to this new era of information. The UK has been noticeably successful in this and has led the world in the Fintech sector Mike has podcasted about for many years. This background along with generosity of time of countless entrepreneurs, NEDS, Angels, Chairmen and Capital Providers that have related to him their stories and experience have enabled this Realpolitik map of the SmallCo Board territory.

Like all entrepreneurs I had to work out this map the hard way, through experience, through trial and error. In terms of making the world a better place the fact that the entrepreneurs of the future now have a map of the territory cannot be anything other than a great leap forwards for entrepreneurialism and, therefore, the economy.

Brian Basham
June 2019

Introduction

"Not only is there something of a shortage of good published material relating to small business, but in addition it is by no means certain that – despite much lip service from government, media, academia, and professional organizations, and despite the herculean efforts of such bodies as the Federation of Small Businesses – the essential characteristics, needs, priorities, and vulnerabilities of SMEs are properly understood by those who advise, sustain, or harangue them!"[1]

Have you noticed how one thing leads to another? And that sometimes several things come together at one place and time, which leads to some new thing very different from the original things themselves? Sun, rain and fertile soil combine and create the ideal circumstances for something to come into the world that wasn't there before. Before you know it you are eating ripe mangoes from a tree where before there was, apparently, only bare earth.

Creation and creativity are mysterious. In our all too often prosaic and practical culture, one has to go back to the Ancient Greeks to get more poetic considerations of what mysteries lie unseen beyond the realms of our senses.

But, whatever its true nature, it is this creativity which has created the world in which we live today. This creativity is mankind's God-like mysterious power to bring into existence things that never existed before. Not only things in themselves but things that produce other things. All of the countless thousands of products we interact with every day (think of all the component parts in a car, train or plane) have been created by *Companies*. Companies which themselves never existed before they too were brought into the world by someone who was visited by the Muse

---

[1] Smithson "The Role of the Non-Executive Director in the Small to Medium Sized Businesses" 2004

and who took that inspiration [etymology ~1300 "immediate influence of God or a god"[2]] and *created* – translated an idea into a thing. From that point forwards, for all the successful companies that create our physical and virtual worlds today, that creation met with enough sun, rain and fertile soil until it became a huge strong tree.

In this book we examine that sun, rain and fertile soil. It turns out that a well-constructed Board can be an immense source of all three for you and for your creation. A poor Board will be a heavy grey cloud in the sky hanging over your head, draining your energy and sinking your mood.

When the Muse drops the seed of an idea into your mind is something beyond your control. In your control, however, is *what* you do with it. Do you plant it? How do you nurture it? How do you protect it from disease?

In a business context when you have that inspiration to make a change in the world, to create a new good or service, or a new twist on an old one, in all probability you very soon have to create A Company. What role does the Board have to play? How can you do it well? How can you avoid doing it badly? What do you do when it has gone wrong?

All good questions we shall answer. First, however, let me contextualise by giving you some context about how this book came into existence which will help you understand what it is you have in your hands or on your screen.

There were two very different research processes. The first was speaking to the living and the second was researching what their business ancestors did.

Let me start with a tale of Muses and creation that led me, in a way I could never have imagined at the time, to both the living and the dead. Some five years ago the Muse woke me in the middle of the night and I "suddenly" "thought" "oh, there is no podcast on Fintech".[3] A strange thought indeed. I planted the seed. Five years later the London Fintech Podcast (LFP) has over 150 episodes with half a million downloads in 190 countries – nigh on the entire world. I have been

---

2   www.etymonline.com

3   At the time no-one cared much. I was going to choose the twitter handle @LondonFintechPodcast but realised that would take up far too many characters so I opted for the simpler @LondonFintech which was available precisely as no-one cared back then. It was all super-new.

privileged to have conversations with the leading creators and founders of the super-hot and innovative "Fintech" sector – the product of the interaction of the "digital" world (mobile phone/interweb) with FS (Financial Services). Inter alia I have also been fortunate to speak not just to the new poachers but some of the key gamekeepers of Financial Services. Lord Turner was not only the last Chairman of the FSA but chaired one of the two committees that created Basel III, the current global banking regulation. Sir Paul Tucker had a lifetime at the Bank of England ending as Deputy Governor, now chairs the Systemic Risk Council and is a research fellow at Harvard. He joined me to discuss his magnum opus, which he spent four years writing, on the "unelected power" of the regulatory state. Understanding the gamekeepers' perspective is super-important in a hyper-regulated world. I have also spoken to wise academics. Economist John Kay had a long pedigree before his better-known incarnation as a journalist. Professor William Lazonick wrote the HBR best article of 2014 and deconstructed the shareholder value ideology.

Podcasting is all fine and dandy but, back to noticing that one thing leads to another, what I hadn't noticed was that this created "thing" would itself become the field of potential for a new creation.

In the summer of 2017 I spoke to a few folks about being a Non-Executive-Director (NED) in the Fintech sector. Podcasting is a great privilege but it is something of a cross between being Sisyphus ("that was a great episode Mike, what's the next one?") and Clint Eastwood riding into a new town every two weeks and then moving on. Working with the same team on an ongoing basis seemed the ideal antidote to a life of being Sisyphus Eastwood. Being slow on the uptake I was also behind my old City chums who long since had "gone portfolio" and taken up Boarding. At this point I would love to make the joke about "it's better than working" – but, as we shall see, if it was better in the past it is certainly a very different trip these days.

As I have often found, having had a relatively broad career within Financial Services, folks' perceptions of me differed markedly. If one thought I was a risk expert the next thought I was a strategy expert, the next an indie media guy and the next a project turnround specialist and so on. But that wasn't the interesting thing. Having been independent for twenty years I was used to this identification of me with one facet of my career history. Rather the far more fascinating thing was that what slowly dawned on me was not the essence of the Sufi story of blind men grasping different parts of an elephant and so defining the elephant as rather different things.

Rather what dawned on me was that the folks I spoke to all had some wildly differing underlying assumptions about what SmallCo Boards were and what role they had.

Not "legally" – that's all written down – but practically.

How curious.

Fortunately the seed of my curiosity met the field of potential that was by now a fat rolodex of some of London's most creative businessmen/women bar none operating in one of the fastest growing, most competitive sectors.

I sent an initial email to a dozen key founders/CEOs asking what they thought about this Board topic, promptly forgot about it, and went off to bed. To my astonishment they all came back within two days. This in itself was amazing as, if I had written to them saying I owed them fifty quid, it would take them weeks to reply – not as they wouldn't want the money, but because they are super-busy. Not only did the CEOs respond but they all considered this a fascinating topic that they had never been educated in but had learned about the hard way – by trial and error, by good fortune, by bad, by falling over and by picking themselves up again.

And so started my conversations. For many this was rather like a therapy session – a third reason for the prompt response being the often pent-up and not-entirely-shared emotional pressure that many had experienced. It can be an incredibly lonely business leading confidently from the front when crossing territories which are dangerous and difficult through which you yourself do not know the way.

This territory has been much crossed but never mapped, at least not in a *realpolitik* way.[4] There is plenty of legal advice out there about What You Must Do. That's all fine and dandy. And necessary – after all being locked up in the slammer will impede your business somewhat.[5]

---

[4] One super-experienced NED, himself a published business author, had been on small companies for over forty years and said *"Gosh, you are right, there is no such book for the founders/Board as a whole."*

[5] The UK's greatest Startup had exactly this problem in 1600 to which we shall return.

However, the legal aspect is just one side of the coin. The other side of the coin from "Law" is the world of flesh and blood. The world of what really goes down. Naturally I promised anonymity which meant that, especially in a world where the regulator is always watching, interviewees could be honest. In some cases brutally honest and self-critical. They were kind enough to trust that my word is my bond and told it to me like it is, warts and all.

The archetypal example of Realpolitik, of what happens in the real world, is best summed-up in a quote from a founder/CEO – *"my Board meetings are shit". This* is the world of realpolitik. Life doesn't always work out right does it? What do you do then? As we noted one thing leads to another. What in this case, and many others, were the "things" that had led to this outcome for his Board? What were the possible "things" that might lead out of this?

I interviewed not just founders/CEOs but other Boarders and "surround": Chairmen, SmallCo and BigCo NEDs, Angels, VCs, headhunters and yet more. Over time my initial few dozen, long tour d'horizon conversations became more focused. I was no longer sketching out the whole map but zooming into areas that needed more definition. As one might imagine serial-entrepreneurs and experienced NEDs were super-useful in this phase. But even then, as is typical of perhaps all fields, those who know the most are most conscious that they do not know it all. Indeed this is a key element in the fascination of the Art of Boarding, some interviewees had thirty, forty years of Board experience, but know that tomorrow can always present them with something different.

By now I have spoken to around eighty Board folk whose combined experience is well over a thousand, and I expect thousands of man-years on Boards (NEDs need to have several simultaneous roles as it is a part-time activity). Just over half the interviewees were founder/CEOs so if there is a skew in the narrative it is towards their perspective. This is less problematic than it might sound as NewCo and, for some time, SmallCo *is* the founder/CEO. Thus, understanding the needs, prejudices and challenges of the founder/CEO is at the heart of SmallCo. As part of conveying this perspective I often slip into speaking to you, the reader, as a founder/CEO (and occasionally other roles) – after all many of you may well found companies yourselves one day even if you have not done so already. Even if you do not it is most important to *feel* things from the beating heart of SmallCo.

Although the founders/CEOs were skewed towards Fintech the rest of the Board was more widely drawn, with a slight bias towards FS. Board issues being high-level business are almost entirely generic as confirmed by those NEDs who were experienced across multiple sectors.

There are perhaps three biases from my study group compared to the average UK SmallCo which are worth noting.

First, Fintech is a high-growth, super-competitive sector, with relatively readily available pools of capital. This means that, as it were, "time goes faster" in these companies than in the average UK SmallCo. In a sense all Tech companies are FastCos compared to SlowerCos in more "old economy" sectors. FastCos burn through the money faster, raise money more frequently and meet death or glory sooner. SlowerCos may not have such dramatic lifestyles but will experience similar issues over longer timescales. Furthermore possibly the majority of SmallCos by numbers are perhaps not actually trying to grow. These days even independent consultants need a company wrapper (a legal not substantive thing). One grade above indies are lifestyle businesses where the founder's priority is to do what he wants and to have some resources around him. Such businesses are always likely to stop short of raising VC/institutional funds to avoid any substantive external pressures or need for high returns and liquidity events. They probably don't even bother with substantive Boards – that's fine. This book is for those who do (even if some don't realise it until a little later than is ideal).

Secondly, FS is a sector in which you cannot get it badly wrong and recover. Launch a new beta chat app which fails and your business can bounce back. Launch a new beta FS app that loses folks' money and it's Game Over. Trust is super-important. This bias means that for many *Fintech* unlike simpler *Tech* products and services, your first version really must work out of the box. This bias means that, along with other sectors (Biotech? Engineering?) the lead-time to first market contact and hence, all-important for capital-raising, "market validation" is perhaps longer than average.

Thirdly, FS is super-heavily regulated. The average UK SmallCo is less heavily regulated although as we shall see, regulation is A Big Thing across the whole economy these days.

From man-days-worth of interviews I ended up with thousands of quotes from interviewees on SmallCo Boards. Having mapped these interviews into six thematic chapters it appeared that I had completed the project. I felt however that there was something missing which led to Chapters One to Three.

At a simple level reproducing short quotes led to losing the *context-uality* of what I was hearing – I was reporting founders' and Boarders' quotes accurately but stripping them from the deeply informative context of much longer, richer conversations. This I fixed by coming up with Chapter One – eight essences of a SmallCo Board which infused all of my conversations. This is not elementary stuff no matter how "obvious" or "basic" the points may sound. Let me make a comparison with golf. You can teach a beginner the grip and he says "sure, got that, let's move on" but the expert is far more aware of its importance and that it is (prepare to groan) never fully grasped. Furthermore, for example, no inter-viewee explicitly outlined the vital distinction between the "Corporate Governance" (aka bureaucratic State's) conceptualisation of governance and the predominant realpolitik of SmallCo governance which I came to label as "Closely Controlled Companies" governance.

At this point I had finished compiling interview *content* as well as conveying the bigger picture interview *context*. Job done surely?

If I had been wiser I would have drawn stumps and the book would have been finished a good deal earlier (albeit with half the number of interviews and rather less detail). However, I still rather felt something was missing. What it was was hard to put my finger on.

The clue to what was missing, when nothing that had been said – content or context – was omitted, came when I thought more about language. The project's genesis had been that the single word "Board" meant many things to many people. I then started to wonder where The Board came from. What historically was a Board? What historically was a Company? How did Governance work back in the day? In my interviews we were discussing "today" but surely we needed to under-stand a little bit about yesterday to get some perspective? Otherwise we would be like mayflies seeing only days but never seasons. If we don't know where we have come from how do we know where we are going? How did Boards work well or badly in the past? How did Companies work well or badly in the past? What can we learn from all this? Where indeed did this weird "Corporate Governance" thing come from? Why has it "suddenly" arisen, seemingly from nowhere?

I realised that all these questions, these invisible ghosts, were always present in my interviews. Always out of sight, always out of mind – SmallCo and BigCo businessmen are nothing if not supremely practical and focused on today and tomorrow not yesterday. However, now and then these ghosts shook their gory locks at us and sentences tailed off with nowhere to go. Surely we should learn from our ancestors' intentions and challenges when they designed the Company and the Board and from their successes and failures?

I know, I thought, I'll fix this by having a second contextualising chapter on the history of the Company and the Board and a third about where we are now. How hard can it be?

Well, that's another story for another day, but for now I'll just say that it proved to involve spending a lot of time down a very deep rabbit warren. I eventually re-emerged *over two years* later, rather less sane, nigh on frozen in a seated position and rather fatter from endless months of super-early starts, tea and biscuits during the day and gin in the evening to keep me going through the tedium of much of the exploration of dead-ends and ill-constructed passageways. However, after wandering the labyrinths I emerged with some fascinating traveller's tales both unknown and quite unlike what you might have been led to believe.

Time and again these overflowed the constraints of fitting into a relatively small part of a book that is after all about the realpolitik of *today's* Board. Time and again I culled and culled. Eventually I realised that it was not the history of the Company that really mattered to today's entrepreneurs and SmallCo Boarders but the historical experiences and designs of *governing the Company*. After all, this book is not about The Small Company but *Governing* The Small Company. **Governing SmallCo, or more formally UnlistedCo, which is what most companies have been throughout history, is not something that appeared out of thin air but rather is the result of a long and complex historical process.** This in itself (sadly from the perspective of the time it would take to research) could only be understood with reference to what the Company was doing, what challenges it was meeting and how the State intervened in it over the centuries. And so began my investigation of what our business ancestors were up to. Which wasn't as simple as I had imagined (read a few books and have it done in a few weeks). Ha! The wonders of innocence without which many a Bilbo Baggins would have stayed in their hobbit hole and without which many an adventure, project or SmallCo would never have seen the light of day.

As far as I am concerned I have an even longer book than this sitting on my hard drive to finalise. As far as you are concerned you have a ludicrously over-researched Chapter Two[6] in which we cover five centuries of the English/British Company and how they were governed. Read this and, unless you have very weird friends (or they've read this book too), you will know more than anyone you know about the history of governing the Company. You will never again be stuck for small talk at sherry parties and will for sure know vastly more than Cadbury, the father of UK Corporate Governance (although to be fair to him, as I know more than anyone, the history of governance ain't easy to piece together in a world of infinite information).

Chapter Two encapsulates the experiences of our entrepreneurial ancestors. We look at how the Board came into being and how it worked in the past. The V1 Company – the Chartered Company, was created in England in the 16[th]C and was dependent on Monarchical, and later Parliamentary, approval. In the 19[th]C the V2 Company – the Company Law Company – was created which, after quite a few updates, is the legal pro forma we use today. This was far more easily available (via Companies House which was created for this purpose) but was soon granted a very curious and new-fangled thing – "limited liability" – which immediately led to disasters as it does to this day. In 1855 when created it actually *was* limited liability but after some time it mutated into the "zero or transferred" liability company we have today (even if we, bizarrely, still call it "limited liability"). A second "great Victorian invention" was inferior company governance. The governance of V1 was *owner-centric* but that of V2 was *management-centric*.

In Chapter Three we continue with the context to SmallCo Boarding in the 21[st]C. This has seen the emergence of unprecedented hyper-detailed regulation of *all* businesses and the emergence of the V3 Company – the Corporate Governanced Company – whose governance, rather eccentrically, has been taken out of the hands of both owners and management

---

[6] It's the tip of the iceberg of the draft book on Company History whose bibliography currently refers to more than 300 publications.

and been handed over to people whose defining characteristic is that they are *disconnected* from the company. They are neither owners nor management. They are also issued a large paint-by-numbers guide on How To Govern provided by the State, hardly a paragon of good governance itself, that they have to follow. All in all V3 is a rather curious tale which our business ancestors would have found incredible (in the literal sense). Although rates of listings and delistings are subject to many winds and tides, it is "far from clear" that this new V3 form of the Company is catching-on. Between 2000 and 2018 publicly-listed companies in the US fell by an astonishing number from 7,000 to around 4,000.[7]

Even if, over the past half a millennium, the governance of the Company has deteriorated significantly, SmallCo governing is still however far more flexible and far better attuned to the needs of business than BigCo governance. SmallCo remains a V2 Company (although in 2019 with the Wates Principles in the UK Corporate Governance has, for the first time, started flooding into SmallCo land). As SmallCo is a V2 Company the management and Board have considerable freedom to govern as they see fit – and after absorbing this map of the territory they will hopefully be better able so to do.

Having started with three contextual chapters, we turn to the practical details of managing your Board. In Chapter Four we look at the Board as a whole and then in subsequent Chapters cover the CEO/Founder(s), the Chairman, NEDs and Capital Providers, before turning to the all-important aspect of Fixing Broken Boards. Not to end on a negative note we have a final section focusing on the fact that there has never been a better time to be an entrepreneur.

In the Epilogue, having related countless stories of past and present, we wind-down by reflecting on the importance of stories in creating the people and societies on which businesses critically depend (try having a great business in a failed State). Traditional cultures knew that preserving and protecting stories is super-important. This is something we have rather forgotten.

One of the biggest headaches for modern businesses is the phenomenal amount of rules and regulations. In Appendix A we have a brief

---

[7]   This will of course be multi-factorial but the Corporate Governanced Board is a "plus" in the mind of no BigCo NED I have ever spoken to – quite the reverse. Stat from Tett "The Surprising Rise Of Private Capital" FT 20/5/19

look at how regulation worked 4,000 and 1,000 years ago to provide some historic context to the topic.

Last but not least I should spell out some important conventions which serve to make the narrative easier to read.

I generally use the abbreviation "SmallCo" although to be more precise I was asking interviewees about the Board of *unlisted* companies which are very different from Boards of *listed* companies. An alternative to SmallCo would be SME – but I find this clunky, overly-technical and a term I have rarely heard in conversation. Furthermore it doesn't necessarily connote "unlisted". "SmallCo" and "BigCo" are not accurate terms – some "SmallCos" in my terms are larger than some "BigCos".[8] Many of the SmallCos I spoke to have raised capital of tens (and some hundreds) of millions of dollars. That isn't so "small". I could have used private and public firms – that would be accurate and not too awkward but it's also kind of too technical a vocabulary, it's not that common in everyday usage. So, in order to improve readability, SmallCo/BigCo it is. Besides, interviewees tended to default to that vocabulary anyway.

In a similar way, other than where I drill-down deeper, I use the acronym NED to cover all non-executive, independent, not-independent, outside, external, or investment Directors. I use founder/founder(s)/CEO loosely and interchangeably other than when I drill-down in more detail. I use "man" and so forth rather than "man/woman" throughout – no genderism is implied it just reads easier. I also use the ungainly word "folks" quite often to mitigate gendered implications.

Sometimes where I feel the role of my interviewee is important in the context of a given quote I mention it, otherwise I do not. Any quotes that are not clearly attributed or footnoted are quotes from my interviewees. I am glad to say that they had a wide range of views and any apparent difference in views and perspectives is quite real and not to be ironed out.

Like all books you can use it for education or entertainment. However for those of you immersed in SmallCo Boards right now do consider using it in its most important way – as a **practical guide**. Highlight, turn over page corners, whatever. No one person can have

---

[8] In terms of LFP guests eg Augmentum Fintech, a PLC, hence BigCo in my terms, are smaller in terms, say, of square metres of office space, than many other "SmallCo" guest firms.

had all the experiences or all the ideas quoted in this book. Even if they have, hearing them explained in a different way can also be stimulating. Less experienced founders and NEDs will find too much to implement in one go, so take the key points. Even the most experienced Boarder should be able to find a quote or two worth reflecting on. The Board is so important that literally implementing one idea contained in a single quote can make a huge difference to outcomes.

We will catch-up after dinner for some port and cigars in the Epilogue. In the meantime let's go into the Boardroom and have a short PowerPoint on the essence of SmallCos followed by a short documentary on how our ancestors governed their businesses, an update on the 21stC climate for Boards from a friendly consultant before turning the spotlight on the seats around the Boardroom table. Finally, after a visit from the Company Doctor, we will have a short visit from a motivational coach to make you glad to be entrepreneuring today not back in the day.

1. Eight Essential Aspects of Small Company Boards

OVERVIEW

As I mentioned earlier many of these essences might seem "obvious" and "basic". However they are also fundamental and it's not enough to "know" them, they really have to inform your thinking in terms of other thoughts of yours being consistent with them. Some interviewees I spoke to would say they know some of these points but still have other ideas which de facto go against them – they hadn't fully embedded these essences in their thinking. Thus in this section you may think there is some repetition. There is. However, if there is madness in my method there is also method in my madness. In Martial Arts one spends an inordinate amount of time practising the basics – but at least that way the basics are fully embedded or in that case embodied.

One. The most important task of a NewCo Board is to grow something fragile – a small fire will not grow and spread without a lot of assistance.

Two. The SmallCo Board is not a small BigCo Board – in fact it is nearer to being the antithesis of a BigCo Board. In a SmallCo an unattended fire will most likely go out. In a BigCo it will most likely rage out of control or cause explosions. Hence the principal focus of SmallCo Boards has always been on **Promethean Corporate Creativity** whereas in BigCo Boards it has been more on **Fire Safety Officers and Corporate Control.**

Three. If historically this change in Board emphasis can be seen simply through a growth lens, **the advent of codified Corporate Governance for BigCos** has meant that the BigCo Board is not just a more mature SmallCo Board but a very different beast altogether. Thus attempting to be a small BigCo Board, which crops up in guises such as "doing the

Board thing right", where right implicitly means "as the grown-ups do it", is *doubly* dangerous for the modern SmallCo.

FOUR. There is a lack of clarity around the difference between governing companies and "Corporate Governance". The former has taken place for centuries whilst the latter is a late 20[th]C/early 21[st]C Statist response to contemporary ListedCo governance challenges. However the governance challenges of 21[st]C SmallCos are very different. **SmallCos are much closer in this regard to a very different longstanding governance model – "Concentrated Control Companies" (CCCs).**

FIVE. Boards can be good, bad or indifferent for the Company. **It is a major role of the founder to create them well.** There are many ways to "do" your SmallCo Board – many styles, motivations and mentalities. You need to find a way that works for you the founder.

SIX. **SmallCos and SmallCo Boards are founder/CEO-centric unlike BigCo Boards which are Chairman-centric.** In a SmallCo the spark/small fire and the founder are inseparable for quite some time.

SEVEN. **Boards can be cauldrons of emotion** and by no means as bloodless as all the legal stuff makes it sound.

EIGHT. We all read this now and again but can still easily forget it given the media focus on BigCos – the **SmallCo is a vital economic and societal construct.** The world would be stuffed without them. Let's view them positively not just as a smaller version of something else. There are vastly more UnlistedCos than there are ListedCos in the world.

ESSENCE 1 – THE TOP PRIORITY IS GROWTH AND A GOOD BOARD HELPS YOU TO GROW

Starting up is an act of creation that needs nourishing, it needs nurturing, it needs growth and feeding without which it will die.

Regardless of which economic sector you are in, which country you are in, it all starts the same way. You have an idea. An idea about a product or service. An idea about a gap in the vast panoply of provisions already available. Naturally there are very few gaps in mature economies. Some of the greatest entrepreneurs create a gap in the market that never appeared to be there, or even create a market that didn't exist before. Having had your idea you also need to have the desire to go out there and make it happen. And then the journey begins.

The inception of every company in the world, no matter how small or how large, was the same. At conception the fertilisation of a field of infinite potential occurs when a spark of light, a dawning of a new idea, enters. This is a very mysterious process – the prosaic descriptions of finding gaps in the market doesn't even start to describe the moment of impulse. What is it in the human being that enables them to produce something that never existed before? After all, your idea didn't exist before you had it and nor did your Company before you created it.

Based on my many conversations with real disruptors the Ancient Greek description of a visit from the Muse is a more accurate description than any MBA course's "mark scheme" answer.

After the light enters your mind the next stage is turning it from a thought, from potentiality, into something real. At this point the Muses hand over to Prometheus.

The founder needs to bang rocks together to instantiate that Promethean spark and then use this to light a tiny fire on some dry tinder and then spread that fire.

The Startup phase is all about nurturing your newborn infant, that tiny spark, helping it to grow bigger and stronger and more robust. You need to surround that tiny spark, or sparks, as you keep banging the rocks together, with yet more tinder and combustible materials and take it from being something which will die if left unattended to a robust fire burning bright.

The founder needs to build a Company around him to help this fire spread. **A vital part of this Company is the Board and a good SmallCo Board will, simply put, help that fire grow well and sustainably.**

Incidentally, fire as a metaphor for business creation, growth and control links nicely into the observation of the relative environments for SmallCos in the US and in the UK. Many of you will have heard the observation that, if you have a small fire in the US, they will throw petrol on it to see if it can make a huge fire, whereas in the UK they will throw cold water on it to see if it can survive.

Either way, whether you are being doused with petrol or water, *you* need to manage the whole show.

But what is the show?

ESSENCE 2 – THE SMALLCO BOARD IS NOT A SMALL BIGCO BOARD

That Companies change over time is so apparent that it barely merits mentioning. However, its corollary – that the Board needs actively managing – can all too often be neglected.

At inception when the Muse drops an idea into your mind you are the show of course. For substantive ideas you will need to build a team below you and a Board around you to help you nurture your tiny infant and grow it into a safe strong adult.

SmallCo and BigCo Boards have always differed substantially due to the nature of development. This applies whether a company or a child – the ratio of nurturing to controlling is very high in a newborn and rather lower by the time they are a teenager. The newborn needs constant support and attention to stay alive, the teenager can already cause enough havoc to need a greater control function.

All Boards have two main functions – **creativity** and **control**. The Startup to ListedCo Board journey has always involved a gradual movement of emphasis from **Corporate Creativity** to **Corporate Control**, from **Prometheus** to **Fire Safety Officers**.

On Day1 of NewCo you will be unlikely to have a Board. At some point you will have a real Board. Not just a legal, box-ticking, de minimis effort but a real one. Naturally in Startups the emphasis is all on *creativity* – Promethean talents of creating a bigger fire. The Board is there to support and enable that Promethean act of creating fire in the Startup, sustaining it, spreading it and making it ever bigger and ever stronger.

Increasingly, as your fire grows the Board has to keep more than half an eye on avoiding explosions and the control element increases. By the time you and your Board become a BigCo the principal perspective on "fire" per se is utterly reversed from *creativity* to *control*. The Board has mutated from folks offering shelter from winds, directions for finding kindling, and advice on how to build kilns to being much more akin to Fire Safety Officers. The Board frets far less about fires going out or fuel running out and becomes far more concerned with raging fires burning out of control or causing explosions.

It is for this reason of the nature of growth itself – even if "Corporate Governance" had never been created – that the early stage Board is *antithetical* **to a mature Board.**

In a rocket the first stage, second stage and third stage booster are all engineered differently. Ditto a growing SmallCo Board – you need different Board designs, different Board members, for the stages along your journey. **Failure to understand this point means that you will neglect actively managing your Board which will be to the detriment of your Company.**

ESSENCE 3 – IN THE 21STC THE SMALLCO BOARD IS A DIFFERENT SPECIES FROM THE BIGCO BOARD

Not only are SmallCo Boards not small BigCo Boards, these days they are radically different from 21stC BigCo Boards. Thus to imitate BigCo Boards is now doubly in error – compounding the impact of a Company's growth on Board focus by now applying an inappropriate solution to an entirely different challenge.

SmallCo Boards were always somewhat antithetical to BigCo Boards but this gap has been magnified by the introduction of what goes under the rubric of "Corporate Governance". Before this revolution/experiment one could have justifiably said that a SmallCo was a caterpillar and BigCo a mature butterfly. Now it would not be pushing a point too far to say that in the 21stC if the SmallCo Board is a butterfly then the BigCo Board is a caterpillar – an entirely different beast indeed.

The changes wrought to BigCo Boards in recent decades by Corporate Governance are so substantial that they amount to the creation of a new type of Company as we shall see in the next chapter. Three features of the "Corporate Governanced BigCo" leap out that are radically different from SmallCo: (i) excessive *State-defined* bureaucracy, processes and procedures, (ii) a hugely imbalanced emphasis on control and (iii) the centrality of independent NEDs. By contrast (i) most of the conduct of a SmallCo Board, beyond the basics, is up to the private citizen not the State, (ii) the focus needs as we have seen to be on creativity, and (iii) you do not need to have any independent NEDs if you don't want to let alone centre your Board around them.

The genetic roots of the problem, to which Corporate Governance is a very ad hoc application of bandages to attempt to staunch the bleeding, go back a long way as we shall see in the next chapter. Corporate Governance in the codified sense we mean it today is, historically speaking, an unprecedented experiment – super-recent and super-anomalous.

In the UK it kicked off relatively recently in 1992 with Sir Adrian Cadbury's report. Cadbury appreciated the slightly schizophrenic dual-nature of the Company Board *per se* in terms of the very different roles of creativity and control. However Cadbury's **remit** was only *one part* of governance his report being (emphasis added): "The *Financial* Aspects Of Corporate Governance".

The report started a trend of ever-greater emphasis on control. Its very format, as a "code", started a trend for more codes *all of which focused on what has been called the "conformance" side of the balance compared to the "performance" side.*

Conversely, creativity cannot be codified, business nous cannot be codified – so the more codes (25 and counting) the more that *control* (which can always – *apparently*[1] – be more codified) comes to the fore and the more that *creativity* recedes ever more into the background.

BigCo Boards have been transformed beyond all recognition within the careers of some of my interviewee Directors and have become far *more* antithetical to SmallCo Boards than they ever were. SmallCos have not changed substantially and have thus, in theory (your mileage may vary), remained much more balanced in focus and composition.[2]

The distortions imposed upon the senior governance forum in BigCo are so great that many BigCos are creating "Advisory Boards" to have a Board that actually looks at the always-essential (especially in a new "Information Age") creativity part of the business equation.

Thus for both reasons of (a) the necessity of growth in SmallCo as well as (b) Statist rules for how privately-owned BigCos should conduct their affairs (there are curiously none in passing for how partnerships

---

[1] "*Control is an illusion*" Tom Cruise in "Days of Thunder".
[2] And much more representative of Boards throughout history.

should run their meetings), we find that **the Startup Board is the near opposite of a BigCo Board.**

Failure to understand this point is one of the most crippling mentalities you can have for your SmallCo Board.

The fact that a SmallCo is not a small BigCo might seem obvious – after all no-one thinks their Startup is any version of a BigCo whatsoever. It may be an aspiration to *become* a BigCo but at the beginning it is more like a pipe-dream.

*However, if mistaking a SmallCo for a BigCo is rare indeed, what is not rare, and what was quite common in my conversations with first-time founders, was that their implicit ideas about The Board, were often **unconsciously** based on Listed Companies.*

Firstly, many (most?) first-time founders may never have sat on *any* Board and thus would have zero experience of a Board in the first place let alone the vast difference between SmallCo Board meetings and BigCo Board meetings. How would they guess that the two were so different? After all, the legal blah-blah about Articles of Association, Directors' responsibilities and such are very similar[3] with the differences sounding perhaps as if they were more of degree than substance. The Law must be obeyed – but the Law does not tell you how to create a profitable business! You need the other side of the coin for that – the *realpolitik* of getting results from your Board – you pay these folks money and so you want value-add in return. The NED value-add on SmallCo and BigCo are Venn diagram circles which, at a minimum, don't "entirely overlap".

Secondly, our business world/media is permeated almost entirely with narratives about BigCos and next to none about SmallCos. In addition *some* NEDs (especially those with a control focus) explicitly or implicitly take "Codified Corporate Governance" as "The Right Way To Do A Board Even If We Need To Water It Down A Bit For A SmallCo" rather than the historical anomaly/experiment that it is.

Finally, I researched the history of the Company for a long time without reading anything about this antithetical perspective. Even when I did it was rather implicit. The traditional legal and economic take is that the Company is A Thing which grows over time. **There is nothing**

---

[3] There are trivia such as private companies being a special legal category (eg needing only to produce simplified accounts) but these just serve to reinforce a mentality of comparative smaller/larger versions of the same thing.

that talks about the journey being that of a butterfly which gradually changes into a caterpillar, an entirely different beast.

The result of a lack of clear understanding in general, let alone in the often Board-inexperienced founder, is that when you get round to sketching out your Board you might well assume that there is a "right" way of doing The Company Board – like the grown-ups do – and you do that. That would not have been as toxic thirty years ago as it is today.

Believing that your SmallCo Board is a small BigCo Board is such a huge error in terms of importing growth-chilling Statist bureaucracy that we will return to the topic in the final chapter on Fixing Broken Boards.

ESSENCE 4 – CONCENTRATED CONTROL COMPANIES, NOT LISTEDCOS, ARE THE GOVERNANCE MODEL FOR SMALLCOS

The governance challenge of SmallCos is entirely different from BigCos. However there is a governance model – CCCs which are near ubiquitous, from family firms to Tech giants such as Amazon, Google, Facebook to vast State-owned concerns.

SmallCos are representative of most companies around the world throughout history which were and still are "Concentrated Control Companies" (CCCs).

In the UK/US the predominant governance challenge of BigCo is a widely distributed ownership base far removed from knowledge or control over what the management are up to.

SmallCos are generally CCCs *which have the opposite governance problem* – namely that, generally, majority owners are *in* the Boardroom and hence **there is no "remote owners with neither knowledge nor control" concern.**

Rather **the governance challenge of CCCs is the "tyranny of the majority"** – the majority are capable of disadvantaging the small shareholder which happens all too often.

Screwing the small investor is much harder to do, at least on price, in ListedCos where stockmarket investors all own the same share type and receive the same price on any sale and so forth. Larger investors will get preferential visits from the Chairman/senior team which privilege Joe Sixpack never enjoys. Besides Joe has many investments and has neither the time nor inclination to research his negligible votes on the few issues that the Board deign to put before him. Dispersed shareholders know little about the businesses they invest in and care about little other than their share price performance. Andrew Carnegie recognised this and as he went from being dirt poor to America's richest man and a huge philanthropist he might know a thing or two:

> "Where stock is held by a great number, what is anybody's business is nobody's business."

A misunderstanding of the very different, near opposing, governance challenges between BigCo's remote investors and CCCs/SmallCos in the Boardroom investors is **a third reason** why applying Corporate Governance approaches to SmallCo is such a bad idea.

Apply "Corporate Governance" to SmallCo and you are taking the medicine for a completely different disease!! Not only that but there is zero evidence that the medicine works even for the condition for which it is prescribed and furthermore it has side-effects introducing a very bureaucratic mentality into the Boardroom.

CCCs have always been, are, and will forever be, superior to the zillion rules & regs approach as a form of Governance. It is in effect a form of structural regulation (the best kind and the most common approach throughout history).

There is no better incentive for companies to be governed well than Boardrooms full of people who really care and have serious money at stake (which is the case in SmallCo Boardrooms). It is ironic in this context that once you list on the London Stock Exchange you have to change how you remunerate your NEDs (which presumably was working if you got as far as the listing stage):

> "Remuneration for all non-executive directors should not include share options or other performance-related elements."[4]

In the UK Bob Tricker wrote the first book on "Corporate Governance" (appropriately perhaps in 1984) and has been called the "father of

---

4   FRC UK Corporate Governance Code 2018

Corporate Governance" by Cadbury himself. Writing more recently he talks about how concentrated control changes the whole game:

> "...the Anglo-Saxon system is not the only governance model and some are questioning whether it is necessarily the best. Corporate governance is concerned with the way power is exercised over corporate entities. In other parts of the world, alternative insider-relationship systems exercise power through corporate groups in chains, pyramids or power networks, by dominant families, or by states."[5]

There are many types of CCC – the SmallCo, family businesses, founder-centric businesses, industrial groupings, and State-owned businesses. CCCs are by far the most common types of business in the world.

We don't need to concern ourselves about industrial groupings (German Konzern, Japanese Keiretsu, Korean Chaebol et al) or State-owned businesses other than to notice some of the largest industrial enterprises in the world are also CCCs.

Let's look briefly at the importance of family and founder-centric businesses. SmallCos (at least for quite some time after founding) are a type of "first-generation family firm" and founder-centric businesses.

To my surprise when researching Concentrated Control Companies around the world **family businesses** were and are the predominant business model:

> "In most societies, at most times, it has been the great family which by its wealth, power, prestige, and presumption of permanence has been the outstanding institution in private economic enterprise."[6]

In the National Bureau of Economic Research's 700pp "A History of Corporate Governance around the World: Family Business Groups to Professional Managers", the editor summarises the global state of play:

> "In much of the rest of the world [outside the US], capitalism is a system where a handful of immensely wealthy families control

5   Tricker, Mallin. "Rethinking the Exercise of Power over Corporate Entities" 2010
6   Lane "Venice and History" 1966

almost all of a country's great corporations... Wealthy family domi-
nation of great corporations is not restricted to poor countries but
also characterizes relatively rich economies like Israel, Hong Kong,
and Sweden."

The Economist writing about Italian business points out that many
Italian businesses are dominated by family concerns:

"...most of Italy's medium-large firms [are] still owned and
managed by families: the list runs from Alessi (homeware) to Zegna
(fashion) via Barilla (pasta), Ferrero (chocolates), Lavazza (coffee),
Ferragamo (leather goods) and many more."[7]

The advantage of the model is clearly to narrow the so-called principal-
agent gap between "owners" and "managers" (the prime Corporate
Governance concern ever since Berle and Means seminal tome in
1932[8]) but also:

"For Emma Marcegaglia, president of the national employers' association, and managing director of her own family's steel business,
such firms succeed because of their owners' flexibility, quick decisions and willingness to plan and invest for the long term, even in
bad times. This also wins loyalty from employees."[9]

The global stats are amazing for anyone brought up on a diet of US/UK
business press:

"Worldwide, family enterprises represent anywhere from 80% of all
businesses in developed economies to 98% of all businesses in emerging
economies. (They account for about 90% throughout Latin America,
depending on the country.) They are responsible for anywhere from
64% of the GDP to 75% of the GDP of individual countries."[10]

---

7 Economist "Keeping it in the family – Italian businesses" 10th March 2011
8 "The Modern Corporation and Private Property". Ironically at that time controlling
shareholders were still common. It was not until the 1960s that widely-dispersed
ownership became the predominant model.
9 Ibid.
10 Poza "Family Business" 2009

Nor is the US unexposed to significant degrees of "family capitalism":

> "[In the US] family ownership is both prevalent and substantial; families are present in one-third of the S&P 500 and account for 18 percent of outstanding equity."[11]

The most common device for effecting family control is the pyramidal group which is ubiquitous outside the US/UK. Here the apex shareholder(s) control a single company which has controlling voting blocks in the companies below it which in turn control the companies below them and so on. They can contain hundreds of firms and ensure that small numbers of people can control vast swathes of the economy.

To SmallCos and FamilyCos we must also add another super-important type of CCC – **founder-centric companies** – which, along with frequent use of mechanisms such as "super-voting stock", are actually **the predominant Tech/high-growth model**. Think Bezos at Amazon, Zuckerberg at Facebook, Jobs at Apple, Gates at Microsoft, Page and Brin at Google, Elon Musk at Tesla, Reed Hastings at Netflix.

The founder-centric model is more widely applied than just in "Tech", the Murdoch media empire springs to mind (and here founder-centrism starts to mutate into family-business). Another leading example of founder-centrism (and control) is Berkshire Hathaway the phenomenally successful investment vehicle of Warren Buffett.

These phenomenally successful founders did not grow mega-businesses by allowing their control to become diffused. Dispersed ownership and dispersed control might be the "textbook" model of a US firm but the "Tech Titans" don't fall for that kinda "Business PC" thinking nor submit excessively to Statist/PC dot-to-dot Corporate Governance, full of do-gooders' rules and regulations written by politicians, bureaucrats or businessmen who never created anything from scratch.

There is no end to this game of "Spot the CCC". Morck points out that in Germany apparently widely-owned companies are actually narrowly-controlled by banks in the larger companies and families in the smaller companies. Even in the US in 2017 the largest 50 institutional

---

[11] Anderson, Reeb "Founding-Family Ownership and Firm Performance: Evidence from the S&P 500" 2003

shareholders own 44% of the shares of listed companies[12]. This is hardly "widely-dispersed ownership" and much more akin to the allegedly very different German "bank capitalism" model than generally assumed.

One can also include the 19thC heyday of the exponential rise to predominance of the US economy when it overtook Britain as another prime example of CCCs, where a small number of individuals dominated industry:

> "Between 1890 and 1904, huge waves of consolidation left most of the country's industrial base in the hands of around fifty organizations... The merger era produced some of the most powerful companies of their time, including U.S. Steel, American Cotton, National Biscuit, American Tobacco, General Electric, International Harvester, AT&T, and United Fruit. Two people are synonymous with the trust era: Rockefeller and J. P. Morgan."[13]

Despite the occasional successful move to break up huge businesses – notably Standard Oil and American Tobacco, both in 1911, concentrated ownership lasted for quite some time until the Great Depression.

Dispersed-ownership Listed BigCos and Corporate Governance are historically and presently hugely anomalous.

Conversely, SmallCos map much more closely onto almost every business that has existed since records began some four thousand years ago – the first recorded businesses (in Old Assyria) were CCCs.

SmallCos map closely onto the predominant global model today – FamilyCos.

They map closely onto the giant Tech firms that have had such phenomenal success in recent decades.

They even map closely onto huge business groups – Konzern, Keiretsu, Chaebol – or onto German bank capitalism or State ownership around the world.

SmallCos are in no sense whatsoever anomalies to be reined in to "grown up/real company" models.

---

[12] Bebchuk et al "The Agency Problems of Institutional Investors" 2017

[13] Micklethwait, Wooldridge "The Company A Short History of a Revolutionary Idea" 2003

Vice versa they are representative of *the* most successful model over millennia of successful growth and meaningful control of management by owners.

It is no surprise that the UK/US models have seen the greatest numbers of BigCo failures. Other countries predominantly rely on Boards comprised of people who have serious skin in the game and so *really* care – personally as well as professionally.

Concentrated Control Companies are not only *the* dominant model but the model which has been shown in recent decades to surpass all others in terms of ability to turn a concept into a product and scale rapidly without excessive numbers of disasters.

Be proud of your SmallCo! You, and your concentrated-control form of governance, are the rule not the exception! Yet another reason not to copy, ape or mimic current BigCos which, far from being a model of good governance, are unprecedented and continue to drop out of the sky. Some of you might even grow up to be ListedCos yet still retain the CCC/family ethos.

Having said that there is an Achilles heel in CCCs – major shareholders may make merry at the expense of the smaller shareholders – an important topic to which we shall return.

ESSENCE 5 – YOUR BOARD IS WHAT YOU MAKE IT – FOR BETTER OR FOR WORSE

Will you consciously create your Board or will it just happen as a result of happenstance and ad hoc pressures from capital providers?

What was/is your guiding concept for your Board? Legal? Administrative? Reluctance? Enthusiasm? How is it working out for you?

I recall one of my better business trips involving a taxi ride through the sugar cane fields of Barbados. I was quizzed over my (at the time single) relationship status. In his deepest Bajan accent my driver said: *"You can run but you can't hide."* Which at the time seemed curious as I was neither running nor hiding. Within two years though I was married so the driver's psychic powers must have been pretty good.

In the same way the founders I interviewed were neither running nor hiding. However, in the blink of an eye, their lives changed too.

The more you succeed, the bigger your SmallCo grows, the more your challenges change and hence what you need from your Board changes.

You start your journey not in sugar cane fields but on the plains – the land of infinite potential but no growth. You decide on your direction and start on the journey of growth and challenge towards your mountain. At the top of the mountain if you so choose you can "level up" and go into a rather different phase of the game.

The most important thing I can emphasise to any founder is that there are many paths towards and up the mountain.

I have spoken to some eighty folks – no two Boards, no two companies ever did everything exactly the same way. That's part of the fun of it. It, like your life, is your journey. Sure there are commonalities such as "wear good footwear", "have a plan and adapt", "beware known pitfalls and traps" and we shall come onto all of those. However there are many routes to success with your Board, many ways of growing your Company. Most importantly if you are the founder then you need to find the intersection of what works for *you* with what works for SmallCo Boards.

Broadly speaking the attitude amongst NewCo founders to The Board ranges from *"ignore this for as long as possible, we have more important things to do"* to *"let's get things right from the start"*.

Both extremes can be perilous. The latter end of the spectrum can all too easily morph into the generally toxic "let's be a micro-BigCo" which is a cardinal sin. The "ignore" extreme is always the pragmatic reality the day after the night before in a pub when you thought up Your Idea. And it will be the reality the day after that and the day after that.

After a while, however, generally after raising external capital, whatever your original inclination your SmallCo will have A Board. If I had to put my conversations into three main pigeon-holes I'd label them "ball and chain", "yawn" and "turbocharger". A fourth pigeon-hole is "noose". If the CEO gets changed it is the Board who bring the gallows.

I spoke to some poor folks for whom their poorly/unfortunately constituted Board was a **ball and chain** around their ankle. Just one more thing that made the journey that much harder, something else to drag along, just one more burden they wished they didn't have.

The **"yawn"**, humdrum, routine, somewhat "who cares?" Board is the kind of neutral point along the spectrum. Generally administrative, generally something of a time-waster, somewhat tick-box. We will pick this up in the Fixing Broken Boards chapter under "stale Boards" as, with all relationships, staleness can creep in at any stage if one just drifts along aimlessly.

I should say at this point that we must be careful not to slip into armchair-critic mode. Founders aim to fix everything *in the long run*. In the short term, however, there are only so many hours in a day and you can't fix everything. Every founder wishes that all parts of his company were like some gleaming BMW factory – but it took BMW quite some time to get there. Along the way there will be plenty of mistakes, like a toddler falling repeatedly until it learns first to walk, then run.

The third type of Board pigeon-hole is **"turbocharger"**. *This was over-represented in businesses founded by serial-entrepreneurs who understand deeply that the SmallCo Board can be the difference between the success and failure of the whole project.* Hence these founders *prioritised* Getting A Great Board as soon as possible not leaving it for mañana.

In extremis there are cases where for the founder/CEO the Board ends up being a **noose** which we shall cover later.

The most important takeaway is: Have A Plan for how *you* wish to handle The Board Thing.

In terms of your priorities never forget that serial-entrepreneurs put A Great Board high on their priority list – **a Great Board will be a tremendous help in growing and nurturing your fire.**

ESSENCE 6 – SMALLCO BOARDS ARE CEO-CENTRIC
NOT CHAIRMAN-CENTRIC

A further substantive difference between SmallCo and BigCo Boards is that SmallCos are founder/CEO-centric whereas BigCo Boards are Chairman-centric. *BigCos easily survive changes of CEO, however, until they have quite some momentum, SmallCos do not readily survive the departure of the founder.*

Power in BigCo ultimately rests with the Chairman, whereas in a SmallCo, for quite some time it is with the founder. This is for two reasons. Firstly, on day one, the NewCo founder has 100% control

– it *is* their company. Only over time does their degree of ownership/ control reduce. Secondly, the founder is the creative driving force in the Company. As one founder put it to me:

> "If you are from Mars and you read the FT about big companies you will believe that the Chairman is the most important person in a company. But this isn't the case in a Startup. If I walk there is no business."

BigCo will keep moving for a long time in absentia a CEO. SmallCos will not. Although the BigCo CEO is a very important figure in the world of business he is nowhere near as vital to the business as the SmallCo CEO/founder. BigCos have sufficient momentum, franchise, deals, resources and structure that whilst the departure of key individuals may make a difference, the BigCo has a life of its own. This is fortunate as the median BigCo CEO tenure in both the UK and US is a mere five years.[14]

In SmallCo land it is generally some considerable period of time before a founder or all the founders can depart from a NewCo without the company dying.

As a result, as a thumbnail sketch, BigCo Boards are somewhat Chairman-centric[15] whereas SmallCo Boards are CEO-centric. The Chairman runs the SmallCo Board meeting (it's their role), however, in crude terms, in SmallCo the CEO tends to fire the Chairman and vice versa in BigCo.

ESSENCE 7 – CAULDRONS OF EMOTION: POWER! BETRAYAL! PLOTTING! DECEIT!

"On one Board a lifelong friend stabbed me in the back."

Boards are comprised of people not robots. This needs emphasising as Board-inexperienced folk can have far too much of a "bloodless" legal/ regulatory concept of the Board.

[14] PwC "UK CEOs have less time than ever to make their mark" 2017
[15] Somewhat as of course BigCos change Chairmen all the time.

If the reality – that one side of the Board coin is "legals" and the other "realpolitik" – was accurately reflected then half the books and courses on the market would be about "emotions" not "logic". Which they manifestly are not.

Given that the Board is seemingly "just a meeting" emotions can run very high. One gentle soul said to me:

> "I am not in the slightest bit violent but the nearest I have ever come to punching someone in the face was at a Board meeting."

I subsequently related that tale to another interviewee (who hadn't expressed that view) who said:

> "I know exactly what he means."

Unsurprisingly you can get pretty much every kind of behaviour imaginable in circumstances relating to money, power and control, passion and politics.

It is, to put it mildly, no easy task to raise a SmallCo from a twinkle in the eye to something that has business volumes measured in billions.

It is equally no easy task to, say, have a divorce from your creation imposed upon you by your Board.

It is no fun having someone ruin your vision that you have lost sleep over for years.

Or to have lifelong friends turn against you.

Many of you will have experienced the emotive aspect of Boards and the rest of you can imagine.

The most important takeaway for those of you who haven't experienced this directly is that Board meetings in growing companies are not some boring, dry, calculation of reason but, are rather, on a bad day, cauldrons of emotion and conflict. A kind of UFC[16] where might rules.

In the fast-changing world of Tech or any 21stC SmallCo there is no time for sleep, no weeks ticking by without some minor crisis of some sort, nor long periods without yet another sine qua non fundraising round.

---

[16] Ultimate Fighting Championship a US Mixed Martial Arts format.

Intra-personal frictions arise in all groups. On the Board this is compounded by the fact that around the table there are folks playing very different roles with very different, and in the long run potentially incompatible, aims and desires.

ESSENCE 8 – THE VITAL ECONOMIC AND SOCIETAL ROLE OF SMALLCOS

In too many of my conversations I felt that there was something of an undertone of "second class citizen" about SmallCos. Why might this arise?

One reason is the entrepreneurial mentality – the desire to grow, the understanding that your business is "young" and needs to mature and sometimes an implicit mentality that "listing" is the ultimate proof of success, of growing up, of leaving school. Another is that, given the pervasive media focus on BigCo land,[17] it is all too easy to think of BigCos as the Real Deal and SmallCos as, well, small fry. Also there is an extent to which the modern BigCo NED can be wary of SmallCo land given the higher risks involved and potential reputational damage (or real damage – being a NED of an insolvent company has huge consequences). Plenty do cross the divide but many are, understandably, also very careful about which gigs they will accept.

We all read the stats – and I'll share a few here – but somehow these don't always kind of sink in in a way they might in the UK. This may be cultural, Germans have always appeared to feel considerable warmth towards their *Mittelstand*.

The numbers of companies in the FTSE100 or FTSE250 pale into insignificance compared to the number of private sector businesses – 5.5 million.[18] Small businesses accounted for an astonishing 99.3% of all private sector businesses at the start of 2016 and 99.9% of those were small or medium-sized (SMEs). Total employment in SMEs was 15.7 million; 60% of all private sector employment in the UK. The combined annual turnover of SMEs was £1.8 trillion, 47% of all private sector turnover in the UK.

---

[17] BigCos are cheaper to follow, have more PRs paid to feed stories to the media and most media firms are BigCos.

[18] All stats in this paragraph from "Department for Business, Energy and Industrial Strategy" 13/10/16

The UK is not alone:

> "...in Germany, 99.3% of all companies are SMEs, employing more than 58% of the private sector's workforce, with a turnover of about 33.6% and about 13.9% investments in R&D. A similar picture can be drawn for the US, where small businesses represent 99.7% of all employer firms, employing 51% of the workforce and accounting for 51% of the private sector output."[19]

In the US most job creation comes from SmallCos:

> "Two out of three new net private sector jobs are created by small businesses. This trend has been reasonably consistent for 25 years... Not only do small businesses create a significant percentage of new jobs, but the jobs they create provide high levels of job satisfaction. It's easier to take pride in your work and to feel as if your contributions make a real difference when you have a direct relationship with your boss, than when your company is owned by millions of shareholders, who live all over the world and the business is run by executives in a distant city."[20]

Innovation is unsurprisingly highest in SmallCos:

> "Given the financial resources available to large businesses, you'd expect them to introduce virtually all the new products that hit the market. According to the SBA, small companies develop more patents per employee than do larger companies. During a recent four-year period, large firms generated 1.7 patents per hundred employees, whereas small firms generated an impressive 26.5 patents per employee"[21]

---

[19] Frietsch, Neuhäusler, Rothengatter "SME patenting: An empirical analysis in nine Countries" 2013

[20] https://smallbusiness.chron.com/reasons-small-businesses-important-54131.html

[21] "Exploring Business" https://doi.org/10.24926/8668.0601

Furthermore many BigCos rely on a huge hinterland of SmallCos:

> "Small firms complement large firms in a number of ways. They supply many of the components needed by big companies. For example, the U.S. automakers depend on more than 1,700 suppliers to provide them with the parts needed to make their cars."[22]

Don't be shy! Don't feel "small" but rather feel like a private company free from all those annoying Corporate Governance constraints. Whilst you need to plan for tomorrow do value your contribution to society today. Look around you – you have created jobs for all those folk. They all pay taxes. You are already doing good for society. Congratulate yourself! Enjoy today as well as planning to take over the world tomorrow :-)

---

[22] Ibid.

2. Governing Companies in the 16ᵗʰ–20ᵗʰC

The fundamental root of the Company is that groups of people have always done business together all over the world. The Company is simply one of the State's legally permissible formats for "doing business together".

Questions of "Which was the first Company?" are dependent on first defining what you mean by a Company. This sounds simple but so is the question "Which was the first chicken?" Even if you define certain characteristics of the chicken or the Company you find that there is a slow morphing rather than sudden emergence of said characteristics. In business we see a co-existence in one "together" structure of older forms and newer forms at the same time.

Simplifying all this complexity, as a low res jpeg, we can say that the Company as we understand it today was an English 16ᵗʰC invention. In its first version (V1) – the *Chartered Company* – it was the only Company form until the 19ᵗʰC invention of the second version (V2) – the *Company Law Company*. From the 1990s onwards we are seeing the birth and evolution of a third version (V3) for listed Companies – the *Corporate Governanced Company* which we shall cover in the next Chapter.

The three versions of The Company **are radically different** and in particular have **radically different governance approaches** and also **failure rates** (which follow on from version design). In simple terms the relative governance philosophies are best summed-up by a phrase I really don't like but which provides a useful simplification: "Who's the Daddy?" In V1 it was the owners, in V2 the management and in V3 – amazingly – it is people who are *neither* owners *nor* management, instructed on what to do and how to do it by unelected State bureaucrats.

One of the most important takeaways from this chapter is that in governing terms, SmallCos – far from being an inferior form, a

developmental stage of BigCo – are actually superior and representative of most businesses throughout history as well as most businesses around the world today as we discussed earlier. CCCs are a cross between owner-centric and management-centric – a cross in many ways between V1 and V2. Governing a company with a bunch of folk who have an important slug of their assets invested in it beats any set of rules, regs and "compliance robots".[1]

Naturally at a more detailed level within each version there were frequent releases and updates: V2.0, V2.1, V2.3 and so forth. Updates is an interesting metaphor as we all have phones which have "updated" themselves and performed worse as a result. A major "update" of V2 was released in 1855 when it was "upgraded" with "limited liability". This was one of those upgrades which one suspects Apple and Google do deliberately to ensure you keep buying new phones. We haven't yet "bought a new phone" but in the 21stC there is plenty of hacking around with the phone's software which so far doesn't exactly seem to be solving the problem.

The English 16thC V1 Company emerged from later enhanced versions of the prior "business together" model, the Guild. Like the Guilds the Company was a community and something of a "mini-State".[2] When it came to the question of "how do we govern ourselves?" governance naturally drew on the governance structure of the Guilds and of the State. Note that it was at first *and for a long time* a question of how do we govern "ourselves", "us together", "us *in company*" not "us in *A Company*" – that abstraction emerged very slowly out of the mist (with many consequences).

I shall use the terms governing, governance, or company governance, to mean *how Companies of all eras were governed* – ie managed at the highest level. I shall use the term "Corporate Governance" purely in the sense of the bureaucracy-fest that is the modus operandi of the V3 Board.

The myopia with which governance per se is considered is truly astounding. The FRC, the body that looks after UK Corporate Governance, has a history of governance on its website that starts in 1992 – "it would,

---

[1] A phrase I heard many times – always used in sadness.
[2] Early Chartered Companies could in some cases create their own coinage, lock people up, bear arms and so forth.

wouldn't it". Equally astonishing is that Cadbury, who started off the whole UK military-industrial-Corporate Governance complex, entirely misunderstood how Chartered companies were governed. This is super-ironic as Chartered Companies had the best governance structures of all the versions of the company that have ever existed.

To ensure that we are not too myopic in considering the governance of the Company we step slightly further back in time than 1992 and have a quick summary of how many of our current business practices were extant 4,000 years ago. But first we step back barely a moment in time to consider the conclusions of the first comparative governance text, Aristotle's *Politika*.

ARISTOTLE AND GOVERNANCE

Governance has always been A Big Thing, indeed one of the biggest. In the deepest sense governance is pre-human in its origins. Primates fight over governance – who has the right to boss everyone else around? But it's way older than primates – ants fight over territory and they date back 150 million years. So the next time you are in a Boardroom brawl or reading about those primates in Westminster fighting for control, remember this all goes back a long long way.

One of the ways that people override their deepest, most core, programming is to have rules limiting their behaviour. From a toddler onwards we are continuously being conditioned to obey. This is immensely effective – most people follow nearly all of the rules, written and unwritten, nearly all of the time. Rules restrain behaviour, overruling our impulse to resolve disputes by bashing the other fellow over the head. Although, as we shall see later when discussing broken Boards, this sentiment is still expressed just in a slightly less physical manner.

The most seminal comparative analysis of governance was written in the 4thC BC by Aristotle – *Politika*, "Politics", matters concerning the *polis* (city-state). As the Company is a mini-State understanding Aristotle on State Governance is more relevant than it might at first appear. Back in the day they really did their homework and Aristotle (with a little help from his friends) documented 158 governance constitutions (which was helpful as many, including Athens', were undocumented).

His principal conclusion from all this comparative governance study was teleological: *governance is always a means to an end*. All communities he said aim at some **good** – the community's goals. Which makes sense.

As Aristotle explains, *the key function* of those governing is to create a good set of governance rules. From these everything else follows:

> "This [constitution] involves enduring laws, customs, and institutions (including a system of moral education) for the citizens. Once the constitution is in place, the politician needs to take the appropriate measures to maintain it, to introduce reforms when he finds them necessary, and to prevent developments which might subvert the political system. This is the province of legislative science, which Aristotle regards as more important than politics as exercised in everyday political activity such as the passing of decrees."[3]

The first sentence above is very important to governance especially if we rephrase it. **Governance equals written rules** (laws, regulations), **unwritten rules** (culture, customs, ethics) and **structures** (institutions is too narrow – there are structures inside and outside of institutions). People need educating in the written rules, unwritten rules and structures. A "system of moral education" is a specific phrasing for being educated about the unwritten rules.

Aristotle classified the 158 constitutions into six categories. Visualise these in spreadsheet terms as two rows of three columns:

> "…the government, which is the supreme authority in states, must be in the hands of one, or of a few, or of the many [the columns]. The true forms of government [row one], therefore, are those in which the one, or the few, or the many, govern with a view to the common interest; but governments which rule with a view to the private interest [row two], whether of the one or of the few, or of the many, are perversions."[4]

---

3   Stanford Encyclopedia of Philosophy "Aristotle's Political Theory" 1/7/98
4   "Politics by Aristotle – Book III Section VII" classicalwisdom.com

Aristotle's true (or "straight") forms of government were **kingship, aristocracy** and **polity** [etymologies being from the Greek: *monos, archein*: one, to rule; *aristos, kratos*: best, power; *polites*, citizen].

The perversions (or "divergent") forms of government where the one/few/many rule for their own, not the general, good were respectively **tyranny, oligarchy** and **democracy** [*tyrranos*: an absolute ruler unlimited by law or constitution; *oligos, archein*: few, to rule; *demos, kratos*: the people, power].

Aristotle uses polity for the rule of the people for the benefit of all and reserves the word democracy as the divergent form of rule – a "tyranny of the majority" when they rule for the good of the majority not that of the overall community.

The "straight" forms of government are self-explanatory. With the "divergent" systems, tyranny is clear and:

> "…the real difference between democracy and oligarchy is poverty and wealth. Wherever men rule by reason of their wealth, whether they be few or many, that is an oligarchy, and where the poor rule, that is a democracy."[5]

Moving on from Aristotle's spreadsheet of 158 constitutions, not unsurprisingly one cannot rely on self-description of systems – divergent systems will never self-identify as such. Thus what a governance system is *called* ("allegedly") may well differ from what a governance system *is* ("actually").

As an example you may have heard that *allegedly* the US is a democracy. However, as former US President Carter (who might know a thing or two) said, using Aristotle's definitions correctly, *actually* the US is *"an oligarchy with unlimited political bribery"* which has created *"a complete subversion of our political system as a payoff to major contributors."*[6]

The UK is *allegedly* a democracy (using the word in our terms, being somewhere along Aristotle's polity-democracy spectrum) but the Athenians simply wouldn't have recognised us as such. In 1976 Lord Hailsham said that we are *actually* an "elective dictatorship"

---

5   Ibid. Book III Section VIII
6   Thom Hartmann Program "President Jimmy Carter: The United States is an Oligarchy…" YouTube 28/7/15

(kingship/tyranny to Aristotle). Given how, since Hailsham spoke, governance power has been seeping away from the elected politician we are a combination of "elective dictatorship" and something Aristotle probably didn't encounter back in the day – bureaucracy (or as we shall see in the next Chapter in a different model "soft despotism"). Bureaucracy not in the more modern sense of as a tediously complex process (that is merely a device of bureaucrats) but as rule by administrators. Eg John Stuart Mill:

> "That vast net-work of administrative tyranny ... that system of bureaucracy, which leaves no free agent in all France, except for the man at Paris who pulls the wires."[7]

As well as the allegedly/actually distinction there is the super-important consideration of *"how effectively does the governance system achieve its goals?"*

The UK's national governance system ("the State") has spent zillions of public funds "deciding" (or more accurately, "not deciding", rather having complex "enquiries" and producing countless "reports") on matters such as a third runway at Heathrow. This has been ongoing since 2001! Frankly by now a superior governance approach would have been to toss a bloody coin and, if it came down heads, sharing the zillions not paid out to consultants/lawyers/et al amongst those affected by the development. This would have compensated them many times over. It is a supreme example of massive *governance ineffectiveness*, the failure of governance to achieve core goals. One LFP podcast guest pointed out that, in the last year that the Heathrow runway decision was kicked into long grass, China *built* fifty runways. China is criticised by the West for its *means*, its State Governance structures. However, in terms of *ends* – meeting one of State Governance's key *goals* – the provision of infrastructure for the good of the citizen as well as as a mechanism to increase trade, business and wealth creation (it's done a bloody amazing job with high speed railways too), it's clearly infinitely more successful than our State Governance. Royaume-Uni nul points, la Chine douze points.

---

7   John Stuart Mill "Westminster Review XXVIII" 1837

The results of the sempiternal competition between tribes or nations have always depended and will always depend on the tribe's/nation's comparative *governance effectiveness*.[8] It's *comparative* not absolute effectiveness that counts just as, when a lion is chasing you and another guy, you do not have to out-run the lion you just have to out-run the other guy. Tribe/national governance can be decomposed into three key areas – State Governance effectiveness, Military Governance effectiveness and Business Governance effectiveness. From the 16ᵗʰC onwards England's great leaps forwards in *Business Governance effectiveness* (and later State Governance effectiveness and Naval Governance effectiveness?) drove it from irrelevance to ruling a quarter of the world as recently as when my parents were born.

Aristotle drew much of his philosophy from a close observation of nature – his teleology, which he applied to ethics as much as to governance, is precisely driven by the observation of nature. In this spirit we can consider 150 million years of ant evolution. It's clearly been super-successful as the little buggers occupy almost every niche on the planet. In our excessively reductionist, physical materialist and socially-atomised times the focus is on "genes". However, at a higher level ants are a social insect and competition between ant societies of the same species, between ant societies of different species and between ants and non-ant species was the driving factor. The results of this competition will have been driven by comparative ant societies governance effectiveness – State Governance (colony organisation, caste systems and division of labour[9]), Military Governance (ant wars, organisation and weaponry) and Business Governance (sourcing raw materials, construction, production and distribution).

---

8 Along with technological innovation, arguably a product of how a State is governed (which includes educating the citizens). However, for innovation to be used needs production and distribution which is covered by Business Governance.

9 antwiki.org: *"It is common for young, newly emerged workers to remain in the nest and tend eggs, larvae and pupae. As the workers age, they may shift their activities away from tending brood and begin to undertake nest construction and excavation. Finally, later in life they may become foragers, leaving the nest to search for food. In contrast to this, some workers may perform the same activities throughout their lives, or in other cases, all workers may undertake all activities of the colony, performing any given activity for a few days before switching to another … This cooperation and division of labour, combined with their well-developed communication systems, has allowed ants to utilise their environment in ways approached by few other animals."*

Thus whether we consider nations, businesses or ants we see that governance is of supreme importance in outcomes. Thus over two thousand years later we can confirm Aristotle's conclusion that *the* most important task for societies at any level is designing effective governance systems. There is nothing more important for an ant colony, a business or a nation. The only difference is that ants can't "think about it" which means that even if they can't improve it at least they can't cock-up a winning formula. And with a formula that has evolved over a long time random changes are more likely to be detrimental than positive.

On the other hand we can change our governance systems and in business we are – *massively* – within all our careers. Not only this but we no longer have (as in the 16ᵗʰC) the cream of London's successful businessmen gently and slowly evolving a winning formula (the Guild), nor in the 19ᵗʰC Gladstone et al, but it has been left to a semi-autonomous "off-balance sheet" civil service department to do so (with some inputs from businessmen – but businessmen hand-picked for the purpose (ie desired outcome[10]) by the Administrative State). Are we mad?

More broadly, at the level of State Governance modern political theatre appears designed to distract the demos from focusing on how many eggs the chicken lays to focusing on its plumage and personality.[11]

Scholarship candidates can write an essay on "To what extent is Corporate Governance political theatre? Is it focusing on plumage rather than egg-laying?"

Before leaping two thousand years forwards to look at the dawn of the Company it might be a useful reference point to briefly see how Athens was run.

"Slightly" compressing the history, in 508BC Cleisthenes woke up with a bright idea which he called *demokratia* and hey presto Athens was democratic (and as Aristotle wasn't born until over a century later they only had one row in their spreadsheet – rule by one, a few or all). Along with *demokratia* came/developed another super-bright idea: *isonomia,* the principle of equal political rights for all. Athens also

---

[10] I am reminded of a Latin lesson involving the word "nonne" which signposts a question which anticipates the answer "yes". In the same way the Administrative State always carefully selects "independent chairs" who won't come up with the "wrong" answer.

[11] Maybe the chicken is getting old and so no longer lays many eggs? Or non-metaphorically maybe the theatre is to distract us from an oligarchical system which governs in its own interests not that of the demos as a whole?

invented a principal we should definitely revive – *ostracism*, a democratic vote to exile the person who has been the biggest pain in the arse. This would be far more effective and efficient than waiting for the 1922 Committee or the next general election to oust tyrants.

All Athenian-born males over 18 had the right to attend the *Ecclesia* (Assembly) which met every nine days and discussed how Athens should be run:

> "So the people decided, for example, to declare war (or peace), levy taxes, repair the shipyards, build the Parthenon, put X into a position of power, or remove Y from his."[12]

The day's agenda was prepared by the *Boule* (Council), which consisted of 500 of their number (drawn 50 each from the 10 tribes). How are we doing so far? Remind you of your country's so-called "democracy"? No, me neither. Each Councillor served for one year only and could never serve more than two in total. The Council managed the practicalities and any actions were put to the Assembly to debate. Executive posts (cf our civil service) were drawn by lot (which practice still persists in our jury trials). As to the Law, bliss was it to be in those days alive! No courts, no judges, no barristers, no solicitors, just a few hundred of the citizenry, able to decide as they saw fit, hearing one prosecution and one defence speech and then voting.

Athenian democracy died in 322BC when Macedonia abolished it for them and it was *"never repeated in the history of the world."*[13]

Or was it?

GOVERNING THE VERSION 1 COMPANY (16TH C–19TH C) – OWNER-CENTRISM

> "Government within the trading companies, in other words, should essentially do what government of the commonwealth did: preserve order and enable prosperity."[14]

---

12 Jones "Ancient And Modern" 1999
13 Jones op. cit.
14 Mishra "A Business of State – Commerce, Politics and the Birth of the East India Company" 2018

In the tsunami of Corporate Governance literature one sees remarkably little about what we can learn from history and in particular *why* things worked better in the pre-Company Law Company past. A notable exception to not looking back in time is Cadbury himself who in "Corporate Governance and Chairmanship: A Personal View" 2002 starts with correctly referencing the East India Company (EIC) as *the* most influential company in terms of the evolution of the Company and its governance but states that *"the governance structure ... was therefore little different from that of a company today"* which couldn't be more wrong. **That such a seminal figure in the creation of UK (and global to an extent) Corporate Governance could completely misunderstand the original company governance structures speaks volumes:** (a) if you don't know where you have been how can you possibly know where you should go? and (b) to the complete failure of Academia to have provided him with a book that he could have read to find out the truth. I don't blame him as a person in the slightest, he was a FTSE Chairman not a historian, how was he supposed to find out? Piecing together the picture for myself has taken far longer than his committee sat for.

The earliest surviving written records of any sort are cuneiform tablets from Mesopotamia ~3200BC by which time civilisations had demonstrably existed in that area for some two thousand years. Tablets were predominantly used for record keeping and the earliest records are, amazingly enough, about business transactions.[15] We have an astonishing archive of 23,000 records from Old Assyria some four thousand years ago which show that much of what you use today as business elements existed then: merchants, contracts, markets, marketplaces, monetary exchange, money-lenders, return on capital, business law and regulation, jointly-owned business structures and partnerships. Indeed, with the exception of The Company and so-called Limited Liability, in terms of business pretty much everything existed long before records began.

A thousand years ago the Italian merchant states of Florence, Venice, Genoa et al were far ahead in business. They utilised *Commenda* and *Societas*, partnership structures[16] that date all the way back to Old

---

[15] In a 2019 British Library exhibition there is an astonishing 5,000 year old tablet (none of our records are likely to survive that long) recording the payment of farm labourers in barley.

[16] In the Commenda one party provides the capital and the other manages. In the Societas both provide capital and one manages.

Assyria. Italian businesses/banks were present in London as far back as 1284. However due to "reasons"[17] their influence waned in the 14thC and thus didn't commend (groan) their business forms as a great example of business structure. England relied on Guilds, amongst many other uses, for trading and the management of crafts. Guilds had no shared P&L and, in simplified terms, were a combination of trade/craft self-regulation and a membership club of sole traders. In the 16ᵗʰC unless you lived there England was utterly inconsequential. It was less than 2% of global GDP[18] and only grew wool which it traded for everything else with the near-Continent. The desire to trade further afield required far greater capital investment and a consequent upgrade in business structures. This led to the invention of "The Company" which at first was a kind of "joint P&L Guild" (eg you had to first become a member in order to invest).

To create a V1 Company you needed the Monarch's permission – a Charter.[19] This Charter was the Constitution of the company and defined how you would *govern* it – principally the powers of the Adventurers (shareholders in our terms[20]) and the role of Committees[21] (Executive Directors to us – those who were "committed" to carrying out their duties[22]). Charters were Anglo-Saxon devices[23] used to record *privileges* (from Latin *privus* (private) +*lex* (law) – something that applies just to you). There was no standard Charter for Companies, each one differed (as they were *privileges*) even if a common governance pattern was recognisable. V1 Companies and Adventurers had unlimited liability.[24]

---

[17] The over-extension of Florentine banking credit to Edward III (for what became the Hundred Years War) in the 1330s followed by Edward repudiating his debts, the King of Naples defaulting and the King of France exiling them and confiscating their businesses, bankrupted the Bardi and Peruzzi family banks. They were the largest Florentine banks of all time – the Medicis never came close – and their failure caused economic chaos and depression. Kunal "The Crash of the European Financial System in 1345" 2013

[18] In 1600 Britain accounted for less than 2% of Global GDP, France 6%, India 22% and China 29%. In 1700 Britain was just under 3%, India 24% and China 22%. It wasn't until the late 19ᵗʰC that British GDP had leaped up to 9% driven by Britain having created the Industrial Revolution. Maddison "The World Economy" OECD Paris 2001

[19] The BBC is a Chartered Company to this day.

[20] Surely a superior term to this day for investors in SmallCos?

[21] Only much later did this phrase evolve into the modern meaning of a way of whiling away the hours and avoiding making decisions.

[22] Note the interesting change in vocabulary then to now…

[23] The oldest surviving examples are from the 7ᵗʰC.

[24] At first funding was on a per-voyage basis so "unlimited liability" generally meant having to put your hand in your pocket when what was left of a voyage limped home and, having blown all the money en route, the surviving sailors needed paying.

The totality of the Adventurers constituted a powerful "Court of Proprietors" or "General Court".[25] This functioned as a **legislature,** approving all major decisions, as well as an **electorate** which voted for Committees drawn from themselves to a "Court of Committees" (an **Executive Committee** in our terms).

It is ironic that what is these days perceived as "uniquely Continental" – two-tier Boards – is actually a direct import of the English Chartered Company's governance structure. The East India Company's governing structure was copied (with one important change namely that the General Court became a subset not a totality of owners) by the Dutch East India Company (the VOC) in the early 17thC from where the model diffused around Europe.

This simple, clear and powerful split of **legislature** and **executive** mirrored concepts of how to govern the State. The fact that the legislature/executive split has remained one of the most powerful State Governance models speaks volumes to its strength in any governance context.

If we take the example of the most important company of them all – the East India Company (EIC), the Court of Proprietors met four or five times a year, or more if necessary. In the crisis period of 1770–1773 before its capture by the British State the Court of Proprietors met on average *twenty-two* times per annum.

The Court of Proprietors had substantial powers and involvement in the governance of the EIC. As an example, once a year they met for the reading of the "Lawes"/Standing Orders – the internal bylaws/rules of the Company[26] – as well as for a meeting with the auditors who provided information on the actual execution of the rules set in the Orders.[27] Disaffected employees or those alleging corruption could air their grievances at the Court. Adventurers were actively involved in the Court of Proprietors. Certainly in the early decades all major capital

---

[25] From which we get the "G" in AGM/EGM.

[26] Lawe XXXII emphasises the need to address all comments in Court to the Governor or his Deputy and not directly to anyone else – which is a protocol that still holds today in formal circumstances. This lawe also required that anyone speaking shall be bareheaded which is also excellent advice and is widely followed in our times.

[27] Order CXLIX "[No] more then two pence in Beere to one man euery day at breakfast, and betwixt Meales" continues to echo. I recall Berry's Ordinary Claret being removed by the philistines from Kleinworts' managers' dining room tables. A while back I read about WeWork trailing a way to limit the free beer in their offices so EIC Order CXLIX is returning mut. mut.

expenditure (eg and esp voyages) needed approval by the Court of Proprietors. Even a century after its foundation it was not uncommon for 1,000 people, highly diversified by wealth, gender and class, to vote at East India House[28] in the annual elections for the Committees or on such matters as dividend rates and relations with the government.

These days shareholders do not meet with the auditors, *nor* do they hear how well the company is complying with its own rules, *nor* do they hear from disaffected employees. In our era such matters have effectively been hidden from the Company's owners and made private to "the Company", which really means "the Board" in this context. Auditors and internal compliance are dealt with by a sub-committee of the Board so that not even the whole Board hear from them directly. Disaffected employees are not even heard at the Board let alone by shareholders.

Furthermore, in the V1 Company, Adventurers (and all Committees were Adventurers) had, unlike today, unlimited liability. Which focused the mind somewhat.

The abolition of the superior governance *structures* of Chartered Companies cannot be remedied by rules, codes or regulations.

The V1 Company, had owner-centric governance with a two-tiered Board and no NEDs.

Now perhaps you can see why Cadbury was so wrong – V1 was utterly unlike the modern British Company. In fact it could not have been more different. He also writes about the EIC's CEO – which they did not have. Chartered Companies (ChartCos) had a Governor *who chaired both Courts*. No separation of Chairman and CEO there (one of Cadbury's recommendations being to split these roles[29]).

ChartCos were also **single-purpose** (even if this could be a complex purpose eg the EIC's mission was "trade with Asia"). The single-purpose Charter made ChartCo that much easier to govern compared to modern MegaCos which have so many business lines that no-one can possibly have a feel for them all. ChartCos could not "own" other ChartCos or have "subsidiaries"[30] once again meaning that a V1 Company had a

---

[28] On the site of the current Lloyd's of London insurance building (bizarrely no blue plaque as far as I can see).

[29] The Bank of England notably still has a Governor. Equally the Prime Minister's role is not split. The State imposes upon the private sector what it will not itself do.

[30] In a notable example in the 17thC the Muscovy Company gave birth (in a complex fashion) to a separate Greenland (which in those days meant Spitsbergen) Company for whaling.

much simpler structure and consequent ease of governance than later versions of the Company which would become too complex to govern effectively. Charters needed periodic reissue which also helped keep powerful companies to heel.[31]

ChartCo's governance model also proved to be an excellent governance model in the US where it was generally believed, and most textbooks avow, that the boom in company formation was a post Civil War (1861–65) phenomenon. However, Robert Wright's scrupulous and meticulous work[32] has shown that this is not the case with *over twenty thousand* US corporations chartered between 1790 and 1860. These companies had, as directly inherited from Britain, ChartCo governance structures and were thus heavily restricted in focus compared to modern companies. They also had a strong element of partnership culture with a far lower divide between "owner" and "manager" and consequently, as Wright shows, *were far better governed than modern US companies.*

We must remember that there was no such thing as our ChartCo "Platonic" abstraction but rather countless ChartCos covering hundreds of years. No two were identical and even in any given ChartCo the governance rules (written and unwritten) were not static. Over time the governance of ChartCos, as measured by new charters, was deteriorating[33] in part as the geographic dispersion of shareholders increased. A further systematic factor behind much of the weakening was the increasingly intermediated relationships between owners and management notably around audit and accounting. We start to see ideas of "management accounts" (as in "for management's eyes only and not those pesky owners") and "public accounts" (for everyone else). The further one got away from the Guild mentality, a single society/tribe of *members*[34] – the ethos in the original ChartCos[35] – the more things

---

[31] The likes of Microsoft, Google, Facebook never need to "return to base" which makes controlling them when they get over-mighty rather more challenging.

[32] Wright "Corporation Nation" November 2013

[33] Freeman, Pearson, Taylor "Shareholder Democracies?: Corporate Governance in Britain and Ireland Before 1850" 2011

[34] In the early Chartered Companies you had to first be accepted as a member (which cost money) and only then could you invest in voyages or later buy shares. The EIC only had permanent capital from 1657 – the better part of two generations after it was founded.

[35] To the earlier point about forms of "together" overlapping. The early ChartCos were more like Guilds in being membership organisations with subsets of members funding different voyages.

morphed over time into a more arms-length relationship between two *different* tribes – management and owners.

However, slow drifts in the governance challenges of ChartCos were, curiously, rather unimportant to the creation of the V2 Company. Indeed, bizarrely, so were ChartCos.

GOVERNING THE VERSION 2 COMPANY (19ᵀᴴC–21ˢᵀC)
– MANAGEMENT-CENTRISM

> "'This is the age of public companies': We receive our educa-
> tion in schools and colleges founded by public companies. We
> commence active life by opening an account with a banking
> company. We insure our lives and our property with an insurance
> company. We avail ourselves of docks, and harbours, and bridges,
> and canals, constructed by public companies. One company paves
> our streets, another supplies us with water, and a third enlightens
> us with gas And if we wish to travel, there are railway compa-
> nies, and steam boat companies, and navigation companies,
> ready to whirl us to every part of the earth. And when, after all
> this turmoil, we arrive at our journey's end, cemetery companies
> wait to receive our remains, and take charge of our bones."[36]
> [written in 1856]

It is hard to imagine now but back in the day people neither texted nor tweeted. Their lives were thus rather more peaceful but conversely they used words without the slightest sense of restraint. Thus in 1720 *"An Act for better securing certain powers and privileges intended to be granted by His Majesty by two charters for assurance of ships and merchandizes at sea: and for lending money upon bottomry; and for restraining several extravagant and unwarrantable practices therein mentioned"* was passed. This Act incorporated the Royal Exchange and London Assurance Corporation and was designed to stop the creation of so-called "unincorporated companies" (UnincorpCos). Its parliamentary process began *before* what we now call the South

---

[36] Gilbart "The Moral And Religious Duties Of Public Companies" 1856

Sea Bubble[37] notwithstanding which in the 19ᵗʰC our untweetable Act became known as the "Bubble Act". Contrary to received wisdom Freeman et al show that neither the Act nor the (separate) Bubble inhibited the formation of illegal UnincorpCos. Lawyers have always had ways of following the letter, but not the spirit, of the Law (you may have noticed).

In the 19ᵗʰC there was considerable liberalisation and roll-back of the British State. Taxation post-Napoleonic Wars was 20% of GNP in 1799 but by the start of WW1 was down to 10%. As part of this liberalisation, the V2 Company, the Company Law Company (CoLawCo), was created in 1844 which, with frequent updates, is the legal form we use today. Companies House was created and anyone with £5[38] to spare could form a company without needing monarchical or parliamentary approval.

Crucially CoLawCo was *not* (as sometimes glossed/assumed) a "democratisation" of ChartCo but rather a way of bringing into the fold near-illegal UnincorpCos *which had long suffered far higher rates of fraud and mishap and were a destabilising impact on the economy*.

These post-1720 UnincorpCos used partnership structures (or sometimes trusts) to simulate much of the nature of a company – especially tradeable and transferable shares. As partnerships their constitutions were *partner-centric* with external capital being granted specific rights which were unsurprisingly inferior to those of the partners. Partnership agreements were never legally conceived of as applying to anyone other than the partners, *thus they were never designed with any "shareholder" in mind and hence never gave them anything like the power, precedence and priority that they enjoyed in the Chartered Company*. As Freeman et al show in their impressively detailed work,[39] the need

---

[37] The South Seas (in those days South America not Pacific) Chartered Company had, like the Mississippi Company in France, got heavily involved in consolidating national debt (both countries suffering from war-related debts). Which didn't go well. By 1719 it owned half the national debt. Its shareprice rose ten-fold in 1720 – inflation-adjusted it became the third largest Company ever – before collapsing back to its issue price. The economic consequences were more severe than the 1920s/30s Great Depression or 2008 Financial Crisis.

[38] According to measuringworth.com this is the equivalent of between £500–£20,000 today depending on your inflation benchmark.

[39] Op. cit. They measured 90 governance parameters in 507 companies (290 Chartered, 207 unincorporated).

to avoid straying too much into the illegal "Company" territory led to many of the developments in the "General Meeting", UnincorpCo's equivalent of ChartCo's Court of Proprietors (aka General Court). In essence if you were legally a partnership or a trust or any other clever legal rinky-dink you could not stray too far away from that structure without legally ceasing to be one of those and straying into becoming something that a Law court would say is an illegal Company under the 1720 Bubble Act. Thus UnincorpCos had to maintain clear blue water between themselves and ChartCos – *which naturally kept them far from having a powerful General Court.* Freeman et al found that 10% of UnincorpCos did not even allow shareholders to see any accounts at all!

It is this "bringing in from the cold" unofficial "Unincorporated Companies" with their self-designed "management-centric" governance approaches (in stark contrast to State-mimicking ChartCo Governance structures) that led to a significant degeneration in Company govern-ance which presents us with significant challenges to this day.

CoLawCo was not a child of ChartCo and thus did not inherit its well-thought-through legislature/executive model based on centuries of governance experience but rather inherited a model which had been empirically proven to lead to greater failure rates.

Governance was still, in principle, two-tier although the legislature, the new General Court, qua AGM/EGM, was almost entirely neutered. *It met far less frequently* and *had far fewer powers* than ChartCos' General Courts. The Court of Committees had over time been reworded as a Board of Directors and in its 19thC CoLawCo context had substan-tive powers – in essence it held most of the cards.

In 1849/50 the recently-created Companies House Registrar, Whitmarsh, produced thirty-eight pages of suggested improvements to CoLawCos. None of which were adopted.

This liberalisation/lowering of standards (delete as applicable) is not just an eccentricity of the 19thC "night-watchman" State. Witness this emailed comment by an experienced Angel/NED/businessman:

"Incidentally, are you aware of the government provisions for minimal disclosure docs provided by private companies to their shareholders has been severely pared down? (Happened two years ago [2017]). Now we receive so little information, I do not bother to go to AGMs. How can government propose to support small enterprises when they reduce shareholder visibility?"

The inferior governance of CoLawCo, the V2 Company, would alone have led to many of the BigCo problems we see today – especially if we compound it with a disastrously mismanaged by the State failure of the audit/accounting marketplace[40] (most of my interviewees who were Chartered Accountants commented on this in the context of BigCo failures).

However, if the V2 Company's parents were from the wrong side of the tracks, yet more genetic damage was about to strike it in its youth as we shall see in the next section with the introduction of "limited liability".

The 16[th]C State creators of ChartCo, the V1 Company, created a robust[41] vehicle and left private matters to private owners and gave the owners strong constitutional powers.

The 19[th]C State creators of CoLawCo, the V2 Company, utilised the provenly weak governance structures of near-illegal UnincorpCos. They kept their faith in the shareholder to control management (who else would?). However, the much diminished constitutional powers led to de facto management-centrism. For owners, trying to control management via a solitary and very weak AGM was, and is, a bit like trying to paint your house through the letterbox.

These dynamics were of course recognised at the time:

"...as the case now stands, directors have practically all the power, whether for good or evil; shareholders have none."[42]

As a result General Meetings became more sparsely attended in the 19[th]C and **shareholders became more interested in purely financial returns**. Hubert Spencer, best known for the expression "survival of

---

[40] See especially Brooks "Bean Counters: The Triumph of the Accountants and How They Broke Capitalism" 2018

[41] If monopolistic but that's another story. Both the EIC and its much larger competitor the Dutch VOC replaced individual efforts which were problematic/ineffective. These businesses should be seen as the two nations' NASAs with the difference being that 16[th]C/17[th]C global business was far more dangerous than the 1960s moonshots.

[42] Railway Record 24/7/1852

the fittest", was bemoaning shareholder apathy about GMs by the mid 19ᵗʰC. Investors increasingly diversified their investments – a relatively new phenomenon[43] – and thus reduced their level of interest/commitment to any particular investment. This was facilitated by the rise of the stockmarket making the mechanics of buying and selling shares easier.

Shareholders became more distant and the simple "single-purpose" nature of ChartCo started mutating into the vast sprawling groups that we know today. We shall turn to the evolution of the NED later when we look at their role on SmallCo Boards. However, they were of no real importance in the 19ᵗʰC and of no consequence governance-wise. You don't even need to know the history to appreciate this – no legal category was created for them then or now despite a management Director being in reality very different to a non-executive Director. The former knows the business intimately the latter far far less. Yet they bear the same legal responsibilities – albeit in V3 the "panacea" NED has a whole lot of *additional* governance responsibility heaped on their shoulders.

The CoLawCo Board became more focused on *property* (the Company's assets) and less on *people* (the owners). In the late 19ᵗʰC financial journalism arose to fill the information gap for these increasingly remote and pushed-away owners but this too led to a retreat by Directors from the public domain into a private realm.

Where did this leave the owners? Amazingly "not even owning" is the strict legal answer. The House of Lords confirmed in 2003 that a shareholder in a limited company is legally not actually, as one imagines, an "owner" of the Company.[44] How curious, albeit reflective of this "pushing away" of Adventurers as owners, as the prime drivers and shuffling them to capital-provider status or, in the case of listed BigCos, folks who buy and sell a piece of paper and may never actually contribute any capital whatsoever.

---

[43] Although Adventurers in the early ChartCos were often invested in a few companies, previously you could only belong to one Guild and many UnincorpCos banned investors from investing elsewhere.

[44] *"The Court of Appeal declared in 1948 that "shareholders are not, in the eyes of the law, part owners of the company". In 2003, the House of Lords reaffirmed that ruling, in unequivocal terms... So who does own a company? The answer is that no one does, any more than anyone owns the river Thames, the National Gallery, the streets of London, or the air we breathe."* John Kay "Is it meaningful to talk about the ownership of companies?" FT 11/10/05

This "pushing away" of owners continues unabated its extreme form being "stakeholderism" – the notion that companies have duties not simply to their shareholders (or even employees) but to most everyone under the sun.

In the V3 Company the pushing-away has been reversed for *some* categories of shareholder where, as we shall see, the State insists that they must vote on the tiny number of matters put to AGMs. In the 21ˢᵗC V2 Company pushing-away of owners continues unabated. Following the 2006 Companies Act Private Companies (UnlistedCos) were no longer required to hold AGMs.

This means that in half a millennium The Company has gone full-circle from "the Daddy" being the Adventurer/Shareholder to today "Daddy" being divorced and living in a bedsit with no contact with his offspring (unless its guardians deign to grant him very limited access by holding an AGM). I doubt that a single 17ᵗʰC Adventurer would invest in a 21ˢᵗC V2 Company – they insisted on parental rights of full access and involvement.

CoLawCo's governance challenges and complexity only increased as the decades went by. One key example of 19ᵗʰC rule changes that increased the challenge of governing was that in 1850 CoLawCos could not change their Memorandum of Association[45] which, just as Charters had, set out what the company could do. Shareholders could sue for *ultra vires* if the company went outside its Memorandum. This was eroded over time to the point today where today the Memorandum is entirely vestigial saying nothing of governance importance. In effect, CoLawCos could eventually do *"anything"* as opposed to ChartCos which were formed only to do *"something"*. Governing entities that can do *anything* is far harder than those that are legally obliged to stick to their knitting. This is a key cause of today's **"too Complex To Understand"** which is another tap-root of modern corporate collapse.

The subsequent development of CoLawCo was driven by competitive pressures between States and between nations which led to CoLawCo as we know it today. Already in the early 19ᵗʰC US States had competed for chartering revenue by scurrying to introduce various forms of limited liability – New York in 1811, New Hampshire in 1816

---

[45] They could change their Articles of Association.

and Connecticut in 1818. The phrase **"race to the bottom"** was origi-
nally used (notably by Justice Brandeis) to refer to competing US States'
deliberate lowering **of corporate standards and significant widening of
company purposes.**

By the late 19thC the US was leading the way in the "development"
of the Company. A notable tweak to CoLawCo was the 1889 evolu-
tion/standard-lowering (take your pick) by New Jersey which allowed
"holding companies", a phase shift in notions of the company that
persists to this day as *the* way of structuring vast groups. A holding
company is not a company, unlike all prior, designed to do some *thing*
– or even things – it merely acts as an umbrella company that owns
a controlling percentage of subsidiary companies. This was the onset
of corporate groups that are **"too Big To Understand"** – a fatal flaw
in MegaCos today. It doesn't matter who you have on the Board or
what rules they are supposed to follow, no-one can possibly understand
MegaCo.[46] Witness the UK Parliament's report on 2008:

> "The incentives for banks to become and remain too big and
> complex are largely still in place. As well as reinforcing the distort-
> ing effects of the implicit taxpayer guarantee, this makes banks as
> currently constituted very difficult to manage. Incentives to pursue
> rapid growth have contributed to the adoption by banks of complex,
> federal organisational structures insulated against effective central
> oversight and strategic control. These incentives were reinforced
> as rival banks grew through acquisitions of firms whose standards
> and culture they scarcely understood. Many of the consequences
> of unchecked pre-crisis expansion and consolidation remain, as do
> the perverse incentives that promoted it. As a result, many banks
> remain too big and too complex to manage effectively."[47]

Further "updates" to CoLawCo continued to increase the governance
challenge – notably in the SmallCo context the invention and expansion

---

[46] The argument can be made that they are not there to understand it but to govern it.
That is all fine until the point at which the proverbial hits the fan when politicians
fall over themselves to "blame the Board" and haul Directors over the coals at Select
Committees.

[47] House of Lords/House of Commons "Changing banking for good" Report of the
Parliamentary Commission on Banking Standards 2013

of "alphabet shares" – all those share classes (A shares, B shares...) that create a multi-class (sic) society with the upper class ruling the roost. Many a naive investor might be fooled by the word "shares" (as per the 1862 Act) or its modern form "equity" – very close to the word "equitable". However, some shares are fairer than others, some equity is more equal than others. What this means is that even on the few items put before the shareholder the vestigial Polity in the V2 Company is easily turned into an Oligarchy by the higher share classes.

THE V2 COMPANY – FROM UNLIMITED TO LIMITED TO ZERO LIABILITY

If one had to pick one key feature of the modern Company it would be its so-called "limited liability" nature.

ChartCos were unlimited liability,[48] as had every "together" business vehicle everywhere everywhen including UnincorpCos (as they were partnerships). The first CoLawCos from 1844 were unlimited liability. To make this "liability" issue concrete let's start with a brief "compare and contrast" of the failure of two very important 19thC banks – one limited liability, the other unlimited liability.

In June 1878, the City of Glasgow Bank (established in 1839) reported that it now had 133 branches, that business was booming and that a dividend of 12 per cent would be paid. In October 1878, when it had the third largest branch network in Britain it went bust. Which was unfortunate. It was especially unfortunate for its shareholders as it was unlimited liability. **When it went bankrupt (causing two other Banks to collapse) its Directors were jailed and its 1,200 shareholders,** *not depositors,* **were responsible for the debts of (adjusted for inflation) getting on for half a billion pounds. Around one-fifth of the shareholders went bankrupt.**

Overend Gurney, known as "the bankers' bank", was a limited liability company when it went bust. Having been formed in 1800 and

---

[48] Legal angles (which can be reflected in business treatments) often place limited liability far back (eg with monasteries). These are mostly academic/legal arguments and easily fool the unwary in particular by using the term in many different technical ways (eg protecting the company from claims on a shareholder's assets). In practice in ChartCos Adventurers coughed-up time and time again and Debtors Prison was a scary thing as late as the 19thC.

been a key player in the market for discounting bills of exchange it had ended up with riskier longer-term assets such as railway shares. Attempting to solve its liquidity problems it converted to limited liability in 1865.[49] Its 1866 collapse, with twice the debts of the City of Glasgow Bank, caused a run on banks, several others failed, and the Bank of England had to raise interest rates to 10% for several months to stem banking outflows. It was seminal in the then private Bank of England becoming "lender of last resort". **Just as we see today prosecuting Directors involved in complex situations is easier in theory than in practice. Tried at the Old Bailey for fraud based on the 1865 share offer prospectus Lord Chief Justice Cockburn found them guilty of "grave error" not criminal behaviour, and they were acquitted.**

Nothing new eh? The ne plus ultra of this trend was reached in 2008 when *citizens* were forced to cough-up for banking failure whilst bankers paid themselves big bonuses and shareholders soon saw their asset-prices recover due to specifically-designed monetary policies.

So where did this limited liability lark come from? And why is it called "limited" when it's clearly zero?

You would think that the question of *why* limited liability arose was a simple question with a known answer wouldn't you? After all, it is *the* heart of the Company, and the State, or rather taxpayers like you and I, pour billions into universities every year as well as management/business studies having gone through the roof in recent decades.

In practice "why?" is complex and amazingly no-one has a simple answer. Any simple answers you may have heard are all easily refutable. In 2016 Julia Chaplin[50] completed a whole PhD on the simple question of "why?" and, although she dives into much detail about *what* happened, she came up with no smoking gun that had been missed in prior investigations. Certainly as per Cottrell[51] it led to English Company Law being the "most permissive" in Europe.

In 1855/56 **Limited Liability** *of an unprecedented and unforeseen type* – namely for both management *and* shareholders – was introduced. **The continental "Commenda" system**, by then big in France and

---

[49] Although the partners had guaranteed the assets transferred into the LtdCo.

[50] Chaplin "The Origins of the 1855/6 Introduction of General Limited Liability in England" 2016

[51] Cottrell "Industrial Finance 1830–1914" 1980

Germany, was of **limited liability for investors but unlimited liability for management**. This Commenda version of limited liability had been Parliament's focus earlier in the 1850s and indeed was introduced as a Bill to Parliament. If this Bill, rather than the full limited liability Bill (which was something of a bolt from the blue), had passed, company history would have been very different to this day, the British Empire being very powerful in spreading its ways around the globe at that time. In a parallel universe I guess it did get passed – I think we can assume that unlimited liability for management would have rather reduced Company failure rates in that universe.

However, the Commenda was no perfect form itself. Passive shareholders had exactly the same problems that plagued shareholders in the Dutch VOC in the early 1600s which led to their two decades long campaign for "proper" governance structures (ie those of the EIC). Shareholders put their money into Commenda but were then at the mercy of management over whom they had no control. As per (a different) Freeman[52] the management were often guilty of financial manipulations for their own benefit and other fraudulent practices. Their sole legal responsibility was to send the passive shareholders financial reports. Shareholder meetings were limited to discussing accounts and any too-clever approach to attempt to "look through" the accounts to the management of the company (of which there were plenty) would trip into investors losing the limited liability that they enjoyed. Plenty of naughty things happened leading to booms and busts in France in the late 1830s and mid 1850s leading to widespread demands for suppression or curbing of their version of Commenda (Société en Commandite).

Unsurprisingly in the UK, limited liability for both management and shareholders led to corporate failures going through the roof. **More than 30% of the public companies formed between 1856 and 1883 went bust.** An astonishing twenty percent of Victorian novels feature bankruptcy[53] as it was so novel and unfamiliar a concept – paying your debts had been essential throughout history and Debtors Prisons were still A Thing in the 19th C. Gilbert and Sullivan mocked the new Limited Liability Company in an operetta:

---

[52] Freeman "Joint-Stock Business Organization in France, 1807–1867" 1965

[53] Taylor "Creating Capitalism – Joint-Stock Enterprise In British Politics And Culture 1800–1970" 2006

"That's called their Capital; if they are wary
They will not quote it at a sum immense.
The figure's immaterial – it may vary
From eighteen million down to eighteen pence.
…They then proceed to trade with all who'll trust 'em
Quite irrespective of their capital.
…You can't embark on trading too tremendous
It's strictly fair, and based on common sense
If you succeed, your profits are stupendous
And if you fail, pop goes your eighteen pence."[54]

Astonishingly I have never read a single accurate description of limited liability in over thirty years in and around FS. The first thing to appreciate is that a liability is – of course – something you might be liable for. Walk your dog through a field of sheep off the lead and you are going to be liable for the damages *if* your dog savages the sheep. You are going to have to cough up *in the future if something comes to pass*.[55] If you own something then that is an asset – and like all assets its value will change – or even go to zero. That shareholders might lose the value of their investment is not "limited liability" any more than the possibility that a valuable picture you own might turn out to be fake and worthless.

What we today call "limited liability" is nothing of the sort and furthermore is not what was created in the 19thC. What we have today is de facto **zero liability** for shareholders (in all circs) and management (in almost all circs).

As consequences never disappear the version of "limited liability" we have today is worse than zero liability – it is a State-sponsored reallocation, a transfer of liability – from the guilty parties to innocent bystanders.

The "bill for the meal" always has to be paid and a tough waiter (the State) who doesn't take no for an answer splits it between some other patrons of the restaurant who weren't sitting at the table which got up and walked out: *"'ere, 'cos I saw you talkin' to 'em, you're*

---

[54] Gilbert & Sullivan "Utopia Limited or The Flowers of Progress" 1893

[55] OK so in accounting terms a liability is something you owe someone now – but I'm not interested in accounting terms but in the principle. Something you owe someone now is what we all call in everyday life "a debt". Something you might have to fork out for in the future *if* something happens is, in real life, a liability.

pickin' up part of the tab for those geezers on that table over there who just did a runner".

One often hears canards around limited liability. One is "look at what progress it has led to!" This is the worst kind of post hoc ergo propter hoc. Given the technological changes and economic impacts of two world wars (the 1930s weren't looking so great) – communications, aeroplanes, computers and so forth, you'd be hard-pressed to evidence any statement that it was the structure of the V2 Company per se that led to progress. Another canard is that "limited liability is required for risk taking". This is palpable nonsense – people took far greater risks in the past under unlimited liability. Long-distance Assyrian trade was super-risky. Most of the crew of early ChartCo trading voyages died! *The whole industrial revolution happened and was virtually over before limited liability came in* (including building a huge canal network and much of the railway system). Furthermore, I have never seen an assessment of the alleged "benefit" of business gambling that offsets it with a calculation of the cost of the injuries that have been transferred to innocent parties (including bankrupting them or their businesses).

So what was Limited Liability when it – er – *was* Limited Liability? There were two mechanisms.

ONE. *Some* (ie "limited") liability for shareholders was retained via the convention that shares be issued partly-paid. Shareholders provided funds but could always be called upon for more funds in the future, on pain of forfeiture (1856 Act) if they didn't cough up. This element could be highly-substantive – banks in particular used 20–25% paid-up shares[56] – which means that *shareholders were liable for four to five times more than they had already given to the company.*[57] **That** is "limited liability".

Over time this partly-paid protection was gradually eroded away to zero although even by 1881/2 the percentage paid-up was still averaging in the low 20%s. **"Limited" liability thus started out as *limited* (ie some) liability but eventually became zero liability if you are a**

---

[56] All partly-paid stats Cottrell (op. cit.).

[57] This was mitigated over time within a given company as companies did call on this partly-paid capital after their establishment as and when they needed it.

shareholder, and, unless you are completely irresponsible,[58] no liability for Directors.[59]

The fact that it *was* limited liability is clear in the first Act labelled a Companies Act – 1862 (which also allowed for Unlimited Liability Companies such as the City of Glasgow Bank):

> "7. The liability of the members of a company formed under this Act may, according to the Memorandum of Association, be limited either to the amount, if any, unpaid on the shares respectively held by them ["a Company limited by Shares"], or to such amount as the members may respectively undertake by the Memorandum of Association to contribute to the assets of the company in the event of its being wound up ["a Company limited by Guarantee"]."[60]

Two. There was an interesting clause relating to mandatory capital buffers in the 1855 Act which sheds an interesting light on the "were they mad?" question. In essence Game Over came, not as today when your capital runs out, but when 75% of it has run out:

> "XIII. In the Case of any Company which has obtained a Certificate of Limited Liability, whenever, on taking the yearly Accounts of such Company, or by any Report of the Auditors thereof, it appears that Three Fourths of the subscribed Capital Stock of the Company has been lost, or has become unavailable in the Course of Trade, from the Insolvency of Shareholders [NB re them being on risk], or from any other Cause, the Trading and Business of such Company shall forthwith cease, or shall be carried on for the sole Purpose of winding up its Affairs; and the Directors of such Company shall forthwith take proper Steps for the Dissolution of such Company, and for the winding up of its Affairs, either by Petition to the Court of Chancery, or by Exercise of the Powers

---

[58] Eg paying a dividend when insolvent – 1855 Act Clause IX.

[59] Elements of Corporate Governance aim to change this but with very limited success. Directors' statutory legal duties exist but other than outright fraud it is hard to prosecute in this context in most corporate collapses.

[60] Pulebook "The Companies Act, 1862, With Analytical References, And Copious Index" 1865

of the Deed of Settlement, or by such other lawful Course as they may think most fit."[61]

As bankruptcies were so high we must assume that measuring capital annually (and with some delay as accounts take time to compile) was too infrequent and/or that the companies "crashed at a lower speed" with lower debts than they otherwise would have had.

The subsequent disappearance of *real* shareholder liability in V2 means that our current 21stC CoLawCos are actually far more dangerous vehicles than the 19thC early subversions of V2 CoLawCo.

One often hears well-intentioned calls for "more ethics training" in business which always makes me recall a great comment below such an FT article stating that *"if you haven't learned ethics by the age of five then the chances are it's too late"*. Certainly the idea that you send say 50-somethings or 60-somethings on courses to teach them the difference between good and evil always seemed ludicrous to me. **Rather the seeds of the genuine ethical problem at the heart of the modern Company were sown by the State in 1854/55 and, after further watering, fully flowered.**

Go to an ice-hockey match and you'll see grown-men punching the lights out of each other with impunity. Go to a football match and you will not – or if players do, stern action will be taken. Would you solve ice-hockey players' bad behaviour by sending them on "ethics courses" having declared them to be morally bankrupt?

Is it the players who are to blame or those who set the rules of the game?

"Limited" Liability as we know it today has been described as *"a construct which institutionalises irresponsibility"*.[62] Its development led to a persistent schism between morality and business – *"the economic domain was relieved of its moral component"*.[63]

Limited liability is, as we saw, a **State-created *transfer* of liability** *away* from the bad boys and girls to the good boys and girls, from owners and Directors of malfeasant/mismanaged firms to those unlucky enough to be dealing with them (or in extremis all citizens). As we all

---

[61] www.legislation.gov.uk "The Limited Liability Act 1855"

[62] Ireland "Limited liability, shareholder rights and the problem of corporate irresponsibility" 2008

[63] Poovey "Making A Social Body: British Cultural Formation 1830–64" 1995

learned at school being made to pick up the tab for your own behaviour is the best way to ensure good behaviour. Furthermore there is understandable outrage when the innocent get the blame. **Zero liability is akin to a school punishing other kids when you do something wrong.** Lucky for you maybe, but not for them.

Zero liability spreads the cost of failure across society, far away from those who historically, all the way back to Old Assyria four thousand years ago, would have been held – quite rightly – responsible. "Corporate Governance" as A Thing first started in the US with the 1970 collapse of Penn Central. This was estimated to have impacted 100,000 creditors.[64] The 2008 Banking/Finance crisis affected everyone in all economies. In this case zero liability (and the mismanagement of the banking sector by players and rule-makers) literally spread the failures of a tiny few across the whole planet.

The Victorians spotted all these things too – hence not creating zero liability. Even their experiment with limited liability was strongly opposed and caused chaos. Gladstone was a 19thC political colossus. He chaired the Select Committee that led to the 1844 Act, was four times Chancellor of the Exchequer and four times Prime Minister so we can assume he knew a thing or two. It says a lot that, according to Chaplin, he was still calling the 1856 Act a mistake in 1893.

Partnerships were seen as following natural law – I pick up my tab, you pick up your tab, if we work together we share the tab. Limited liability was seen as a dangerous, "un-English" doctrine.[65]

To this day companies keep collapsing for reasons *entirely foreseen* in 19thC Parliamentary debates. The reaction to these collapses has been the creation, driven by the US and UK, of the concept of "Corporate Governance". This would appear to be the birth of the V3 Company – it is a way of governing companies that would be entirely unrecognisable to the 16thC and 19thC creators of V1 and V2.

---

[64] And 118,000 shareholders.
[65] Taylor "Creating Capitalism – Joint-Stock Enterprise In British Politics And Culture 1800–1970" 2006

3. Governing Companies in the 21ˢᵗC

The massive expansion of the role of the State and creation of hundreds of "regulators" started in the late 20ᵗʰC but for the sake of neatness we cover it all under this century. It is where we are now that matters to SmallCo and its Board, not what happened precisely when in the past three decades.

We start by having a look at three important angles on "why Palpatine was right", why the bureaucrats have taken over – neurological, sociological and philosophical. As it has huge political implications (did anyone ever ask you whether you wanted to be hyper-regulated?) we then move on to the political angle of State-centrist micromanagement. This apparently limitless hyper-regulation affects companies of all sizes but disproportionately impacts SmallCos (you may have noticed).

The philosophical mentality of all three versions of the Company was dictated by the philosophy of who was in power. Elizabeth I was quite happy that successful merchants who had her trust went off and sorted stuff out. Gladstone et al brought the dubiously legal/illegal UnincorpCos in from the cold and left private individuals to sort out their own affairs. Within an overall pattern V2s had considerable leeway to create specific governance rules for themselves. In the 21ˢᵗC the ruling unelected bureaucrat naturally creates a zillion rules all of vich must be obeyed at all times by all ze V3s. The Conquest of Abundance.

V3's governance is truly bizarre. **The idea that the highest governing body in a company is staffed by people who *neither* have significant stakes in the company *nor* are actively involved in managing it (and hence don't know that much about it) would have been inconceivable to generations of businessmen and the State for over five centuries.** Indeed it was inconceivable at the start of some of my interviewees' careers as NEDs.

Why should people who are – by design – "independent" rule over shareholders' property and management? No "independent" comes into your house and tells you how to run your family or your home so why should they tell you how to run your business? What is the difference? What is your answer to this super-important question?

This fundamental issue is responsible for many of the behaviours we see in BigCo around Boards. If you have to have someone coming into your house and bossing you and your family around of course you are going to choose someone as "amenable" as possible; as Brian characterises it in the Foreword "the person that most people least object to". There is a real tension here. You don't want someone bossing you round in your home but vice versa the State sends them in as a kind of PC Plod to stop "criminal" (literally or figuratively) actions. In V3 the BigCo NED is something of a "piggie in the middle".[1]

Corporate Governance is a bureaucrat's response to a real problem – excessive rates of collapse of BigCos which are a genuine problem for society. This is particularly true in the US/UK which might make one pause to consider why then it is that their Corporate Governance approaches are being pushed out worldwide.

Corporate Governance was always intended to be the way in which *listed* companies were governed. Sadly and without pushback Corporate Governance in 2019 moved out of its ListedCo V3 territory and into larger SmallCos.

Recent decades have also seen the *goals* of The Company become a political football. We look at what the Company's goals were in the 16ᵗʰ-20ᵗʰC and then how four philosophies have impacted them in recent decades – "neoliberalism" ("anything legal goes, the market sorts everything"), "third-way stakeholderism" ("consider your impact on everything and everyone all the time before you think of your shareholders"), the Church of the Woke ("your pre-birth biochemistry will affect your Board career"[2]) and most recently flirtations with old-style

---

[1] When the proverbial hits the fan and said NED is up in front of grandstanding Select Committees I've never seen them have much sympathy for the challenge of being the piggie in the middle. Nor of course do said committees ever acknowledge *that it is the very design of V3 by their State that has created this position.*

[2] The last two UK Corporate Governance reports were focused on immutable characteristics you had in the womb – Hampton-Alexander (gender) and Parker (ethnicity), PM M-y always found virtue-signalling so much easier than governing. 1970s anti-discrimination laws are so old-hat.

anti-private-enterprise Socialism. We have a very quick look at how a future V4 Company might fix all the challenges of the V2/V3 Companies.

This "footballing" of The Company's goals leaves its mark. Much of Corporate Governance is no longer in codes that, if you are forced to, you just pay lip-service to, much is enshrined in Company Law. Thus as we shall see most notably Section 172 of the 2006 Companies Act which increases Director's responsibilities enshrining the political fashion of that time. I'm not a lawyer but I'd hazard a guess that ignoring Company Law isn't the best career move for Directors.

Having covered the V1, V2 and V3 Companies we ask how Aristotle would have ranked their governance. Prior to the practicalities of the rest of the book we wrap-up by emphasising that whilst I have drawn a distinction between Company Governance which has always applied and Corporate Governance (which is super-new) everyone else does not (yet). Thus when one of your Boarders talks about Corporate Governance you need to find out which of several meanings he is using it as a placeholder for.

EMPEROR PALPATINE WAS RIGHT

"The bureaucrats are in charge now."

Before we consider Corporate Governance – a phrase which the Economist magazine never used before the 1990s – and the creation of the V3 Company we must tune into the zeitgeist which has given it birth.

Palpatine's comment about bureaucrats is for me the most apposite summary of late 20[th]C governance of the whole of society (Lucas drew inspiration from his own indie film-maker battles against the big corporate studios and their entrenched bureaucracies). But where does the mechanistic, bureaucratic, controlling, reductionist mentality come from? And to this *allegedly* democratic but *actually* oligarchical society we all live in I assume no one asked you to vote for it either?

Let's touch briefly on three authors to show how deep are the roots of the phenomenon we experience as Corporate Governance.

The deepest roots of the bureaucratisation of life, and the wider phenomenon of ideological possession, lie in our neuroanatomy as brilliantly explained by the super-smart Iain McGilchrist in "The Master and His Emissary: The Divided Brain and the Making of the Western World".[3]

Animals have lateralised hemispheric brains. Early views about how this works in humans are long discredited – language in this hemisphere, maths in that etc – all computation is spread across the brain. **The difference lies not in *what* the hemispheres do but in *how* they do it.** In all animals the left hemisphere has a *local*, precise mode of attention – a pigeon needs an instant decision as to whether what it is pecking is a piece of grit or a seed. However, if it only does that it risks being eaten while it is eating and thus the right hemisphere has an imprecise but all-encompassing *global* mode of attention.

In all creatures the left hemisphere is about detail, precision, pieces, it is Newtonian, atomistic, it only sees what it expects to see and is very clear about its conclusion. *It is not in touch with reality but only with its representation of reality which it mistakes for reality and which turns out to be remarkably self-enclosed.*

The right hemisphere is about context, whole, flow, modern quantum, in principle uncertain, impossible to entirely isolate components from each other, things change according to context and the way they are observed, sustaining an idea over time, uniqueness, human beings (ever flowing, ever-changing), ambiguity, indirect, implicit – non-verbal, metaphors, tone of voice. It has a feel for "everything" but knows "everything" can never be pinned down, defined, constrained, categorised. It is wise but knows that you can never define wisdom.

The bureaucratic takeover of society parallels the servant hemisphere becoming the master, as per Einstein:

> "The intuitive mind is a sacred gift and the rational mind is a faithful servant. We have created a society that honors the servant and has forgotten the gift."

Importantly our society *as a whole* (the real significance of IMcG's book[4]) has been going increasingly in the direction of becoming a paranoid, controlling, machine – which is very much a left-hemispheric

---

[3]   Shorter summaries: McGilchrist "The Divided Brain and the Search for Meaning" 2012, YouTube "RSA Animate: The Divided Brain" 2011 (~2 million views).

[4]   Part I covers the neuroscience, Part II the long-term Western cultural trends.

world. Palpatine was right and we see this all over the place, we are increasingly surveilled and controlled.

The irony of a left-hemispheric society is that the left hemisphere sees least yet is the most convinced that all it sees is all there is. A key "tell" is that, faced with contradiction, the left-brain cheats/lies/ avoids (we'll see an example of that later with the denial-mode re lack of empirical data in support of the V3 Company having any different outcomes from the V2).

Before we move on, a tale IMcG relates[5] underlines that this is no abstract topic. A correspondent had read his book and wanted to pass on her experience. She had needed no convincing of the book's thesis. One day she had been called to the hospital to identify the body of her brother in the morgue. When she touched it she said: *"but it's warm!"* The nurse replied: *"no, don't worry dear, he's dead, it says so on this piece of paper"*. The woman protested to no avail and rushed out into the corridor screaming for help. She found a doctor who immediately injected her brother in the heart with adrenalin who lived as a result.

Sociologically, a century ago Max Weber thought deeply about **"rationalisation"** in modern society which he saw as trapping people in an **"iron cage"**, in systems based purely on teleological efficiency, rational calculation and control. A man not afraid of multiple metaphors he also wrote about the **"polar night of icy darkness"**. Furthermore he fretted that this would lead to the rise of dictatorship – a system of "command and control" being, as it were ripe for being commanded and controlled. This is of course what Palpatine did and today this "command and control" mentality extends far beyond the bureaucrats in the regulatory and administrative State, to the government and the Law (Kritarchy is not, as often spun, "the rule of Law" but the "rule of lawyers/judges"). They are all on the make.

Weber was obviously on the money in terms of the rise of communism (which dominated east of Austria to Vladivostok for quite some time) and fascism (Spain/Portugal are often neglected in that regard, far longer running than Germany/Italy). He is clearly right about the Law – have a system that Must Be Obeyed At All Times, massively increase its reach and hey – no one can object.

---

5   ConsciousTV "Iain McGilchrist 'The Divided Brain' Interview By Iain McNay" YouTube 2014

Weber saw the roots of "rationalisation" as lying in the scientific revolution, in Protestantism, and in business. The "factoryisation" of society saw the industrial era move from small-scale crafts to large factories with people playing smaller and smaller roles and more micro-controlled from on high.

Aldous Huxley was a great fan[6] of French philosopher/sociologist Jacques Ellul who published "La Technique ou l'Enjeu du Siècle" ("Technique or the dilemma of the century") in 1954. Poorly entitled in its English translation as "The Technological Society" in 1954, Ellul was much more focused on how we make *technique* sacred – be it in technology or in domains such as government or psychotherapy – rationalisation and factoryisation in my terms. This worship of technique has political and governance consequences as he spelled out in the book:

> "Consequently, the opposition between technicians and politicians places the politician squarely before a truly decisive dilemma. Either the politician will remain what he is in a democracy, in which case his role is fated to become less and less important in comparison to the role of technicians of all sorts (a state of affairs already evident in the financial sphere); or the politician will take the road of political technique, in which case the crisis of adaptation will inevitably arise. If the politician really wishes to continue to exist, he must choose the second solution as the only possible one. The existence of techniques in all other spheres forces him to this choice. Even so, little by little he is being stripped of any real power and reduced to the role of a figurehead."

Ellul would have recognised modern focus groups, opinion polls and the many many obligatory political techniques we see across the western world as "adaptation". Prophetic stuff given how long ago he was writing. Talking of prophecies and rule by unelected technocrat/bureaucrat, Ellul wrote:

> "It is not conceivable that the normal operation of democracy would be acceptable to those who exercise this technical monopoly

---

6 Ellul was "making the case I tried to make in Brave New World."

– which, moreover, is a hidden monopoly in the sense that its practitioners are unknown to the masses."

Do iron cages and polar nights of icy darkness sound familiar to any of you BigCo NEDs? Do you feel that some hidden monopoly tells you what you must do in ever more detail? Rationalisation is tied-up with concerns about efficiency, predictability, calculability – which rather remind me of Dave Lister's girlfriend troubles.[7] The overall impact of rationalisation is **dehumanization** and **disenchantment**. Dehumanization a century after Weber's writings springs to mind as being precisely what lies behind Chairmen and senior NEDs talking to me about "compliance robots". It is the *factoryisation of the Boardroom*. If Ford and other businessmen factoryised the craftsmen now all-powerful State bureaucrats factoryise the businessmen.[8]

I should emphasise that I mean no offence to folk working in regulation. Everyone needs a job, most people try and do theirs well and none of us choose the world we live in. I am absolutely criticising the *game* here, not the vast majority of the *players*.

STATE GOVERNANCE VIA HYPER-REGULATION: "SOFT DESPOTISM"

"Thus, after having thus successively taken each member of the community in its powerful grasp and fashioned him at will, the supreme power then extends its arm over the whole community. It covers the surface of society with a network of small complicated rules, minute and uniform, through which the most original minds and the most energetic characters cannot penetrate, to rise above the crowd. The will of man is not shattered, but softened, bent, and guided; men are seldom forced by it to act, but they are constantly restrained from acting. Such a power does not destroy, but it prevents existence; it does not tyrannize, but it compresses,

---

[7] Red Dwarf "Stasis Leak". Dave was bemoaning the fact that, and failing to understand why, women always left him for men who were *"reliable, sensible, dependable and lots of others words that end in '-ible'."*

[8] No one needs to factoryise the bureaucrat as they are already factoryised. Ellul would argue though that all these players – workers, businessmen and State – are rather slaves to *technique* which is the real master, or rather, false God.

enervates, extinguishes, and stupefies a people, till each nation is reduced to nothing better than a flock of timid and industrious animals, of which the government is the shepherd."[9]

Almost two centuries ago de Tocqueville foresaw the danger to democracy of what one might call "hyper-regulation" leading to his concern above which has been summarised as, soft despotism or soft totalitarianism.

It is most ironic that it happens in Britain, on balance leaders for centuries in delegating governance – to individuals,[10] business (Companies), Law (Common Law created in courts). Now, in the blink of an eye, we are world-leaders in de Tocqueville's soft despotism. We are a long way along "The Road To Serfdom" in which Hayek in 1944 seminally linked political freedom and economic freedom (hyper-regulation of course depriving you of much economic freedom). He argued against both Stalinist State-centralism and its mirror image in WW2-British State-centralism, in the latter case warning that democracy and Statism are incompatible (which brings us back to de Tocqueville and Ellul a few years later and perhaps where we have reached today). He made a compelling case for the importance of "profit" as a signal that enables countless human beings to self-organise their businesses. So important were his arguments deemed to be that Conservative Central Office contributed 1.5 tons of their 1945 election paper ration so that more copies of the "The Road To Serfdom" could be printed.

Notwithstanding which Hayek, whose influence on radical-Conservative thinking would return with Thatcher (and her mentor Joseph) much inspired by his arguments, was not, however, a Conservative as:

"It may succeed by its resistance to current tendencies in slowing down undesirable developments, but, since it does not indicate another direction, it cannot prevent their continuance. It has, for this reason, invariably been the fate of conservatism to be dragged along a path not of its own choosing. The tug of war between

---

[9]   de Tocqueville "Democracy in America" 1838

[10] Gradually improving from Magna Carta in 1215. *"Until August 1914 a sensible, law-abiding Englishman could pass through life and hardly notice the existence of the state, beyond the post office and the policeman."* AJP Taylor "English History 1914–1945" 1965

conservatives and progressives can only affect the speed, not the direction, of contemporary developments."[11]

We can see that a powerful centre will, in absentia figures such as Gladstone and Thatcher (did she reduce the size of the State?[12]), always take more power for itself. Computers and communications advances though have utterly super-charged the speed at which it can do so.

Early in my career Kleinworts invented the BT privatisation and under Thatcher huge chunks of industry were moved from the State to the private sector. In the 1990s the collapse of the Soviet Union reinforced the empirical superiority of the *delegation* of the organisation of the sourcing of raw materials, construction, production and distribution to the people. Delegation fitted our history well – it was only the Normans, possibly the Republic (but that was short-lived), and the WW1 and WW2 States that over-centralised and over-controlled everything. Until now.

The UK's membership of the EU has radically increased State-centralism and soft despotism. To put British business delegation (which is at the very heart of "can you do what you want on your Board or not?") into some historic context it might be interesting to have a quick look at the different philosophies of various European EICs.

The Portuguese "Casa da India" effectively went bust despite having had a monopoly for a century. The Dutch VOC was half-trader, half-State imperialist from the get-go (it exported one million Dutch to settle in Asia). The French East India Company was also a strange beast, being founded and re-founded several times after its inception in 1664. The French were rather late to the Chartered Company experiment compared to the English and Dutch and never quite got into the spirit of it. The French, like the Spanish and Portuguese, were very state-centric and the FEIC's method of funding was in notable contrast to both the EIC and VOC. Louis XIV wrote to 119 towns ordering merchants to get together and subscribe to the FEIC. Many refused and by 1668 the King was the

---

[11] Hayek "The Constitution Of Liberty" 1960

[12] In only two of her twelve years did public spending fall in real terms, on average it increased 1.1%pa. When she entered office State spending was 44.6% and *it wasn't until her eighth year of office* that it dropped below this. When she left it was 39.2%. The recent low was under Labour: 34.5% (2000–01) who then put pedal to the metal with it reaching 47.7% in 2009–10 (impacted by 2008). New Statesman "How public spending rose under Thatcher" 8/4/18

biggest investor. Other players were less consequential (then as now). The Danish EIC (1616) was more successful than the early EIC (which struggled) although European wars led to bankruptcy. Sweden was the last European nation out of the blocks (1731–1813) and together with a re-formed Danish EIC (1670–1729) smuggled more tea into England than the EIC imported. As to the Scottish (always admirers of the continent – my enemy's enemy and all that) their East India Company was such a disaster that it drained the country of a quarter of its liquid assets and hastened Scotland into union with England in 1707.

The British were not just minarchistic at home but also in the Empire which was a patchwork of different structures with various degrees of delegation (Dominions having the most) and where less than a thousand Brits ruled a Raj of hundreds of millions.[13] Our ancestors must be spinning in their graves as we are well on the road to maxarchism. A century ago the government spent 10% of GNP now it's 40%[14] and that's before we count the number of regulations now compared to a century ago.

The results of delegation and minarchism (two sides of the same coin) and (relative) incorruptibility (a cultural, unwritten governance rule) were proven successful. The Cato Institutes' huge (406pp) annual research project "The Human Freedom Index"[15] measures 79 indicators of personal, civil and economic freedom, in 162 countries around the world. In the aggregate table an astonishing six of the top nine countries[16] were formerly in the British Empire, a staggering testimony

---

13   Anyone reading only contemporary narratives might assume that we rivalled Mao, Genghis Khan and Stalin. Hence a quick evidencing of this "superior governance" claim. Kartar Lalvani was born in the Raj and is now one of Britain's finest entrepreneurs (founding Vitabiotics in 1971) with a net worth now in nine figures. To the governance point of CCCs and family businesses Vitabiotics remains an UnlistedCo and his son now runs the business. In his spare time he spent twenty-five years (!!) researching and then writing a chunky tome on the detailed development of India's infrastructure [Lalvani "The Making of India – The Untold Story of British Enterprise" 2016]. Lalvani said that in sixty years of living in this country he had never heard any Brit say anything positive about their contribution to India yet: *"Far from looting India, British governance promoted education, fostered enterprise, revolutionised transport, created an impartial judicial system, nurtured intellectual debate and tackled barbarism."* Lalvani "If our ignorant academics really understood history they'd be proud of the British Empire" *Daily Mail* 20/12/17

14   Even in the US it was 38% in 2016.

15   Cato Institute 2018

16   The Top 9 being: New Zealand, Switzerland, Hong Kong, Australia, Canada, Netherlands, Denmark, Ireland, United Kingdom. The US in passing is 17th. Not to stretch a point but under Cnut we were in the Danish Empire (1013–42). William of Orange was King of England and we invented mountaineering and skiing. So we'll call that 9 out of 9.

to the legacy of governance ideas we left behind. Vice versa to disregard or in extremis, invert, those principles – *with State or Company Governance* – as the modern British State is doing – proves deleterious to disastrous.[17]

LIMITLESS HYPER-REGULATION: NEVER MIND THE QUALITY FEEL THE THICKNESS

"The end result has been that government has become a self-generating monstrosity. Abraham Lincoln talked about a government of the people, by the people, for the people. What we now have is a government of the people, by the bureaucrats, including the legislators who have become bureaucrats, for the bureaucrats."[18]

Soft despotism is not just an expenditure question, or percentage share of the economy, it's a "rules & regs gone mad" question. The limitless word in the title is heartfelt. *There is no limit.*

Back in the day there was a limit. Hammurabi's law code, much of it commercial regulation, was carved on a four-ton slab of long-lasting and super-hard to carve hard stone. Technology led to brevity. Now technology only accelerates complexity, verbosity and prolixity.

The UK tax code is 21,000 pages long and at ten million words now has 12.5 times the number of words in the Bible.[19] It has increased *sixfold* in the past twenty years (threefold under Brown and then Osbourne, who came in to "simplify" it, doubled it again).[20] Who does that serve? Not the majority of the people or the majority of businesses that's for sure.

---

[17] Aristotle would no doubt be fascinated with this index which would merely seek to confirm his thesis about the supreme importance of governance. The people in those countries whose post-colonial rulers rejected almost the whole British package of governance ideas suffered greatly whereas those who kept the key ideas prospered in relative and absolute terms. Thus we see for example that Botswana (which was one of the poorest and least developed places in the world upon its independence in 1966) is 63rd yet its neighbour (far more wealthy at independence) Zimbabwe is 146th. India is 102nd yet Pakistan 141st and Burma 144th.

[18] Friedman "Why Government is the Problem" 1993

[19] As any techie will tell you anything that long and complex contains plenty of bugs (loopholes). These, to put it mildly, "don't exactly benefit the poor".

[20] Frisby "Daylight Robbery" 2019

**Value-creating businesses are ever more tied down like Gulliver by
a million ropes** and require increasing armies of internal "compliance"
(the word says a lot), internal and external accountants and lawyers,
almost entirely to add no value other than dealing with State-created
and State-imposed bureaucracy. On the podcast guests talk about
having to provide ever greater volumes of data to regulators. Why?
Why should regulators be allowed *without limit* to ask for ever more
data? Which of course they will use for their next cycle of regulations, ever-finer control and yet more data. *All of which is anti-wealth
creation; we should never forget that without wealth-creation every
society ever would have been stuffed.*

In the UK the National Audit Office[21] states that there are 90 regulators which cost **£4bn** to run with an estimated cost to business to
implement the regulations of **£100bn p.a.** A recent UK report by
Professor Sikka for the Shadow Cabinet counted rather differently and
enumerated the scale and complexity of the extra-parliamentary sources
of regulation:

> "The UK has nearly 700 overlapping regulatory bodies. There are
> 41 regulators for the financial sector alone and at least 14 [now
> 15[22]] dealing with accounting, auditing, insolvency and some
> aspects of corporate governance."[23]

Regulators are generally deeply unconstitutional as former Deputy
Governor of the Bank of England Sir Paul Tucker has made clear in his
2018 magnum opus.[24] They are unelected, beyond democratic control
or influence, and are an extra-parliamentary source of law-making:

> "We shouldn't refer to them as regulations we should refer to them
> as laws because that's what they are."[25]

---

[21] National Audit Office 2017

[22] Since Sikka's report ARGA has been created.

[23] Sikka "The regulators of corporate Britain have been too timid for too long. It's time
for a new approach" 2019

[24] "Unelected Power – The Quest for Legitimacy in Central Banking and the Regulatory
State"

[25] LFP113 "Regulators – Unelected Power & Uncertain Constitutional Position w/Sir Paul
Tucker former Deputy Governor Bank of England"

Centuries of English and British liberation of the citizen from the arbitrary direction of untouchable figures ruling over them from the iconic Magna Carta in 1215 to the full voting franchise of the early 20thC are being rapidly reversed. The decay in State Governance matches, and indeed is creating, the decay in the governance of the Company.

In both the US and UK it has suited politicians to delegate much of their detailed responsibilities to off-balance-sheet civil servants – notwithstanding the point that the Administrative State has no constitutional authority to make laws.[26] This leaves politicians with more time to extend their domain of influence and to virtue-signal – the modern equivalent of kissing babies. Of course whoever you vote for you get a politician and for all the theatre the realpolitik is that the political tribes share much in common and are members of the same class (gilded pensions and all). Politically the authoritarian left (the libertarian left appears to have been AWOL for quite some time) is happy to have private businesses tied down ever more and as per Hayek:

> "A conservative movement, by its very nature, is bound to be a defender of established privilege and to lean on the power of government for the protection of privilege."[27]

Historically, privilege meant the landed classes but now means the Corporatocracy who benefit from privileges in the Anglo-Saxon sense (private law) in terms of regulations whose net effect is to keep them dominant. So both are happy to see more and more rules especially as these rules absolve them of more and more work and responsibility.

In the UK this downwards delegation has been compounded by upwards delegation to the EU and sideways delegation to the Law. *The tiny bit of the State that you are occasionally allowed to vote in and out as an elective dictatorship has given most of its power away.* Thus what you can vote out of office or influence is faaar smaller than in the past. Faaar more of the State and people who have control over you are literally just "doing their own thing" and untouchable by you. It's an oligarchy – and one that is expanding rapidly.

---

[26] And if you don't think they are laws, try disobeying a few regulations. You will soon find yourself deprived of money, livelihood or freedom just as if you had disobeyed a law.

[27] Hayek "The Road To Serfdom" 1944

Moving upwards, the EU's "Mifid II" alone is **one million seven hundred thousand paragraphs long**! Whatever the goal of that it certainly is the wrong means. In that respect the cross-sectoral "horizontal" GDPR, at a mere 55,000 words, is a positively light read, albeit one 20,000 words longer than Shakespeare's Hamlet.

Palpatine's maxim applies more broadly. Medici Research produced a chart of the number of *global* regulatory publications, changes and announcements *purely in FS* between 2008–16. In 2008 it was a staggering 8,704. In 2016 it was an astonishing 52,506. Imagine the cost of merely processing all of these let alone implementing changes in your organisation?!? Yet people/media remain uninformed and are often heard crying out for "more regulation" – *never "better regulation"* – and bemoaning so-called "de-regulation" in FS.

It is a disproportionate burden on SmallCo. In his 2012 Reith lectures Niall Ferguson quoted the **US Small Business Administration Report as having calculated the cost of regulation across all sectors to US small businesses as an astonishing $1.7trn.**

Other "standards" get ever more complex creating a shell game that confounds even the professionally-trained:

> "I'm also very sympathetic to accountant-bashing. Accounts have become so complex [IFRS] that they serve only the accounting profession. The burden on small businesses is disproportionate, and the large businesses have successfully used the complexity to confuse and confound their auditors, so it works for nobody."
> [NED/chartered accountant]

Of course it is not just business that suffers, other sectors are under the cosh of factoryisation, of Statist rules, rules and yet more rules. An oldskool GP I knew, who was also on the Boards of several major London hospitals, retired early about a decade ago. When I asked him whether he had got bored of healing the sick he said:

> "On the contrary that's the bit I enjoy. It's the bureaucracy I can't stand. You can save someone's life but if you haven't filled out the right forms you will be in big trouble. Vice versa you can saw their wrong leg off but as long as you have the right forms nothing will come of it."

Former Supreme Court Judge Lord Sumption in his 2019 Reith Lectures stated that, in 2010, 700 new criminal offences were created, three-quarters of them by government regulation (!) and that whereas in 1911 there was one solicitor for every 3,000 people, now there is one for every 400 individuals. Any non-lawyers (or non-parents of lawyers lol) think that's a good idea?

> "The standard modern edition of the English statutes fills about 50 stout volumes, with more than 30 volumes of supplements. In addition, there are currently about 21,000 regulations made by ministers under statutory powers and nearly 12,000 regulations made by the European Union, which will continue to apply unless and until they are repealed or replaced by domestic legislation."[28]

The answer to "do we really need all this?" is clearly no. Every society in history had orders of magnitude less. In Appendix A we have a brief look at regulation 4,000 and 1,000 years ago. It was better.

And before any of you dares to peep up with "but Sir, the world is more complex" review your biology notes. Does a chicken lay an egg or an egg lay a chicken? Society is principally "more complex" as lawyers', regulators' and governments' printing presses are running 24x7. Back to our section lead-in quote from de Tocqueville it is a system of soft despotism.

Here's a simple question: *what do you think will ever put a limit on, let alone set into retreat the ever-expanding empires of the bureaucracy, government and judiciary?"*

Or do you think in a century (or less at this rate) there will be one lawyer per 40 individuals and in another century one per 4?

Corporate Governance has become a conduit into the Boardroom for the State and an ever-growing State *overall* (which is the real issue) can *always* think of more it wants the people to do and how it wants them to do it. The State has reconceptualised its role and no longer just provides re-directs funds (benefits) and "infrastructure" whether hardware (bridges/roads/hospitals) or software (laws), rather it instructs us in how to live our lives as well as manage our

---

[28] Sumption "Trials of the State: Law and the Decline of Politics" 2019

businesses (as if it knew anything about that, it doesn't even do State governance well).

"Again, let me emphasize, the problem is not that bureaucrats are bad people. The problem, as the Marxists would say, is with the system, not with the people. The self-interest of people in government leads them to behave in a way that is against the self-interest of the rest of us. You remember Adam Smith's famous law of the invisible hand: People who intend only to seek their own benefit are "led by an invisible hand to serve a public interest which was no part of their intention". I say that there is a reverse invisible hand: People who intend to serve only the public interest are led by an invisible hand to serve private interests which was no part of their intention."[29]

Whatever the problems of the V2 Company, the 21stC approach to overly-frequent BigCo/MegaCo collapses was always going to involve a whole pile of bureaucracy.

As we saw the V2 Company was born genetically weak. Its parents were from the wrong side of the tracks which gave it poor governance and, due to a freak mutation and poor care over time, zero liability (which has only spread since, LLPs qv). Rather like a magic car where, whatever speed you crash it at, you are guaranteed to walk away with only small bruises, it gets driven too fast, too irresponsibly and crashes all too often. **Only the innocent bystanders get hurt.**

All this was evident in the 19thC. **"Corporate Governance" is an ad hoc bureaucratic attempt to try and staunch the bleeding caused by a genetic defect in V2 and by an utterly defective accounting/audit market.** But applying bandages neither cures haemophilia nor fixes the accounting and audit market.[30]

---

[29] Friedman "Why Government is the Problem" 1993

[30] But don't worry one regulator has been sacked from this role and another regulator (ARGA) has been created. That should fix it.

Corporate Governance as we use the phrase now had been on a slow-burn in the US since the 1970s. It kicked-off in the UK in 1992 with Cadbury which was the first of an astonishing 25 "codes" to date.[31] In the US Enron was Fortune magazine's "America's Most Innovative Company" from 1996 to 2001. That's impressive. Less impressively for both in 2001 Enron collapsed although the extent of its accounting malpractices remained impressive. Shareholders lost $74bn in "America's Most Innovative Company". Not good! The following year WorldCom collapsed spectacularly having inflated its assets by a mere $11bn. Investors lost $180bn and 30,000 employees lost their jobs. Bad! To round off the trio it was little surprise that the auditors of both – Arthur Anderson (who had also signed off on a prior earnings misstatement scandal of $1.7bn for Waste Management in 1998) – disappeared. Henceforth the "Big 5" turned into "the Big 4" – an even smaller oligopoly strengthened by proportionately more "Too Few To Fail"-osity. As a consequence in 2002 the biggest change in US Corporate Governance since the 1930s, the Sarbanes-Oxley Act (SOX) was introduced.

Fast forward to 2018 – after twenty-six years of relentless growth of the military-industrial-Corporate-Governance complex in the UK, Carillion, a government supplier, collapsed and became the UK's largest ever trading liquidation, with the biggest hit ever on the UK's Pension Protection Fund. That's unlucky. Or maybe it wasn't bad luck at all? Maybe it was entirely foreseen nigh on two hundred years ago and the State has failed to fix the problem despite having issued 25 (!) Corporate Governance codes and many Company Law changes?

The whole UK Corporate Governance bandwagon started gathering momentum in large part due to concerns over excessive executive

---

[31] The Watkinson Committee (1973, BigCos should have NEDs), Bullock Report (1977, also called the "Report of the committee of inquiry on industrial democracy" worker representation on Boards), Cadbury Committee (more formally, and interestingly "The Financial Aspects Of Corporate Governance", 1992), Rutterman Report (1994), Greenbury Report (1995), Hampel Report (1998), Combined Code (1998), Turnbull Report (1999), Myners Review (2001), Smith Report (2003), Higgs Report (2003 defines "Independence" for NEDs, recommends senior independent NED), Smith Report (2003), Tyson Report (2003, recruitment and development of NEDs), revised Code (2003), Turnbull (2004), re-revised Code (2006), re-re-revised Code (2008), Turner (2009, financial crisis), Walker Report (2009, Banks only), re-re-re-revised Code (2010), Stewardship Code (2012, on asset managers but impacts companies), Hampton-Alexander review (2016, more women on Boards), Parker review (2016 ethnic diversity of Boards), re-re-re-re-revised Code (2018), Wates Principles (2019, "The Wates Principles on Corporate Governance for Large Private Companies").

compensation. Well I guess dozens of codes sorted that. Nope, that too has spiralled out of control.

That the V3 Company (CorpGovCo) is radically different from the V2 Company should be readily apparent – the simplest slam-dunk in this regard is that the V2 Board was dominated by management. On the other hand the V3 Board has been transformed beyond all recognition and denuded of executive management. In 2013 85% of all Directors were "independent" and in the US super-majority Boards with only one executive – the CEO – were widespread.[32] V3 Boards are dominated by fetishised NEDs whose role is increasingly framed as some sort of PC Plod – there to police an untrustworthy management.

We shall return to the strange history of NEDs later but we should note that **the creators of the V3 Company put their faith in the very recently invented "independent NED" as panacea – someone neither owner (indeed economic exposure to the company is strictly controlled) nor manager. That's odd. Other than in Nazi Germany[33] it has no precedent, and there is zero empirical evidence that it works.**

If your ten-year-old asks you what an "independent NED" is you will no doubt say something along the lines of: *"someone who does not own any of the company, who doesn't go there much, who doesn't know much about it in detail, who doesn't manage it and who increasingly has to follow a bunch of rules made by people in the government."*

To which your ten-year-old would no doubt reply: *"that sounds very strange Daddy(/Mummy)."*

Throughout the whole of history, in non-totalitarian countries with private businesses, how owners and managers operated their businesses was unsurprisingly completely a matter for them.

Why should the State assume to itself the power to tell you what to do in your Boardroom any more than it should tell you what to do in your Bedroom? After all it is not as if State Governance is in the

---

[32] Puchniak, Baum, Nottage "Independent Directors in Asia – A Historical, Contextual and Comparative Approach" 2017

[33] Nazi Germany put State representatives on Company Boards. Whilst we do not do that today the State has commanded that "independent NEDs" be on Boards and told them what to do – a difference perhaps of degree but not principle – the principle being "State tells privately owned Company Boards what to do". See Morck "A History of Corporate Governance around the World: Family Business Groups to Professional Managers" 2007

slightest bit impressive these days and super-impressive State-wallahs are simply sharing their superior governance insights and wisdom.

In CorpGovCo world the State hasn't even stopped there. The State goes into major owners' houses and tells them that they *must – whether they want to or not* – vote at your AGM. The consequence of that is even more bizarre and dysfunctional. Although all interviewees had, naturally, heard of Corporate Governance some had not heard of Proxy (ie AGM Voting) Advisers. Most fund managers can't afford to research all the votes for all the companies they own so outsource this task to so-called Proxy Advisers. Estimates are that the two market leaders (ISS and Glass-Lewis) **control 97% of the market.** It's very scary indeed – shockingly undemocratic. Monarchical levels of power over companies all over the world. There are no shortage of troubling issues to be addressed – this summary is from 2012:

"The proxy advisory industry has come under fire for a range of alleged transgressions, such as:

i) providing misguided and ill-informed vote recommendations;

ii) suffering from various conflicts of interests;

iii) operating in a virtual black-box bereft of transparency and free from regulatory oversight or any external monitoring [Ha! The irony!];

iv) taking a one-size-fits-all approach to corporate governance and certain key voting issues, such as executive compensation, without taking into account the specifics of each company;

v) making decisions that affect a company's vote outcome even though these proxy advisors, unlike company managers, owe no fiduciary duties to the company or its shareholders who are affected by their decisions [!!!];

vi) making substantial voting decisions without bearing a concomitant share of the risk; and

vii) wielding significant influence over the vote outcomes of billions of shares at company shareholder meetings both in the U.S. and abroad."[34]

---

[34] Belinfanti "Re: Comments on Concept Release on the U.S. Proxy System; File No. S7-14-10 letter to SEC" 2012

As per (iv) above the Proxy Advisers can't research all the issues so just apply yet more cookie-cutter, business-PC templates to issues. Doh! Proxy Advisers are agents of neo-liberal neo-colonialism, forcing their one-size-fits-all perspectives upon nations around the world far more aggressively than the EIC who for a century and a half merely traded (and even after that strongly resisted the British government's desire to change Indian social customs). In a notable case involving India's largest mortgage lender HDFC two Board members were forced to step-down[35] as they did not meet ISS's dot-to-dot manual of What Is Right.

The sheer weight of regulation and State intrusion into *how* you conduct your Board meetings and now into what *institutional owners* Must Do would have been utterly inconceivable to any of our business ancestors over the past four thousand years. As an interviewee bemoaned:

> "It has become a religion there is no way you can criticise it." [BigCo/SmallCo NED]

Religions of all sorts give history a good makeover, and much counter-Cadbury comment is well and truly buried by now. In some cases one cannot even find the original critiques just summaries of the critiques (here is some samzidat to read behind the bike sheds[36]).

---

[35] See Sinha "Proxy advisors: Boon or bane for corporate governance?" 2018

[36] One of the most substantive was that it was a determined and successful attempt to draw fire away from auditors. Another angle is that it created Angels and Villains. The following abstracts FTSE CEO John Corrin's article "A blatant slur on executive directors' integrity" [Corrin in "Accountancy" April 1993]: *"This article presents the author's view on the Cadbury report on corporate governance in Great Britain. It is a political document designed to provide a convenient whitewash for some embarrassing failures by a number of people and institutions in an area that has become known as corporate governance, and is so removed from reality that it can only be the predictable weight of establishment acceptance that has muted criticism. It is, I have say, a blatant slur on the integrity of the hard-working, committed and dedicated executive director. The whole report is like a script for a soap where the non-executive director is cast as saint, the auditor is a tarnished guardian angel, and the executive director is a villain. Yet such a notion has no basis in reality or research. Every single corporate scandal that gave rise to the need for the report in the first place was riddled with non-executive directors. Some of the highest salaries have been fixed by remuneration committees. In fact, salaries tend to be higher where a remuneration committee operates. Yet the suggestion that remuneration committees are essential to good corporate governance does not surprise me: it is in line with implication that executive directors are far too irresponsible to review their own salaries or to make any proper decision whatsoever."* http://connection.ebscohost.com/c/articles/6075992/blatant-slur-executive-directors-integrity

As to the codes themselves:

> "I have a lot of sympathy with the view that the Code is obeyed by people who are carrying on in business with integrity anyway, and ignored or implemented superficially by those who are not." [experienced NED]

Maybe another few dozen codes will fix it? After all we have only had 25 codes to date. Maybe another hundred regulators. Maybe more Statism will finally lead to Stalin's wet dream, the ability of the centre to pull all the strings of everyone as puppets. Maybe. Or maybe not.

In the meantime maybe V3 is not catching on? The 2019 Milken Institute's Conference presented data showing that between 2000 and 2018 Private Equity-backed companies in the US rose from 2,000 to just under 8,000 whilst publicly-listed companies fell by an astonishing amount from 7,000 to around 4,000.[37]

My money is on the V4 Company to fix all this. However, as it requires a Queen to be on the throne to ensure the creation of new versions of The Company (to date Elizabeth I, Victoria, Elizabeth II) we may have to wait some time.

Constitutionally, what the governance structure amounts to in V3 is utterly unclear to me. What is the constitutional role of the Board in a V3 Company?

ChartCo had a legislature which was *solely* about owners with substantial powers and direct sources of information not filtered by management, voting on the direction of the company. ChartCo had an executive which was *solely* about Directors managing the business. There was a clear separation of roles (even if, as you can imagine, over the centuries plenty of boundary disputes).

V2/V3 Boards are constitutionally a very strange interstitial beast being neither fish nor fowl. The modern V2/V3 Board is almost but not quite a *legislature* as the AGM, as well as being an (ill-informed) electorate, retains vestigial legislative powers for super-big-picture decisions. Nor is the Board an *executive* – the Court of Committees ran the EIC day-to-day they didn't just cover a few super-high-level business topics now and then.

---

[37] Tett "The Surprising Rise Of Private Capital" FT 20/5/19

In so-called "super-majority" Boards, in essence, you have a Prime Minister (CEO) in front of the National Audit Office but a NAO with powers to sack the PM. There is an extent to which "constitutional confusion" applies in today's V3 Company in a similar way to the constitutional confusion surrounding the position of regulators – are they under the traditional triangle of legislature/executive/judiciary or are they a fourth corner in a new square?[38]

We can also note that *some* of V3's development is being taken-up by some current V2s. One key example for maturing SmallCos is "sub-committee-isation" – splitting off matters such as Audit, Remuneration, Risk et al into Board sub-committees. In a century or two it will be easier to look back and make a simple "good/bad idea" assessment. In practice in your SmallCo today these may or may not help. On the upside sub-committee-isation ensures that Corporate Control functions are not clogging up the main agenda which should always have a very large dash of Corporate Creativity. On the downside it does mean that all Directors are not directly exposed to key conversations and information.

Corporate Governance was never something UnlistedCos needed to worry about until they started to approach the Floating World. However in the UK in 2019 the bureaucrats' landing craft arrived on the shores of SmallCo land.

UK CORPORATE GOVERNANCE REACHES INTO UNLISTED COMPANIES

"The ever-increasing burden of regulation." [Chairman, not in Fintech]

Eisenberg's 1976 "The Structure of the Corporation: A Legal Analysis" was seminal in the creation of Corporate Governance. **It held that closely controlled unlisted companies were fundamentally different from the widely-diversified-ownership pattern of listed companies** *and thus should be governed differently*. This is a view that has held for decades. However the FRC,[39] recently fired from overseeing account-ing after doing an appallingly bad job, says "nah" to all that and the

---

[38] Empirically it varies – some act as if they are under the triangle, others act as part of a square.

[39] The Financial Reporting Council – i/c UK Corporate Governance.

2019 Wates Code covers both ListedCos and "large" UnlistedCos. The ever-expanding self-created remit of the Administrative State.

The following interviewee comment is super-ironic given that accountancy and auditing failures are at the heart of many (most/all?) of the collapses that led to the creation of the Corporate Governance supernova:

> "[Wates is] all the rage with accountants doing frequent presentations on it hoping for consultancy work to comply. I think the accountants are complaining about the lack of new complex regulations since GDPR, nothing to sink their teeth into or their hands into business' pockets." [NED who is a Chartered Accountant]

Despite the usual protestations that the report writers "conferred widely" it was clearly not wide enough to catch this super-busy and super-successful founder:

> "Had not heard of it. Just Googled and read it. What a lot of old waffle." [founder/CEO]

The Wates Code has six principles: "Purpose and Leadership", "Board Composition", "Directors' Responsibilities", "Opportunity and Risk", "Remuneration", "Stakeholder Relationships and Engagement".

Companies captured by the Wates Code must report on their Corporate Governance Code compliance, on their engagement with "stakeholders" and with employees.

Amazingly – or amusingly if you are in wry-mode – it doesn't just define "large" UnlistedCos in one way but *three different ways*! Who makes this stuff up?

"Large" in the context of *needing to report on how you engage with your employees* is "any company with more than 250 employees".

Re reporting on *your governance arrangements* "large" means either (i) more than 2,000 employees *or* (ii) a turnover of more than £200 million, and a balance sheet of more than £2 billion.

Re reporting on *how you consider stakeholders* you are "large" unless you meet two out of three of the following criteria: (i) turnover under £36m, (ii) balance sheet under £18m, (iii) fewer than 250 employees.

I hope you've remembered all that.

But hang on what's this "stakeholder" lark? Where did that come from and what's it got to do with my SmallCo? Good question well presented.

Stakeholder engagement is a requirement under Section 172 (S172) of the 2006 Companies Act. Under Wates large (well the third way of measuring large) SmallCos are obliged to do it. It's one of the most pernicious leaks of Corporate Governance into SmallCo land. The power of the unelected bureaucrat to tinker with the means of production *for the whole economy* is truly staggering.

It isn't just codes you have to watch out for thus for example "The Companies (Miscellaneous Reporting) Regulations 2018" amends CosAct2006 and so is in effect A New Law (to which the Wates Code presents itself as the helpful way of complying).

Let's just have a quick look at S172:

> "S172 ... imposes on a director the duty to 'act in a way he considers, in good faith, would be most likely to promote the success of the company for the benefit of its members as a whole' and, in so doing, to have regard to a series of factors listed in the section which refer to the promotion of social, environmental and governance objectives."[40]

The IOD outline how S172 de facto *legally redefines of the goals of The Company per se*. Whether you agree with it or not it is a massive change in what Directors are supposed to be there for (and what the Company is assumed to be there for):

> "S172 is a part of the section of the Act which defines the duties of a company director, and concerns the 'duty to promote the success of the company'. What is noteworthy about S172 is the diverse range of stakeholders whose interests are said to feature in the "success of the company' – shareholders, employees, suppliers and local communities affected by company activities are all included."[41]

---

[40] Tsagas "Section 172 of the UK Companies Act 2006: Desperate Times Call for Soft Law Measures" 2017

[41] IOD "Corporate governance reporting under Section 172 of the Companies Act" 2006

S172 is a nightmare but the relevant laws as a whole are a bit of a dog's dinner (imagine my surprise). On the one hand there you are documenting how you have considered Gaia in your latest Directorial decision about photocopiers and the date of the Xmas party yet S172 cannot overrule pre-existing law on Directors responsibilities. As the IOD explain superficially S172 just adds detail to prior requirements that Company Directors be "fit and proper" persons and conduct their business activities fairly, however this is not the case:

> "Having 'Regard' for Stakeholders: S172 defines company success as promoting the interests of shareholders while taking account of a diverse group of stakeholders. From this arises the challenge for a company director to demonstrate regard for stakeholder interests which may conflict with what might be best for shareholders. A simple illustration – A company board concludes that it is in the long term interest of the business to close a production site with 1,000 redundancies. Certainly such a decision may make sense for shareholders, but the 1,000 employees affected will not feel their interests have been served.
>
> Enforcement: The Companies Act 2006 did not change the fact that company directors are (provided they commit no outright criminal act) solely accountable to the company and its members or shareholders. Provided a board can demonstrate that the concerns of various stakeholders are considered as part of a board decision, a class of stakeholders adversely affected by a decision has little recourse against the directors if it cannot secure the support of company members/shareholders."[42]

There is a real tow-truck problem here. The more extraneous content that the non-profit-making, non-entrepreneurial, bureaucratic State chucks in the truck that a company must tow, the slower the company will go as ever more of its resources go into non-profit-making activity and the less profit the company makes. **The principle contribution the Company makes to society is to create wealth for its shareholders and**

---

[42] Ibid.

employees (both of which are taxed) as well as products/services for its customers. Without wealth creation the State would have no tax revenue and no ability to spend all the money that it does.

I recall when ESG[43] reporting came into fashion. I had lunch with a couple of former merchant banking colleagues one of whom was saying what a great thing it was. I was shocked. "Are you mad?", "No" he replied, "I get well-paid, it will go on forever and you get paid great money for a load of waffle." All too often the response to all these things is to just create yet more verbiage for an ever-thickening report and accounts on how you considered the Polar Bear, what used to be called the third world, and whatever else is de rigueur business-PC to care about in every decision.

Despite a zeitgeist of media moaning, which only ever increases as its profits decline and as clickbait mutates into hatebait, about how terrible everything is the opposite is the case. It is easy to overlook the success and impact of technological change and international trade's impact on levelling-up in the past two centuries. If I get elected Global Fascist Dictator I'll have a full inbox and be a busy guy changing stuff, but I would keep in mind that, *compared to every period in the past*, **the current system is succeeding beyond anyone's wildest dreams:**

> "In the last quarter century alone more than 1.25 billion people escaped extreme poverty... In 1820, only 60 million people didn't live in extreme poverty. In 2015, 6.6 billion did not."[44]

Corporate Governance is the child of a regulatory world. **One of the most pernicious aspects of the rules & regs supernova is that the impact falls disproportionately on SmallCos. Regulation is *the single* factor most responsible for keeping Corporatism in place.** When I had to do some tedious economics exam in the 70s the presiding theory was of "dis-economies of scale". Which still exist. However, since then an opposite and greater force has served to keep BigCo ruling the roost.[45] As the

---

[43] Environmental, Social and Governance

[44] www.HumanProgress.org

[45] And lobbying, funding political parties and being involved in the technical creation of yet more laws and regulations. Hey, hang on – do you think all of these might be connected?

Economist[46] pointed out many big firms survive because of government red-tape and regulation whose relative burden is multiples higher on SmallCos. Every time there is a new regulation or code BigCo just hires a few more bodies for its compliance department. SmallCos cannot keep up. The Hampton Report[47] was produced for the Chancellor as far back as 2005 (since when regulation has only ever increased):

> "The regulators ... carry out more than 3 million inspections each year. The national regulators covered send out 2.6 million forms for businesses to complete every year; reliable figures are not at present compiled for local authorities. This burden is felt most heavily in smaller businesses. A recent NatWest survey claimed that a business with two employees spends over six hours per month per employee on Government regulation and paperwork, while a business with over 50 employees spends only two hours per employee. Research by the OECD suggests that the same is true internationally, with businesses with fewer than 20 staff bearing a burden five times greater than businesses with more than 50 staff."

Anyway if you are in SmallCo land I am preaching to the choir – you know what a burden it all is and how costly it is to implement.

I have been immersed for many years in the London world of Tech Startups/ScaleUps. I have spoken to well over a hundred of London's greatest founders and entrepreneurs on the podcast and far more off it. As a result I am intimately acquainted with how *immensely* hard it is to succeed in the modern world and the crazy effort and hours that founders have to put in, often just to avoid going under the water for the third time. Few companies can succeed and in Fintech even those that "succeed" are generally making losses. There is absolutely a complex and nuanced conversation to be had about how one restrains MegaCos and how one makes sure they don't cause social harm. This is a conversation that has been – rightly – going on for centuries and shows no sign of terminating (the 2019 bleeding edge being the imposition by "social" media platforms of their politics on global conversations). However, SmallCos get disproportionately beaten-up by regulation when it is

---

[46] The Economist "Our Schumpeter columnist pens a dark farewell" 20/12/16
[47] Hampton "Reducing administrative burdens: effective inspection and enforcement" 2005

hard enough for them to simply make a profit let alone rescue Gaia and usher in a New Age.

Still it's the realpolitik so we have to proceed regardless – you can always vote for a party that opposes this regulatory supernova, this ever-expanding soft despotism. Or can you?[48]

Back to the Wates Principles – maybe you should become an LLP? After all – utterly bizarrely – although Wates applies to Large Private Companies it does not apply to Large Private LLPs (?!):

> "UK-incorporated companies (but not LLPs) will need to check whether they fall under the relevant tests."[49]

As to the realpolitik of regulation and the new Corporate Governance incursions into your territory:

> "You have to do the Corporate Governance stuff. But if you just do that you will fail your company." [Experienced AIM Chairman]

Even this tiny glimpse gives you an idea of how the State is tightening the noose on SmallCo as well as BigCo in many ways, "Corporate Governance" these days isn't just some "load of old waffle" in "codes" but is increasingly The Law.

Sociologically it is "interesting" how docile people and businesses are these days. Our V1 and V2 predecessors would have thrown a wobbly and stopped all this in its tracks. These days everyone just goes along with ever increasing micromanagement and interference. Trend growth continues to decline in Europe. Which isn't surprising is it?

THE GOALS OF THE COMPANY 16ᵀᴴC–20ᵀᴴC

> "The clauses as to the management of the company I pass over, because the management we leave to the companies themselves.

---

[48] Good luck with that one. Quangos (or as they have been somewhat rebranded, NDPB's – Non-Departmental Public Bodies) in the UK employed 111,000 people in 2009. Cameron came in promising a bonfire of the Quangos (which at the time he said cost the country just under £70bn). The net effect of which was that their number increased.

[49] Linklaters "Corporate governance for private companies" June 2018

Having given them a pattern the State leaves them to manage their own affairs and has no desire to force on these little republics any particular constitution."[50]

Returning to Aristotelian *goals*, "we have companies because...?" is a question that we haven't covered so far. Although it's worth a book of its own let's just sketch out a few simple features of the terrain. For most of the last five centuries the "because" would have been relatively obvious.

The V1 Company had been formed as the needs of long-distance trade required a different form of "business together" from the pre-existing Guilds.[51] The capital investment in voyages around the world required the pooling of capital and ultimately the creation of far-off infrastructure meant that long-term pooling of capital was necessary. This "together" structure and its internal organisation, governance and so forth proved so successful that its use expanded well beyond the initial far-off trade impetus. If you like, it is the same phase shift as that from unicellular to multi-cellular life. Before amoebas had, as it were, banded together but now they formed a new organism per se.

The designers of the V2 Company, liberals in the true 19ᵗʰC sense of the word, had a clear concept in mind for The Company. This section's lead-in quote is from Vice-President of the Board of Trade Lowe's seminal parliamentary speech introducing the concepts of a Memorandum and Articles of Association and the need to produce an annual Balance Sheet. They put their trust and not so much delegated authority to, but left it where it comes from, the people to manage their affairs as they see fit as Lowe explained:

"When those articles appear to the persons who have signed the articles of association to be applicable to the company, they may be adopted bodily without any expense; but if it should turn out that those rules are not applicable to a particular company, the company will have the power of filing a document with their memorandum of association, either specifying the whole code which they have

---

[50] Hansard "Law Of Partnership And Joint- Stock Companies" 1/2/1856

[51] As with the Guild the early Company was used for a wide range of things including notably colonisation. We shall mention in the next section the seminal importance of the Virginia Company's governance.

agreed upon, or enumerating such of the rules as they do not adopt, and giving those which they substitute for them. There is no compulsion, therefore, in the matter. We leave companies to form their constitutions as they please."

"We have Companies because…?" when I started my career would, for most, have had a simple O Level answer such as "Just as with ant societies our societies need the sourcing of raw materials, construction, production and distribution. Empirical results have shown that privately-owned businesses structured as Companies are the most efficient means of this. Furthermore, the profit they generate is taxed and the wages they pay are taxed and these taxes are needed to fund the State and its provision of hospitals, education, the military and so forth." Let's call this the "traditional" view.

The important point to note, much forgotten or ignored as inconvenient in our "nothing wrong with globalisation, move along, move along" times is the importance of social context. *The context of the Company has always been the society it existed within and its culture –* the unwritten rules of governance.

To take a V1 example, the EIC at times were even concerned about the reputation of their investors/members! In many ways it was concern with that old-fashioned word honour:

> "When the court of committees discovered that a Company adventurer was buying pepper and then adulterating it before selling it abroad in Naples, they 'held it to be a great deceit, wrong, and scandal to the Company, disgrace, discredit, and disparagement to this nation.' Despite the merchant's claims that 'he had done the like before, and it was well accepted and went current without any exceptions in those parts where it was sold,' the court of committees, 'to maintain the honor of the kingdom and Company,' impounded his pepper and admonished him to be 'so mindful of his own reputation as not to force those things to public notice.' In other words, lack of consideration of his private reputation would have public consequences for the Company."[52]

---

[52] Mishra "A Business of State – Commerce, Politics and the Birth of the East India Company" 2018

And people have the temerity to attack our ancestors for lack of business ethics! It is we as a society and as some businesses who have abandoned ethics.

When I started my career most UK V2s had as an unwritten governance rule the creation and preservation of employment. In a world of lifetime employment sacking people was bad news for them and a loss of face not a business technique for the company. In the stockmarket I remember being told there were "income shares" and "growth shares". The former just paid a dividend and could never be expected to go anywhere (eg Banks) whilst the latter could be expected to gain in value. All that was about to change with the 1980s seeing the introduction of a much greater focus on "shareholder value" along with the crazy notion that "everything must grow all the time" and employees became "human resources". All of this is a nice simple case study that shows that Companies and their governance *never* exist in a vacuum but always in a cultural context.

THE 21ˢᵗC COMPANY – IF YOU ABANDON CULTURE AND CULTURAL RESTRAINT WHAT THEN?

This shift in the culture was to go further with a "neoliberal"/"globalist" abandonment of seemingly any substantive cultural restraint or even recognition of culture. Not just employees became disposable commodities but there was no need to concern yourself with your customers well-being – after all they make their choices [a weak point in the argument given infinite marketing spend] and the Company is *solely* a mechanism for delivering goods, just a machine.

Brian mentioned in the Foreword the disgraceful behaviour of some 21ˢᵗC Banks – *just to make more money*. 21ˢᵗC food manufacturers design and push junk food *just to make more money* which leads to skyrocketing rates of obesity and diabetes, an appallingly cruel condition in its consequences. Drug manufacturers covered up 40% of the data on SSRIs *just to make more money*. The mainstream media (MSM) treats all but its favourite politicians with hostility and contempt. This ensures that fewer and fewer talented people go into politics and around the world we end up with ever-more thick-skinned, narcissistic and self-righteous politicians sometimes to the point of sociopathy. The MSM foment anger, discord, polarisation and distress in society *just to make more money*. It is not hard to think of examples in many economic sectors where the realpolitik is "it's legal, what's your problem?" *just to make more money*.

Let's have a brief look at the impact of four schools of thought on the traditional view of the goals of the Company – neoliberalism, Corporate Governance, the Church of the Woke and the revival of the socialism word.

On the plus side 1980s **"neoliberalism"** restored a focus on profitability and economic vigour compared to complacent, sleepy post-war managerialism. On the negative side ignoring your impact on society as a whole is the act of a psychopath.

"Neoliberalism" as a globalist concept must de facto ignore the role of culture as pre-neoliberalism corporate culture varied from country to country. It took me some time to spot that "the influence of foreign capital", a phrase often used about the globalisation of the City post Big-Bang, was a euphemism for "those Yanks don't behave like proper chaps". This was super-important as British reliance on unwritten rules, British conventions of behaviour and so forth would no longer work. Naturally, if people won't follow unwritten rules you have to start writing them down. Naturally, as the dominant global empire, US corporate culture has led the way. From the 1980s onwards this meant "profit at all costs" (it was not thus in the 1950s/60s) with corporate raiders, junk bonds, asset stripping and so forth. In extremis the apotheosis of such neoliberalism is the nigh-on evil **Ethicless Corporatism**. MegaCos making loads of money for the management and shareholders but screwing society.

Higher levels of business gambling and consequent collapses led to **Corporate Governance**. This provided a mechanism for easy tinkering with the Company's means and ends. As the V2/V3 Board is unprincipled (it lacks a clear constitutional role) it has proved relatively simple for new governance goals (often in the guise of means) to be written onto the palimpsest. It is thus no surprise that, *compared with every prior version* of the Company, V3 and its governance is becoming a hotchpotch lacking a simple, clear, agreed goal and a simple, clear, effective means towards such. Naturally, the more that later writing on the palimpsest departs from earlier writing the more it is held to be gospel truth of all time. A notable example of this principle is the notion that "a Board exists to monitor management" which is a very new gospel truth indeed.

In regulating, all too often, the means seem to have mutated into becoming the de facto goal. By now whatever was at the heart of the snowball is almost completely irrelevant, the manifest phenomenon is the gathering of ever more snow and ever more size. Corporate Governance is an example – the seed was "oh dear, BigCos appear to be crashing too much, let's beef up the Boardroom". Which was fair enough. But by now Corporate Governance reports are on politically fashionable concerns such as gender and ethnicity – way, way away from the original mandate and concept for Corporate Governance and the Company. In the guise of amending *governance means* the unelected regulators are actually changing *Company ends*. In the case of considering "pre-birth biochemistry" and the Board it moves a long way from "the Company as an efficient means of production" and a long way towards a Stalinist desire to enforce a centrally-approved pattern upon the whole of society.

The **Church of the Woke** educated at US colleges in the art of griev-ance and revolution have found it relatively easy, just like Palpatine to manipulate a maxarchistic State. Many Ethicless Corporates (especially in the US) have been only too keen to sign up for a package that makes them *appear* moral at quite a small cost and no substantive change to their business model. The woke's goal is a post-Marxist centrally-controlled society [relationship to Corporate Governance[53]]. In the case

---

[53] A seminal article was "Socialist Strategy Where next?" (1981) in Marxism Today. Its title says a lot about the *crise de confiance* in the socialist left at that time. Communism everywhere was a clear disaster and children were no longer up chimneys. In the early 80s the radical left needed a new cause. Marxists/post-Marxists were trying to wriggle their way out of the "single-axis framework" (oppressor capitalist, victim worker): *"To what extent has it become necessary to modify the notion of class struggle, in order to be able to deal with the new political subjects – women, national, racial and sexual minorities, anti-nuclear and anti-institutional movements etc – of a clearly anti-capitalist character, but whose identity is not constructed around specific 'class interests'?"*

Anyway you know where it went – the Democrats and Labour party lagged behind socialist theory but eventually caught up – goodbye working man, working-class-based politics, and hello to metropolitan woke middle-class-based politics: hello to race, gender and sexuality-based politics. The above quote presciently points the way to recent Corporate Governance reports! Just as well-meaning regulators probably don't know they are channelling the Nazi Party in their approach to the Board I doubt that they realise they are channelling Marxism Today as well. The commonality is no coincidence, however, as per de Tocqueville's soft despotism all three share the mentality of enforcing central-control upon society upon the *"flock of timid and industrious animals, of which the government is the shepherd"*.

of gender "targets", legally-binding in some countries, strong moral persuasion in others, this amounts to **recasting Companies as a tool for social engineering**. A US-college-course-premised "oppressive patriarchy" must be opposed and a post-/neo-Marxist egalitarian utopia must be created. No concern that utopias have always required coercion and always create more harm than good. Concepts that a decade or so ago were solely confined to US liberal colleges are now in Company Law or Corporate Governance. Some people welcome these developments, some do not. As a father of daughters I do not want them treated differently at work or on Boards because of their gender but only because of their hard work and abilities. It is not just me but all other businessmen/businesswomen I have met with just daughters feel the same (parents with daughters and sons I have met don't want their children treated differently and parents of sons just hang their heads; it is only nonparents that I have met who favour discrimination). Furthermore, this is not some "business" thing, leading second-generation feminists (Greer, Paglia, Hoff-Sommers et al) having been in the vanguard of feminism *qua* "equality of opportunity" for decades strongly oppose third-generation feminism *qua* "State intervention to ensure equality of outcome".

Stakeholderism attempted to address the psychopathic nature of "Ethicless Corporatism": a perfectly sensible notion that "hey companies, you know you exist in society don't you? We want you to make a profit as we need your taxes but please don't fuck the world up to do so." Fine, I get it. But try putting that into rules, laws, regulations and you end up with dogs' dinners like 2006 Companies Act S172.

Which, politically, brings us up to now. The Labour party in the 2019 general elections (and some Democrats in the 2020 primaries) whilst fully on-board with post-Marxism retain (as does post-Marxism and the more "watermelon"[54] green/ecological movements) a rabid dislike of private enterprise. Less than three decades since the Berlin Wall came down and Deng Xiaoping focused on the governance effectiveness of cats[55] there are some Western politicians only too keen to

---

[54] Green on the outside, bright red on the inside. Several of the trendy eco movements right now would destroy the economy overnight given half a chance. The UK government is committed to zero emissions which, barring a deus ex machina, will do the same unless abandoned.

[55] "It doesn't matter whether a cat is black or white, if it catches mice it is a good cat" – ie private enterprise methods work and are therefore good.

show they can do State-socialism "properly" unlike the Russians and Chinese who clearly knew little of real socialism.

In summary, not just the means but the ends, the goals of the Company have become a 21stC political football. Tinkering with governance is rarely a good thing – our 20thC tinkering – such as the transformation from limited liability to zero/transferred liability, removal of compulsory corporate wind-up when 75% of the capital has been blown, and the introduction of "share classes" (groan) have only introduced far more peril for society than existed in Victorian V2s.

Constant messing around with the State's implicit definition of The Company's *ends* cannot do anything but make it harder to generate wealth. One decade it's "profit! profit!", the next it's "stakeholderism!" ("be all things to all men!") and the next its some kind of "let's ignore anti-discrimination laws, over-rule meritocracy and instead create a woke, egalitarian utopia". And in all decades it's "follow ever-more rules". As all entrepreneurs know and as the USSR's businesses ably demonstrated, generating wealth is no trivial matter. The State should be rather more bloody careful with changing the Company's destination every other week, and should be rather less casual about lobbing whatever is currently politically fashionable into the tow-truck that they have added onto the Company.

If we constantly monkey around with The Company then we can expect to economically underperform those countries that don't keep tinkering with their microeconomic structures. Corporate Governance has evolved into a conduit, a mechanism that has enshrined constant monkeying around with The Company. I wonder how much more profit businesses might have made in recent decades if Boards weren't dancing to the State's ever-changing tune instead of simply managing their businesses?

ISSUES FOR THE V4 COMPANY DESIGNERS

The abandonment of what I see as very roughly speaking five centuries of relatively agreed means, ends and goals for the Company, of governance structures, written rules and unwritten rules – is hugely problematic for business, the economy (trend growth, wealth creation) and society.

Businesses need a context, a society in which they operate. Interestingly the two apparently antithetical forces have the same net effect. Both the "acultural"/"neoliberal" "who needs culture, business is only about profit and markets sort everything" (which is wrong) and the postmodern multicultural "cultures are incommensurable"[56] (which is correct) have the same failing. They fail to come up with *a* culture, *a* value-system in which business can operate – one says "business is outside of culture" another says "they are all great, how can we choose?" It's another reason I am sceptical of "ethical training". *Whose* ethics?

We can even make that question as narrow as possible. Let's pick two cultural relatives – the US and the UK – a super-similar and super mutually-influential (aka "Anglo-Saxon") business culture. They are not the same. As we shall see in the last Chapter with the example of Fanduel there are two very different value-systems operating.

It is all part of the koan to be solved in the V4 Company. Your freedom to do what you want with your private property needs restoring. The State should stay out of your business as much as it should stay out of your bedroom. You can make this argument on libertarian grounds or microeconomic efficiency grounds. This (as Friedman thought) would also solve the huge problem of many (but not all) oligopolies which are only held in place by regulation.

A necessary condition for the State to stop throwing a zillion random ropes over Gulliver though is that V4 has some proper gene therapy to correct the weak V2 governance template, restore capital buffers, fix the accounting/audit market failure and "transferred liability" nature of the V2/V3. If I become global fascist dictator tomorrow and replace the current system whereby when your dog savages sheep the farmer pays with one whereby you pay I think we can imagine not just you but the whole world's business owners and management will act very very differently.

So far so good. But we are going to have to scratch our heads on the "unwritten rules" piece *which has always dominated business*. This is the hardest nut to crack and I would argue the deepest challenge.

---

[56] Thomas Kuhn is most associated with reviving/expanding an Ancient Greek concept. You have one paradigm, you have another, you can't line them up in correspondence or measure one against another. Eg Chinese medicine has a one paradigm and Western medicine a very different one yet both may help your health.

When countries had cultures with a strong centripetal force (in England historically Christian ethics and a measure of localism or patriotism) we had that important attribute that the seminal 14thC historiographer/ sociologist Ibn Khaldun called *asabiyyah* – social cohesion. In cultures with strong *asabiyyah* (the old City springs to mind) getting people to conform to social ethics was relatively straightforward. However, now business is "very global", as a world we have no *asabiyyah*. In such circumstances, just as with the competitive lowering of governance standards in the early 19thC we see a race to the bottom – just this time a race to the bottom on ethical standards (Fanduel is archetypal).

More generally, when there was a common moral education to inculcate in citizens the *unwritten rules*, the conventions, the *spirit* of how you play the game it was possible to have ethical businesses (Kleinworts was very ethical). This spirit in business has changed dramatically over my career from (roughly speaking and caricaturing slightly) *"play up, play up, and play the game!"*, to all too often *"fill your boots"* and now *"follow those rules"*.

ARISTOTLE REVISITED – COMPANY GOVERNANCE: FROM DEMOCRACY TO COLONIALISM

"The greater the number of owners, the less the respect for common property. People are much more careful of their personal possessions than of those owned communally; they exercise care over common property only in so far as they are personally affected."[57]

Let's pick up from where we left off with Aristotle, namely Jones' comment that democracy *qua means*, to a degree that Athenians would recognise it as such, was never seen again.

The nearest State example I would suggest is Switzerland where, quite unlike the UK where the people have never been enshrined in the constitution as Top Dog, the Swiss people have been since their 1848 constitution. Swiss citizens have a constitutionally defined need to have to approve any changes to the constitution, can have a referendum

---

[57] Aristotle "Politika"

on any law change and may propose changes to the constitution. In effect this means that the answer to "Quis custodiet?" is "cives seipsos" (the citizens themselves). How cool is that? Compare and contrast this with the UK where one private subject, a by-now well known lady with money, or perhaps funders, and a court at hand, has bound the hands of two consecutive PMs. How is that an improvement on a few Barons and a Monarch sorting stuff out a thousand years ago with the peasantry being an irrelevance?

Turning to the V1 Company does in Aristotelian terms the Court of Proprietors and Court of Committees remind you of anything? The Greek Assembly/Council for example with the former fully involved in all substantive matters and judicial matters?

Additionally, in the early EIC the voting system was "one member one vote". I would say that they actually met Aristotle's idea of polity, and that a *demokratia* was again seen in the world (and in the other V1s too). The only difference was that in Athenian terms the Assembly delegated to the Council the day-to-day management for the sake of efficiency. Furthermore, it was a polity and not a democracy in so far as they elected from their midst the most-able to govern on a day-to-day basis in the general good.

I bet very few of you imagined before embarking upon this chapter that the first English companies in the 16thC were next to the only example of true (using our modern terms) "Athenian democracy" and were far, far more democratically governed than the 21stC UK!

Polity was ironically created by an absolute Monarchy and has been ended by what we call a democracy.

Indeed, in terms of democracy as we understand it now Company Governance was in many ways better than the State's Governance at the time – all members voted and the General Court of the EIC contained women – both quite unlike Parliament at the time. The democratic principles of ChartCo were also super-influential as the first roots of modern US democracy:

"As corporations, the companies were empowered by the Crown to govern themselves, and this right was passed on to the colony following the dissolution of the third Charter in 1621. The Virginia Company failed in 1624, but the right to self-government was not taken from the colony. The principle was thus established that a royal colony should be self-governing, and this formed the genesis of democracy in America."[58]

Compared to those early companies, over five centuries later, democracy in the modern company has all-but disappeared. The list of issues that shareholders get to vote on has plummeted from "almost everything important" in the 16thC to "bugger all" in the 21stC. The vast majority of decisions about their Company are made for them by the company's *aristocrats-oligarchs* (delete as applicable).

V2 companies were, from their birth, almost entirely in Aristotle's "column two" ranging from *aristocracy* (rule by the most able in the general interest) to *oligarchy* (rule by the few in their own interest). In the 2006 "updated" Companies Act, UnlistedCos gained the ability to eradicate any sense of those dangerous Athenian ideas as SmallCos are no longer required to bother having AGMs. Those pesky shareholders, pain in the arse, are finally nigh on banished, ostracised. Phew! As far as corporate democracy is concerned in V2 it is ichabod! RIP unlisted corporate democracy.

Three curious things have happened in V3 Governance.

The first is that individual share ownership has collapsed with the rise of fund managers and the increasing size of pension funds. Thus, in governance terms, even ignoring the far fewer items that owners get to vote on *polity/democracy* has thinned-out enormously to be increasingly replaced by *aristocracy/oligarchy*.

The second curious thing is that countries are increasingly mandating that certain classes of large shareholder must vote. This has led to the super-perverse, if entirely predictable, outcome of concentrating a huge amount of US institutions' (and others) enormous voting power on companies *all over the world* into the hands of two companies who simply don't have the time to make wise decisions but dot-to-dot decisions! I think if we explained that one to Aristotle he would label that as *tyranny*. Not good! Bad!

Thirdly, in terms of the composition of the Board that get to decide upon almost all important matters they have mostly, or almost entirely,

---

become aristocrats/oligarchs *who don't live in the city state that they rule over*! **That governance model is colonialism/imperialism** – rule by people not native to the land. Mind you, even that is a bit inaccurate as, taking the Raj as a prime example, the rulers *didn't* "fly in and out" as do the new rulers of the V3 Company, but did actually live in India and the better ones knew quite a lot about it. Now "not living in the country you govern" is essential! **In the V3 Company, distant imperialism has become the essential Governance model.**

De Bono's idea of different coloured "thinking hats" was fashionable for a time. In terms of ListedCo maybe you should buy your independent NEDs some sola topees and hope you get wise and benign *aristocratic* (in the Aristotelian sense) types and not rapacious and self-serving *oligarchical* types.[59] Even if you get good colonial governors, based on everything these aristocrats of the corporate world tell me, exercising wise aristocratic rule is becoming ever-harder as the ever-centralising State produces more and more dot-to-dot manuals constraining their actions. Wisdom is profoundly situational. The more that, say, Britain's Roman Governor had to follow a bunch of orders and protocols written in Rome by people who had never even visited Britain let alone lived in it, the harder it would have been for him to rule well.

THE PHRASE "CORPORATE GOVERNANCE" IS USED

BY MANY PEOPLE TO MEAN MANY THINGS

"Philosophy is a battle against the bewitchment of our intelligence by means of our language."[60]

So after all that complexity of looking at centuries of The Company let's start to get more practical and keep it simple. One of the simple takeaways from my many conversations about the Board is that folks

---

[59] And for all you BigCo NEDs who don't feel like you lead the life of a Viceroy we do rather project onto history what we expect to see. I have forgotten whom but I do recall reading one Viceroy's letter back to his family complaining about the utter tedium of his role, the sheer mechanical repetition of it, his need to remain separated from those he ruled and that he was only doing it out of a sense of duty. Any of those sound familiar?

[60] Wittgenstein "Philosophical Investigations" 1953

use *the phrase* "Corporate Governance" to mean many different things – and rarely the "actual" Corporate Governance Full Monty Real Deal correct exam answer. So let's have a look at *how* people use the phrase so that you become conscious that when someone says "Corporate Governance" to you they may mean some very different things.

ONE. For the majority Corporate Governance was used as if it were **A Thing**, which it is not. Rather it is a complex mess of rules, regulations, common law, statute, listing rules, the company's Articles of Association, Corporate Governance codes, investor guidelines (eg ABI, NAPF, PIRC) let alone Proxy Advisers dot-to-dot books – and that's before we get to matters such as the release of financial information for listed companies, rules for takeovers, competition authorities et al. No doubt I've forgotten a few categories – ask your lawyer, As to codes, I counted 25, but I may have missed some out (all the sources I consulted had). Very pertinently from our perspective **not one of these codes was written by an entrepreneur who created something out of nothing** and therefore not one of them are informed by our situation and this vital part of any economy – the need to create new businesses.

TWO. Others used it as a term for **What You Must Do On The Board** – but again this is nebulous. Directors have legally defined responsibilities and duties but the broader ramifications of Corporate Governance per se vary significantly depending on, inter alia, the listing stage of your company. As we saw, running a SmallCo along BigCo Corporate Governance lines is dangerous as even the State doesn't say that you should (entirely) do that. If you do the Full Monty Corporate Governance Thing on your SmallCo you will tilt your Board far too far towards the Fire Safety Officer *control* direction and away from the essential Promethean *creativity* direction. You will also risk making your Board excessively bureaucratic and focusing excessively on process rather than content.

THREE. Some (especially significant capital providers) used the **phrase as a proxy for a control focus/mentality**, a pretext/justification for conceptualising the Board as *principally* being "overseers of executive management". This is a super-recent late 20thC conception.

FOUR. Some used it to refer to the "**Combined Code**" (the FRC's list of rules and regs) – in a sense the narrowest usage (as much Corporate Governance is now in statute and the various other desk drawers I mentioned).

FIVE. It was sometimes used as a way of indicating an idea that **NEDs represent shareholders**. We will return to this later in our chapter on NEDs however it is clearly impossible in anything other than trivial examples.

Understandably plenty of folks have not wasted much of their lives reading tomes and tomes of rules. Some know more, some know less. Most folks, curiously, didn't seem entirely au fait with 16ᵗʰC business practice, or 19ᵗʰC and thus failed to differentiate between the absolutely vital need to Govern Your Company and "Corporate Governance" per se. They all know far less than you now do about the big picture unless their lives too have been graced with this tome. **Just be aware that everyone does not mean the same thing when they say "Corporate Governance". Often/generally (unless you are speaking to a lawyer) they are indicating an *implicit concept* about the Board's function in a company rather than referring to the zillion rules.**

4. The Board

Let's have a quick recap of the context.

First we sat through a PowerPoint on the Eight Essences of the SmallCo Board – help in growing; SmallCo Boards are not small BigCo Boards; in the 21stC there is a near-species difference between SmallCo and BigCo Boards; CCCs – Concentrated Control Companies – are the governance model for SmallCos; your Board is what you make it *for better or for worse*; SmallCo Boards are founder/CEO-centric; on a bad day they are cauldrons of emotion and finally we reminded ourselves of the absolutely vital role of SmallCos to the economy – yours might feel small, it might be small, but if all these small things did not exist society would be seriously screwed.

Then we watched a documentary about our business ancestors invention of the V1 Company in the 16thC and subsequent development thereof. In the 19thC the V2 was created which, after many updates (many problematic) is the version you bought from Companies House.

And rounding off the context to our Boardroom today we looked at developments in the 21stC and how they are impacting businesses today.

Now we leave all that behind, we close the Boardroom door on the outside world and dive into what it takes for you to create and manage a Board that becomes a major factor in your Company's success. We start this chapter with three key SmallCo governing challenges that come from the hugely long historical process which led to your Boardroom today, the needs for **responsible driving, creating culture** and **not screwing your small shareholders.**

Then we look at how one cultivates a small fire. What role does The Board have in this? Amidst all the Startup chaos and long hours perhaps the last thing you have on your mind is The Board. When you are so busy is it not just some kind of distraction, something you'll have to report to when at first you'd rather report to no-one, some wet blanket, hindrance or at best tedious dress-rehearsal for when you have floated? Or can you make it a turbocharger for your growth?

> "One of the biggest differences between first time entrepreneurs and serial entrepreneurs is that whilst both know that a Board can be a nuisance the latter group know that a well constructed and well managed Board over time is a huge asset."

This quote nicely summarises the heaven and hell of SmallCo Boards:

> "If you are a founder then a Great Board will help you nourish and spread your fire. This will include nourishing you as well as challenging you. A Bad Board will drain you, distract you from the fire and be a contributor to the fire and your firm dying out."

The Board matters far beyond its "legal" must-do aspect. No matter whether you start real (not pro-forma/tick-box) Boarding early or only on a capital raise – when those giving you a few quid will want someone to check that you aren't spending it all on sweeties or fountains in reception – you will at some point have a substantive Board.

If you *deliberately* focus on making it as great as you can at each stage, and if you manage the transitions between stages, your Board over time will repay you and your company many times over. If you don't, you risk ending up with a big headache and in extremis fired from your own creation.

So let's look in a little more detail at *why* you should take the Board seriously as soon as you can and then move on to the practicalities.

As we noted it is super-important to create a Board (and Company) culture that *you* desire. Even if you select Board members for their complementary value-add, without focusing on having a clear **Board culture** in mind, you will find out what happens when, culturally, a semi-random group of people get together in a room. Good luck with that one. Culture involves communication so we take a look at how the same words mean different things to different people.

The Board is not a "set and forget" – it needs to be consciously managed over time from Startup to ScaleUp to Growth to the pre-IPO Board – and each stage comes with its own challenges.

Advisory Boards are becoming A Thing in BigCo as Corporate Governance forces their main Board to become increasingly dot-to-dot and control-focused. Some SmallCos have Advisory Boards – or frequently simply collections of Advisors. Why do they do that?

THREE KEY SMALLCO GOVERNING CHALLENGES

"Recklessness, hubris and greed pretty much sum up our attitude to our precious planet as a species, so it isn't surprising that they are core values for many businesses also." [NED]

The rest of this book zooms in to detailed SmallCo governing but there are three important high-level challenges which are worth highlighting before we start.

Let's call them **responsible driving, creating culture** and **not screwing your small shareholders.**

The First Governance Challenge – "Responsible Driving"

Although we have said that V2 Companies have zero liability it can sometimes be unwrapped in SmallCo and turned into some liability for management – even for those who didn't invest much of their own money. One way that limited liability can be "unwrapped" is by Banks requesting Directors' personal guarantees for loans to the company. Generally in Tech this is avoided by relying on equity funding. Another is that if you are on the Board of Banks, Insurers and the like there are also "unwrapping" powers that the regulators have in terms of "authorised institutions" and the Orwellian concept of FCA/PRA/et al – "Approved Persons".

Nevertheless, with some attention to avoiding red lining the motor, some boy racers in search of death (for others) or glory (for themselves) can actually drive the darn thing pretty recklessly. Many do. As we saw, the root problem here is that the State created laws that ensured that if you crash your car others suffer not you.

But let's assume that you aren't some boy racer with your pedal to the metal going for death or glory. In most SmallCos the founders are very emotionally committed to keeping their new car shiny and dent-free. However – and this is obviously a mega-challenge for any Board – when you start to slow the car down before a tricky bend can be a matter where reasonable people differ. How many months cashflow should you have before embarking upon a raise? Furthermore, as next to every SmallCo finds out along its journey, some raises are touch and go and you have moments when you think that you will crash unless the Fates intervene on your behalf.

In practice some/many founders can succumb to something of a gambler's mentality: "I've spent so much time, energy, emotion at this game there is no way I can afford to lose". This can cause excessive risk-taking if things are going badly – "hit the hyperspace button" – which is where, ideally, the Board is a useful restraint. We shall discuss later a particular example of once the founders shirts were on the table they decided to just keep gambling. One of my interviewee NEDs was on such a Board – what would you have done in his shoes when it became apparent that "death or glory" was the unspoken motif?

THE SECOND GOVERNANCE CHALLENGE – "CREATING A CULTURE"

Responsible driving is just one example of the importance of culture. Culture is of supreme importance in a society. Multiculturalism is generally these days a substitute word for multiracialism. In the strict sense however all cultures have always been multicultural, the Lords of the Manors would have had a totally different culture from the peasants who worked their estates. For all the current fetishisation of multi-culturism, *asabiyyah*, unity is also of supreme importance. It is the same in your business – your salesmen are likely to have a different culture from your techies but you need to create unity at the company level. I have seen plenty of companies where the centrifugal forces of multi-culturalism set one division against another, one department against another. Vice versa excessive centripetal force – be it "command and control" or groupthink fails to leverage everyone's creative force and will lead to poor adaptability in the face of change. The same applies to the Board which we shall consider in more detail later.

Attitudes to crashing cars – bankruptcy – are culturally-determined. More often than not, *in the UK*, founders' over-investment of blood, sweat and tears makes them avoid crashing their car. However business culture is different in the US where bankruptcy is widely perceived as a learning experience and a "business technique". There are around 50,000 bankruptcies per annum where, due to State-sanctioned techniques, the guilty parties "socialise" (ie fob off) the errors of their ways. Ask the current US President who has filed for bankruptcy for his companies on six occasions.[1]

Another prime example of the supreme importance of Board culture is the simple question "Why did the Corporate Governance revolution start when it did?". After all, the Company did not suddenly change substantially. An FT survey of 20[th]C UK corporate scandals contained *none* from the 1950s and 1960s. In the US, post-WW2, the much-criticised system of "managerialism" worked exceedingly well:

> "...scandals, while not unknown, were the exception to the rule as senior executives of U.S. public companies refrained for the most part from taking personal advantage of their position as stewards of corporate assets."[2]

Why were there no scandals when Boards weren't following *any* of the modern "Business PC" Corporate Governance approaches? Simply put because culture – in this case a post-War "we are all in this together" mentality[3] trumps everything. This was to be replaced by "fill your boots" and Gordon Gekko's "greed is good". In the absence of society (at large or in your company) having a "North Star" it can all too easily drift into every group/man for themselves. Eastern Asian Confucianism offers the countervailing mentality and a clear North Star is an ethos centred on the *responsibilities* to the group not the *rights* of the individual:

> "The eastern experience suggests that board leadership and board-level culture, in other words people and the way they behave, are more important than board structures and structures, rules and regulations."[4]

---

1 www.thoughtco.com/donald-trump-business-bankruptcies-4152019
2 Cheffins "The Rise of Corporate Governance in the U.K.: "When and Why" 2015
3 And possibly more Christian in their value-system?
4 Tricker, Mallin "Rethinking the Exercise of Power over Corporate Entities" 2010

In the EIC the auditors were company *employees*,[5] not "independent" in any modern sense, but did a far better and more honest job than any modern "independent" auditor. How come? Culture.

There is no substitute for a good culture. It has been central through-out history *and is not replaceable by any amount of rules and regs*. It is not replaceable by sending executives on ethics courses.

The great thing about SmallCo land is that *you get to define/create the culture you want* and hire/train/mould in that image.

SmallCo *is* your "mini-kingdom". You create the company's culture and you must create a Board culture too no matter how senior/experienced your NEDs are. One should not be overawed by important NEDs with impressive CVs – they may be great but they have lived in different companies (mini-kingdoms) and the cultures they lived in may or may not overlap more or less with what you are trying to create. As all founders know if you are not proactive at creating your vision and values others will create them for you – they will happen by default not design.

The Third Governance Challenge – "Not Screwing Your Small Shareholders"

If the BigCo governance challenge is stopping management making merry at the expense of widely-dispersed absent owners then in SmallCo the problem is simply the possibility of the tyranny of a majority (ie those with a large measure of control). The majority are most likely represented in the Boardroom, or about to be if contributing significant funds, and thus are in a much stronger position to dictate terms. The Achilles heel of Concentrated Control Company governance is that the little guy can easily get screwed. This happens all too often especially given the invention of "share classes" which allow you to create a feudal society amongst your capital providers. A nice feudal analogy might be the Shogunate in Japan where the A shareholders (the ruling samurai) were allowed to test the sharpness of their swords by chopping the heads off B shareholders (the peasants). If you have been around for a while you will have heard about or seen for yourself such a Shogunate in some parts of SmallCo land.

---

[5]   All employees of the EIC were called servants. We've all been there. From this word we
get the phrase civil servant (as opposed to military servant).

I recall being told in the early days of crowdfunding about C, D shares out there – no doubt one day we will get to Z. It is not as if this is like old-fashioned railway carriages – luxury, acceptable and uncomfortable – *at least they all got to the same destination at the same time.* Vice versa different classes of share may well have different dividends, voting rights, values in a sale, and entitlement on a wind-up.

Share classes are just entry-level jiggery-pokery. There are a whole bunch of clever rinky-dinks as well as pre-emption rights, tag-along/voting-rights/consents and other kinds of sorcery which the professional investor will almost always have but the naive investor who "just bought some shares" may not. It is a prime example that increasing complexity in the Law *always* benefits the rich and powerful.

Now the chances are that if you are reading this you understand many of these things. But for sure most of the population do not. Also busyness is a real issue for the modern person. You may have noticed. As an example I *intended* to look at the terms and conditions of a Monzo crowdfunding raise but I never had time and just invested anyway, *assuming* that they, being relatively blue-chip in the sector wouldn't be excessively screwing me over. But as to pre-emption rights or other rinky-dinks – it would probably take me some time to find out whether I have them or not. An infamous example is that of Eduardo Saverin, an early investor in The Facebook who owned 30% of the company but who lacked pre-emption rights. His tale is depicted in the film "The Social Network". Long story short via the issuance of new shares to new investors he was diluted down to 0.5% whilst Zuckerberg's percentage ownership remained the same.

One example of this which led to super-corny headlines[6] was Camden Brewery. In 2015 it raised £2.3m from 2,127 folks from "the crowd". It then promptly sold a 20% stake to a Belgian family at a valuation one-third lower. This was window-dressed as being at the "same price" but as so often in "special deals for the powerful large shareholders" rinky-dinks meant that the small shareholder was being screwed.

The average punter no doubt takes comfort from the fact that crowdfunding platforms – the principle conduit with over £1bn raised in the UK to date – are regulated. But this assumes that the regulator does

---

6 "A Bitter Taste for Camden Town Brewery Crowdfunders?" altfi.com

what its remit is – protect the consumer. However, to this pre-emption rights point Crowdcube who describe themselves as *"Europe's largest community of equity investors"* not only allow B shares but *"Most companies do not offer pre-emption rights for B Investment Shares."*[7]

Matters such as B shares, which just invite "differential treatment" (ie abuse), are ultimately a regulatory failure. It would be super-simple for the regulator to say "A shares only, boys and girls". If the regulatory problem I have presented to date has been the excess quantity of regulation this in a way indicates the timidity of many/most regulators and reluctance to take simple bold actions. Regulators prefer multiplying minutiae to bold moves. The problem is in this sense one of politics and legitimacy. Politicians in theory should take bold actions – and are voted in or out. Regulators are part of the civil service (in reality if not in name) and act in the same way. Regulators could also ask to see what percentage of the profit forecasts of crowdfunding companies were met – but they don't. The last stat I saw about one platform was something crazy like 99% of companies failed to meet their targets – this is shocking if unsurprising.

A further device which is used to disadvantage the small investor is the SSA (Subscription & Shareholders' Agreement). Let's zoom up to the big picture to see where this fits in. In the Chartered Company the Charter was the constitution of the Company. In a Company Law Company there are three formative documents. A Memorandum of Association, a form IN01 (modern bureaucracy-speak really lacks any sense of poetry) and the most substantive, the Articles of Association. This defines the constitution of your "mini-kingdom". Key constitutional items are the powers of Directors, decision-making processes, appointment and removal, indemnity and insurance, shares, General meetings, Voting Rights and so forth.

The Articles can be changed by a Special Resolution of an AGM/ EGM which gets a 75% vote. This in itself means the small investor is vulnerable and can't take that much comfort from the company's constitution when he invests. This is par for the course. Thus the BVCA[8]:

---

7   www.crowdcube.com/pg/risk-36
8   British Private Equity & Venture Capital Association

"In most cases, a venture capital investment will call for a complex share structure and extensive rights... As such, a venture capital investor will usually require the target company to adopt new articles setting out those rights."[9]

Professional investors don't fall for such ruses:

"As soon as you get savvy shareholders there is usually a shareholder agreement which bungs in all the tag along, drag along stuff, and prevents the inbound VC from cleaning up at their expense." [NED]

SSAs[10] are generally[11] between a large investor, the company and its management but may include other large investors. The SSA, being a legal agreement, binds all parties. In effect it sits on top of the Articles in a sense adding provisions/protections which apply *just to that investor alone* – privileges in the ancient sense. In this way whilst they are not *directly* part of the company's constitutional documents they are legally-binding and legally-enforceable. In effect they say "we, the investor get these special goodies and these special protections and you the company submit to these various restrictions *above and beyond your Articles*".

If crowdfunding and VCs are at one end of the Closely Controlled Company spectrum at the other end are the MegaCo CCCs – a prime example being German Bank Capitalism – I think we can assume that the Banks "don't come off worst" in that system either.

This "not screwing your shareholders" was a challenging question for SmallCo Board members. It was challenging as, as outlined above, "special deals for special categories of investor" – which sounds so much more palatable than "screwing the little guy" – is market practice. Furthermore it is entirely legal. Back to ice hockey players – it is hard to fault folks for operating within the rules/law.

---

[9] "Practical law drafting notes to BVCA articles of association for early stage investments" 2017

[10] Or just Shareholders agreements if the Subscription is handled in a separate document.

[11] Seedrs has a unique crowdfunding model in that it aggregates the crowd's investments in a nominee company and, using the same device as VCs, a shareholders agreement which offers special protections and restrains management. Syndicate Room give "the crowd" the same terms as a lead major investor.

Although this is legally a matter for the Board as a whole, in practice some founders were very clear where the buck stops. I didn't have one conversation where a founder blamed his Board for this phenomenon. One practical point was made by a serial founder/VC-savvy interviewee:

> "All too often in these circumstances [of the small shareholders being done-over] the inexperienced founder does not realise that he has quite a lot of power to push-back. Naive founders often simply do not know they can push-back without risking the deal."

And as we shall see later:

> "VCs are trained negotiators, they have done courses, the average founder is not and has not. This too can be a factor in not adequately defending small shareholders rights."

Another founder was very clear where the buck ultimately stops:

> "Ultimately any problem with screwing small shareholders comes back to the founders either not caring or not preparing well. Ideally raises should be done from a position of strength and if they are not then of course the founders plans haven't worked out which is down to them and no-one else. If you have strength you have leverage in the negotiations."

We shall return to this topic in a later chapter where we look at what role a specifically-tasked NED could possibly play in this – someone who is designated as in charge of putting forward the interests of the minority investors in the circumstances:

> "I think that anything that protects shareholders is a good thing as long as it doesn't get in the way of the company to flourish." [CEO/founder]

In the meantime a key defence is a conscientious CEO/founder:

> "As the small investors are my friends and family, or just former colleagues, even though I am a dominant shareholder I make sure

their interests are looked after – I have no desire to screw them over even if the reality is that sometimes on a big raise we have to concede more generous terms than we would wish."

There is no simple answer (which is often what Boards are there for), raising money on bum terms may be the only way to save a company at a certain point. In principle, the Board as a whole is there to look after what is, after all, owned (well in everyday terms) by the shareholders en masse. In theory/law all of the Board *are* there to look after the interests of the shareholders as a whole. In practice, as we shall see later looking at the Realpolitik, this isn't actually what happens – even Higgs in his review flagged this point. On SmallCos the large investors' appointed NED (generally an employee of the investor) is clearly there to look after his own institution's interests. Thus we are back to where we started that, given Company Law, the Achilles heel of CCCs is looking after the interests of the little guy.

WHY SHOULD YOU TAKE THE BOARD SERIOUSLY?

"The main thing a Board needs is balls … if we hadn't had that we would be sunk by now. That and trust."

For legal and regulatory reasons Of Course You Take The Board Seriously As You Have To. However, away from doing what you are told (or at least pretending to), **a "real Board" gives the company the opportunity to access the experience, knowledge, contacts and general savoir faire of individuals who would never work for that firm full-time and who can significantly help the SmallCo grow faster and more sustainably than it would otherwise.**

After countless interviews I truly believe that even if there were no legal/regulatory requirements to have a Board, not long into its journey a SmallCo would hugely benefit from having a well-constituted Board. Serial entrepreneurs that I met, to a man,[12] all prioritised the Board and understood that it was a vital tool to help them be successful.

---

[12] The "serials" were all men.

For those entrepreneurs amongst you – when did you realise that the Board could be a tool to help you? Most inexperienced super-early stage founders I have met understandably view the Board as terra incognita, a bit scary and a can to be kicked down the road. Some view it as pointless:

"Board and strategy in a Startup is nonsense."

"Boards are poorly used by the venture sector in general. At first they tend to be "investors and mates", later "owned by VCs" and all too often have no real independents."

Even in its earliest, pre-raise, pre-external NED phase a SmallCo will gain benefits from having a regular, specific meeting focusing on The Big Picture and stepping away from the day-to-day "fighting in the trenches". I can vouch for this from personal experience a couple of decades back. When in a product-centric company with an astonishingly high average employee level of charm and talent, albeit a low number of staff (one, me) I found it helpful to once a month write a "Report to the Board" and hire a meeting room and go through the report as if at a Board meeting. This was super-helpful. At one's desk one is generally in tactical mode and the tactical always crowds out the strategic. It's why away-days work (sometimes). De Bono probably had a hat for it.

I entered this process of investigating the inside-track thinking that you have to have Boards and, well, maybe they could be helpful. I came out of this process a passionate believer that done well (and with this map you will be far more likely to do it well) they provide oxygen to your flames.

As why and in the next section, what, who, how, when, where and how much are so important let me step away from abstracting and summarising. Thus in my interviewees' own words:

"A good Board can give you invaluable advice you can't afford to pay for."

"The Board is there to facilitate success from the senior management team."

"[It] force[s] you to stop once a month. Challenges you. Supports you." [from a four-decades-plus NED]

"For a first-time entrepreneur there is a set of real challenges – real [external] experience helps enormously."

"When you start to grow you need someone to help you professionalise the firm."

"Depending how you structure a Startup you'll get a wide range of experience. But there will be gaps, blind spots. You need to cover those – the Board can help immensely."

"I didn't realise how important [the Board was] until I had a crisis; how incredibly well designed [Boards are], not having absolute power [as CEO] is good because arm's-length [a forum rather than an individual] can be helpful."

"If no sectoral experience on day one you can have real problems. You must find someone who does – senior person who can sit on the Board. I came from this sector so am better connected on matters such as regulation."

"A Board brings independent oversight, experience, contacts and help dealing with issues – and there are always issues."

WHAT, WHO, HOW, WHEN, WHERE AND HOW MUCH?

WHAT?

"The Board challenges/oversees, provides value-add (mentorship, support, guidance, contacts, know-how) and has to deal with complexity re shareholders."

"The Board should have an evangelical focus."

"A counsel, a sounding board."

"Critical friends."

"Support the CEO & counsel re senior staff, support you, help you see your strengths and weaknesses."

"Access to experience that must understand the journey and help the business keep focused and provide controls around suppliers/customers/investors."

"Backing management and creating value in their own right – have to leverage networks and be evangelists."

"Not 'just numbers', not just 'corporate governance'."

"There's a delicate balance between mentoring/advice and governance – most books are geared to later stage business and hence too focused on governance."

"Structure + tradition + over-engineering will not lead to success."

"Where business has holes, in this firm marketing and Tech, specific skills can really help fill those gaps [advice to help in identifying/recruiting angles]."

"Board's main task is managing funding. Board should focus on 'what do we need to prove to get to the next round of funding?'"

"Helps with endurance, sustainability, fibre."

"Missing skills, for example your company might even be weak on 'pricing' or 'how to get clients'."

"When my co-founder left I found out why I had a Board and why it could be really valuable to me."

"A strong Board keeps VCs in check."

"Easily underestimated is the need to develop partnerships – for example we had to develop one with a custodian bank for client money. Experience on the Board was invaluable in helping with this, keeping us focused on the salient and knowledgeable about hidden dangers."

"One thing I would recommend re Boards is to actually manage them."

"Manage your Board – for young companies you need different teams at different stages."

WHO?

"A smart entrepreneur will recognise he doesn't know everything. Need older and wiser buddies with different skill sets."

"Should bring a different, broader perspective. Need differing skills on the Board – you should seek these out and get them in. Cf being on the Board simply as you provided money."

"Trust is hugely important – trust in them and their advice."

"Surround yourself with good people."

"Young folks who don't have industry-capital would benefit from bringing in the well-connected."

"Bring in rolodexes, super-connectors."

"Make sure you don't just have 'big dick' guys simply demanding results."

"Successful entrepreneurs are the only ones who really know what it's like to be an entrepreneur."

"You don't need a large Board."

"Five no more, you will kill almost dead if eight to twelve."

You are building a Board not a collection of individuals and need to give some thought to it being a **balanced** forum. As we emphasised when talking about NEDs, there are many different types with many different skillsets. Which skillsets do you want? How many people will it take to get them?

> "Hire a balanced Board, avoid getting too many of the same stereo-type; e.g. if you have an industry figurehead, balance them with an ex-entrepreneur."

However, just as with the Beatles and many successful bands there was a view that:

> "A Board needs cultural tension."

Diversity as a word has become hijacked.[13] However, in the traditional sense it is super-important:

> "You need diversity in the real sense – diversity of opinion, experience, perspective."

How?

It's up to you (and your Chairman) to set the tone – after all, as we shall see later in "Uncultured Boards", if you recruit a bunch of folk to your Board there is no reason to assume they will all march in step or dance to the same tune:

> "Board should balance the skills of the company and be complementary."

> "Balance in the Board's skills – help in not being marched off to jail but also allows you to grow."

---

[13] To refer to "biochemical" diversity only (melanin and testosterone/estrogen) and an ideology where there is no diversity of thought just a Manichean division into #RightThink and #WrongThink.

"Don't use them as a reporting tool. Send the docs in advance."

"My Board is incredibly professional, pretty damn demanding."

An interesting "how" is "how professionally should we do it?" especially in the earlier years. One of the best potential "bangs for the buck" is to consider appointing a professional company secretariat. The small number of interviewees who had done this from an early stage were nigh on evangelical about the benefits.

"My hot tip? Get a professional company secretariat. Serious investors want to see governance minutes – this is enormous re due-diligence which is largely lawyers."

"Do invest a few hours/quid each year in getting basic Company Secretarial right (eg Board minutes, Remuneration Committees), it's a huge tick in the box for future due diligence."

"The regulator was super-impressed we could show them an ordered file of minutes since inception done by a professional firm. The impression it created was worth far more than what it cost. It also made it easier for us to keep the basics [of a Board meeting] in order."

When? and Where?

Re "When?" we shall later examine in more detail the various stages on the journey from NewCo to FTSE.

When, or rather how often, Board meetings are held varied a lot across my interviews from monthly, through quarterly to, in NewCos or early Startups, "not yet" and "not really" with, naturally, more meetings when crises hit:

"When your company is small keep the Board small, eg three NEDs is plenty, and in terms of frequency a quarterly Board meeting is plenty."

Where doesn't really matter – I am sure most postcodes would work fine.[14] The main answers being "at the company", "wherever", "sometimes by phone". Telephone contact with Board members individually or collectively emerged as an important Board management technique. One founder whose Board meetings were generally not ideal noted that:

> "Interestingly, when we have ad hoc phone Board meetings it works much better." [CEO]

So don't have a concept that Boarding means that you either Have A Board Meeting In The Boardroom or you don't. Even if formally/legally a "Board meeting" is digital – one did or didn't happen, in reality in terms of interactions and communications there is a practical spectrum in-between that's worth testing out. A lunch or dinner with all the Board will generally not be A Board Meeting but in certain circumstances it may be helpful to meet more informally, "off the record".

> "It rather depends on the stage and complexity – ours right now are quarterly with monthly updates/telecons."

You certainly need to ensure that:

> "You must keep your Board informed – avoid springing surprises on them in a meeting (unless for some reason you are doing this deliberately)."

How Much?

> "I couldn't believe how much they cost!"

An area that it sometimes takes SmallCos some time to get their heads around is a professional approach to setting remuneration rather than a "souk" negotiation (pick a random number on each side and haggle from there, each side trying to move less than the other). Pre-IPO one will probably be in RemCom (Remuneration Sub-Committee) territory

---

[14] Having said that, despite the alleged "laptop lifestyle", in most sectors the majority of Tech Startups are concentrated in London.

but long before that one needs to have some source of market data/advice. This can be particularly acute as I heard in one case of a Board with a sole "independent NED" and otherwise just founders/VCs on the Board. Here strategic weaknesses around professional remuneration processes not having yet been implemented can end up risking generating counterproductive and unnecessary ill-will.

All SmallCos are not the same and all Board compensation packages are not. Ballpark median/average figures from an excellent survey[15] are, for around eight meetings per annum, compensation packages for a Chairman ~£30–40k pa, 0.5–1.0% equity, 2–3 days per month; NED £25–30k, 0.25–0.5% equity, 1–2 days per month. So depending on how many independent Directors you hire a smallish professional Board at market rates is likely to cost roughly £50–100k pa.

Which brings us to some important advice:

"Use them! They shouldn't be there just to drink the tea."

CREATING A BOARD CULTURE: WORDS MEAN DIFFERENT THINGS TO DIFFERENT PEOPLE

Having carpet-bombed you with quotes let's take a step back for a short interlude – not least of which to give you the proper mindset about quotes in general. The variable usage of "standard" or "common" words was something that became increasingly apparent to me across conversations. You can't assume that people use words in the same way that you do.

We are all conned at school. No doubt in many ways but in particular by being told that the dictionary "defines" words. At some point one wonders what this whole dictionary thing is – how can a dictionary define words by using other words – isn't it all entirely circular?

In the real world everyone uses not "the dictionary" but rather their own internal "personal dictionaries" aggregated and evolved over time. Dictionaries might fool you into thinking that "Boards" or "NEDs" or "strategy" and so forth have clear and unique meanings. However, speak to more than a handful of folk and you will soon find that, at a

---

[15] Erevena Salary Survey 2017

minimum, usage differs somewhat and at a maximum people can mean completely different things when using the same word or phrase as we noted with "Corporate Governance".

This matters immensely in terms of your recruitment of Board members as well as the **all-important creation of the right Board culture for you.** One of the "Broken Board" scenarios which we will collect in the last chapter is the "uncultured Board". As always the best defence against such scenarios is having a deliberate design. *Based on your Company's culture and your answer to why, what, who, how, when and where you need to build your Board in your way.* This of course involves plenty of communication.

Let's pick two examples of "personal dictionaries" in action – "challenge" and "strategy".

People's understanding of the simple word *"challenge"* definitely differs. You might, in a game of football – in your terms – "challenge" me for the ball. Which I might interpret as outrageously kicking me up in the air and deserving of a sending-off.

The following quote implicitly assumes (as many people often do hence emphasising this point) that "proper dictionary definitions" both (a) objectively exist and (b) that everyone uses the same dictionary:

> "You really have to differentiate between 'challenging management' vs 'a Board being difficult' – needless to say a dividing line which is often crossed." [experienced VC/NED]

The basic sentiment is correct in principle although sometimes hard to assess or impossible to assess in practice. One Board member's concept of "value-adding challenge" can be another's concept of "rude and aggressive bastard". We all might think that a Board member has a bee in his bonnet which he unreasonably keeps banging on about and should just drop. But six months later when the building is on fire we might find it is we all who were wrong and he was right.

If it's possible to be too tough (on average, over a period of time) it is also possible to be too gentle (especially when the circumstances necessitate robustness).

I recall many moons ago in a gentler age a Group Chairman being asked to fire the Chairman of a subsidiary. All rather delicate. The meeting was arranged and a conversation duly had. After a couple of weeks no-one saw any change in the subsidiary Chairman's behaviour or indeed any reduced tendency to come into the office. So someone spoke to the Group Chairman. "Did you tell him that he is to leave?" "Oh yes, absolutely, no question." A little later said same person went to speak to the subsidiary Chairman. "How was your conversation with the Group Chairman?" "Very pleasant actually." "Anything in particular in it?" "No nothing at all really, I rather wondered why I was there."

Perhaps those genteel days have passed but perpetual aggressiveness or perpetual gentleness/avoidance are the Scylla and Charybdis to be navigated – as is a dead straight course between them where your behaviour is the same on all days. Sometimes you need to err on the "tough" side and at other times (at least in the early SmallCo) on the "love" side.

The gist of what CEOs said to me was pretty common – they wanted both *support* and *challenge:*

"Too much form over content, little challenge."

Challenge also needs to be relevant – one reason to beware the "abstract" concept of a "general" NED. At least some definitely need up-to-date sectoral knowledge:

"Actually they are generally fairly useless discussions – they don't challenge or ask wrong questions based on old [FS] experience." [CEO talking about his Board]

Few CEOs want to waste precious time with a rubber stamp of a Board, but neither do they want kicking up in the air at every meeting (which some were experiencing):

"It got to the stage where the night before a Board meeting my wife knew one was coming up even if I hadn't mentioned it. It became super-depressing."

This is not to say that pressure on these CEOs from the Board was warranted or unwarranted. An under-fire CEO may be under-fire for valid and important reasons. However CEOs' tone was very much about the style, the culture of their Board meetings, through thick and thin not when they were rightly berated for kicking their football through a plate glass window.

Taking a second example of simple words that mean different things to different people let's have a look at *"strategy"*. Being a great fan of "many paths up the SmallCo mountain" I have no desire to shoehorn feedback into The One True Way. There is also the complicating matter that the Board's focus can be very dependent upon the stage of the journey. Thus, for example, the following comment might be seen as the midpoint of "LargerCo" thinking:

> "I'm a purist – strategy is the job of the Board and the CEO is accountable to deliver that strategy."

> "There are different models of Boards around the world but the commonality is – holding management accountable for the day-to-day running of the company and setting the overall strategy for the company."

The bulk of the SmallCo perspectives on "the Board and strategy" differed from the above:

> "Management is responsible for strategy – it needs to be challenged and sanctioned by the Board – no Board member is in a place to originate it."

> "Board doesn't propose strategy but validate, challenge."

> "The executive team does the strategy."

> "Board is just not good for strategy because generally the Board aren't people who would have created it in the first place! As we discussed, for a new Tech business having a bunch of middle-aged blokes setting the strategy isn't probably going to be a route to interesting innovation. It's also why we're seeing the innovation teams for incumbent insurers being separate from the operating

teams, it's very hard if you've always done something one way to buy into ripping that up and doing things completely differently."

Just to keep us from thinking that there is a simple one-dimensional spectrum of positions on strategy here is a view that strategy is less created than emergent:

"Board is less about strategy – this is more something that evolves on its own as the team meets the real world – it's what works in business."

Finally, wrapping up the need to understand words and phrases as they are *used* – often in different ways – even if two people have the same understanding of, say, "challenge" any instance is always context dependent.

Your best friend might be truly your best friend if one day he gives you a real bollocking about your drinking to excess. It might be the wake up call you need. At other times he might need to be more gentle to help you most. In both cases the context when a message is delivered is also part of defining an "appropriate" challenge – are the two of you with a group of your friends or in a one-to-one? In a Board setting maybe you need to tear a strip off the CEO in private sometimes but on other occasions in the Board meeting.

YOU MUST MANAGE YOUR BOARD'S JOURNEY OVER TIME

To follow-on with a linguistic perspective, one of the deepest ways we English speakers are fooled in communication is by having a noun-based language rather than a verb-based language.[16] Furthermore, European civilisation having thrown Heraclitus[17] into the bin and worshipped excessively at the altar of Plato[18] amplifies this distortion

---

[16] Eg several native American languages are verb-centred.

[17] "No man ever steps in the same river twice, for it's not the same river and he's not the same man."

[18] Fixed eternal "true" forms. Neo-platonism was very influential on Christianity and hence European civilisation as a whole.

considerably compared to say India[19] and China.[20] Noun-centrism is the language and conceptualisation of left-hemispheric cognition – separable, knowable things – not right-hemispheric cognition – a flow of ever-changing ungraspability and interconnection.

What's all this gobbledygook about perchance you ask?

Let's take a simple example. It has been said that the scariest five words are "let's talk about the relationship". But maybe that wouldn't be so scary if it was "let's talk about how we are relating". This latter contains an innate sense of flow and change. How are we *relating* today, yesterday, last week, last month, last year and how might we dance[21] differently to be *relating* better tomorrow?

The idea of God (a noun, a thing) conveys a very different feel to many Native American nations, verbal-languaged "Great *Mysterying*". Many people would have problems with a noun-based concept of God but rather less so at a concept of a sense of mystery that we are here at all and relentlessly experiencing goodness knows what, this experiencing being precisely the content of our lives every day.

If I stop interluding (see what I did there) we can move onto The Board versus Board*ing*. I am quite sure that the noun "The Board" *qua* "thing" is behind a lot of the "set and forget" attitudes that lead to trouble. It's a dangerous mistake akin perhaps to considering your house as a static thing and then being shocked one day when the roof leaks. Treat your Board as A Thing and you will find its roof leaking one day. Sure we don't spend every day worrying about repairing our house and neither do we spend every day worrying about Board-*ing*. However maybe this digression has served to put the Boarding framing in your mind which will remind you now and then. How are you and your Board dancing right now? And last year? How would you wish to be Board-*ing* next year?

Returning to conventional English and focusing on the flow of a very much changing thing over time:

> "The Board is not a "set and forget". You need to manage the Board, its composition, its focus, its phase transitions just as much as you manage the changes in operational structure and composition."

---

[19] The Buddha's first essential characteristic of existence is "change"/"impermanence".

[20] The eternal flowing Tao.

[21] A noun but absolutely suffused with a sense of flow by definition.

"The required skills change over time – at first you need the hustle, hustle, help to grow, but NB client acquisition is down to the bizdev team – your NED is not a replacement for that."

Given that the nature of the SmallCo journey is growth and change it should not surprise you that *by far the most common essential advice from folks with experience* is **You Must Manage Your Board!**

"One thing I would recommend re Boards is to actually manage them!"

"You should manage it!"

"Clean up as you go along."

"Tidy up the Board as you move through the stages – you want to avoid conflicts between Board members from Seed round vs C or D etc."

"You need the right people for different periods – expansion/skills/ watching your back."

Not unsurprisingly a key skill you will need is:

"You need to be OK with getting people on and off!"

This will be made far easier for all concerned if you utilise the Tour of Duty concept we shall cover in "NED Expectations".

This flow over time is a super-important aspect which isn't always handled well in SmallCos, especially those growing rapidly where time is on fast-forward. How, as you grow and grow, do you manage the transition from a Board which needs to start pretty much focused entirely on creation and spreading the fire to, over time, assuming an increasing amount of control and firestorm prevention focus?

"Your Board needs to evolve – over time you will need more Corporate Governance [used in the sense not of All Those Codes but "control"] per se."

The overall journey was nicely metaphored by an experienced Angel who said he could only spare the time for one glass of wine after work. Two bottles later he was texting apologies to his wife. If Corporate Governance is a tedious topic, how to *govern* well is a fascinating topic for all Boarders:

> "Startup – needs help getting them ready for primary school. Your child. Unconditional love, support, guidance, potty training. Startup all about support, helping with the loneliness.
>
> ScaleUp. Working together – primary school teacher now in charge of education. You may not always agree with them but you have to work alongside them. They are like a teenager, growing but still uncoordinated. No one can tell them what to do. But by now they know how to tie their own shoelaces and have to knuckle down and do the work – not wet their pants.
>
> Your job is to get your kid into the right school. Right school equals choosing the right VC.
>
> Once the VC is on the Board you need an independent Chairman who is on your CEO/founder's side."

There are many ways of subdividing the journey from NewCo to world-beating FTSE. To an extent any such schema is arbitrary and stages overlap – after all one day just follows another and then another and then another However there are some phase shifts, especially around funding, which necessitate movement at the Board level even if the rest of the company doesn't notice any sudden changes at all.

The SmallCo/Tech media's model and news is very much funding-centric (simply perhaps as its economics allow little more in most cases than reformatting PR releases and fund-raising is a simple and clear event easy to write about). However whilst important I personally don't find this all that helpful. All these Seed, A, B, C etc raises seem so context-dependent that they promise much and deliver rather less.

Personally I find the developmental stage of the company a more helpful framing. Thus subdividing the journey from NewCo to FTSE into four stages:

i) *Startup* – from an idea to initial product-market fit. The essence of a Startup is faith and hope that "this will/may work" and proof (or product) is slow to arrive. You generally exit this stage when you have sold something to someone – B2C Startups needing far more trans-actions as proof compared to B2B. One client for a B2C is distinctly uninteresting, whereas if my Startup has just signed a global deal with, say, HSBC, then that is a clear validation;

ii) *ScaleUp* – now you have proved your idea works and someone will pay for it (or at least sign up in free/freemium models) then doing far more of the same – *mutatis mutandis* – seems like a good plan;

iii) *GrowthCo* – by now your "thing" is clearly working and you are looking like a real business (*pace* "making a profit" is all too often still a challenge). You start to think that floating at some point, or a real sale for real value, is becoming "a serious possibility" rather than a far-off pipe-dream. At this stage you want to "turn pro" moving from being a cobbled together ad hoc craft to a better engineered, reliable, solid machine;

iv) *IPO/liquidity event.* By this stage you have got a fantastic business. A bonfire which should roar and roar with demonstrable heat and sustainability.[22] Sadly for many you do need to do this tedious thing called a "liquidity event". In simple terms, folks gave you dosh quite some time ago, they are very pleased that you are having a nice time and enjoying yourself but they'd rather like their money back please. Not only that but with a nice return on top by way of thank you. As your pockets are unlikely to be deep enough to just buy them all out you are headed for "Game Over" for SmallCo land and "levelling-up" to BigCo land. This is generally the dreaded/lusted-after IPO but can be a trade sale. You become a BigCo (or a subsidiary of one) with all the regulations or restrictions and tedium – especially at the Board level – that that entails. You are no doubt pleased (or at least your mum is) to suddenly be worth a gazillion but may find yourself not enjoying the BigCo CEO job and pining for the indie days. Once floated your firm starts to have more in keeping with other listed companies in other sectors than it does with your still unlisted chums in your sector.

---

22 Either that or, as per some notable recent floats, something your capital providers are only too keen to hype up and dump onto a gullible market/buyer.

Whatever schema of phases or stages you adopt, the overall idea-to-IPO journey is about as radically different in start and end points as is the journey from fertilised egg to graduation certificate.

THE STARTUP BOARD

"What's their background? Do they appreciate what early stage is all about?"

We can define the essence of a typical Startup as being the inability to raise meaningful funds. There are always exceptions and a Startup founded by previously successful, well-connected entrepreneurs, or at a time when hot money is flowing into a sector, might well jump the queue and go straight to something with meaningful funds. Nevertheless this is the case for only a tiny minority of Startups. I have been struck by the observation that serial entrepreneurs do not put all (or sometimes even much) of their profits from the last one into the next one. I suspect that this is because they have a very realpolitik sense that all Startups, no matter how prestigious the parents, are hugely risky investments.

Many interviewees didn't really bother with anything that could be called a Board in any substantive sense at the Startup stage:

"At the beginning do you even have a Board?"

"In early years we kind of didn't really do Board meetings."

If you do start with a tiny Board bear this point in mind:

"Have more than one NED as otherwise there is just too much pressure on one person."[23]

Others started relatively early driven by the need for regulatory approval before going to market. In Fintech this has increased enormously in recent years compared to a decade ago. The Fintech bit doesn't matter

---

[23] This is something I can vouch for myself having been the last NED standing after a Boardroom power struggle.

– it's a question of whether you are regulated and if so you need to start dancing to the State's tune far earlier than otherwise or at a minimum have "clear and visible control procedures":

> "When do you start? Due to regulation one needs to start earlier in Fintech than elsewhere."

> "What? Some Fintechs didn't prioritise regulation right from the start? How so? Surely it was essential for the Regulator?"

Whatever the timing of Your First Real Board the essence is the same:

> **"In a Startup the CEO/founder and the Vision need supporting."**

Other comments were:

> "Startup – a Board has strategic discussions working out what you do as a company. Not compliance. Not committees. How do we grow the business? A sounding board for ideas."

> "Mentor-based Board, trusted advisors."

> "You need a Board who believe in you and are advocates for the Business."

> "At the beginning 'keep it small, keep it focused'."

> "Be super-lean – three Board members at first."

> "Owners represent themselves. No need for independent represen-tation of shareholder interests but even then it is often useful to have a neutral party at times [who brings perspective and more impartiality]."

The perceived need for some formal measure of control (many folks called it Corporate Governance) to go alongside the centrality of Corporate Creativity varied widely:

"Startup – necessary to have a Board for Corporate Governance [ie "control"] – especially when comes to investors."

In terms of establishing *some* control focus:

"KISS [Keep It Simple Stupid] at first – just hire an accountant."

The final chapter covering broken Boards applies at any stage. Two common comments about frequent errors with Startup Boards were:

"With early stage companies there can be too many matters reserved for the Board rather than delegated to executive management [The 'Waterline In The Wrong Place' Board]."

"Startups err in tending to start with those who bring cash rather than relevant skills [The Unbalanced Board]."

It is important to start as you mean to go on:

"The first appointment is very key. You can end up with a very dysfunctional Board because you admitted anyone at the beginning and then found it was hell to get them off."

The main failing of Startup Boards was seen as the following:

"The main early stage fault? Most don't really have Boards. This is a major weakness, early stagers ought to take [the right type of] NEDs more seriously." [serial entrepreneur]

"Have to take seriously at first even though it may seem like an annoyance. The answer is to keep it very slim early doors." [serial entrepreneur]

THE SCALEUP BOARD

You move from being a Startup to a ScaleUp when you raise a decent amount of non-"friends and family" money. A "decent amount" will naturally vary depending on the sector you are in. However regardless of the amount, if you can get strangers to invest money in you, you must have gone well beyond simply a twinkle in your eye, an idea in your mind (or I guess just be good at hyping and selling).

> **"The secret to ScaleUp is to appoint better people [throughout the company] and to listen to them."**

This is the phase change after which you don't actually really have the option of ignoring the Board:

> "An investor round is a really important point for Board management."

> "For us the big phase change was on a more material fund round. Questions arose re Board structure. The Business focus moved from purely sales and revenue to shareholder interest."

Other markets work differently:

> "The US works very differently."

> "They have a completely different mentality in the US. In early companies they don't fuss about the Board just growth."

The first serious raise is a phase change in the Board and you may need different types of Board member. Careless Startups may have taken whoever they can or whoever insisted, especially "small-a" angels (we'll cover "Angels" vs "angels" later) who might turn up for the love of it, or as they have nothing better to do or to protect a chunky investment but not add value.

As we saw earlier a proper Board can cost you ~£100k per annum and thus you should be getting a lot in return. In the ScaleUp/Growth phases your NEDs are ideally people you could never afford to hire full-time who bring a lot to the party. They are the ones whose connections, savoir faire and experience of the journey can be a major ingredient in continuing along an exponential growth track:

"Replace Boards 3–4 yrs in with more experienced NEDs who are less mentor focused."

"Your Chairman that got you through friends and family and seed rounds may well step off when the VCs come in."

Once others have capital invested they will expect their interests to be represented somehow even if just to check you aren't spending it all on sweeties:

"We just started with a retired accountant known to the shareholders who checks the numbers, report and accounts. A small acquisition subsequently focused the mind on process."

"When you raise money you become accountable. Investors will expect a management team around the founder which includes an appropriate Board."

The Board itself is shuffling along the spectrum from "Corporate Creativity" to "Corporate Control" and later even a flavour of V3 Corporate Governance concepts start to creep in:

"We started sub-committee-ing with Audit and Remcom as VCs and the regulators were always asking what we did in this area."

"You need someone who can "do all that stuff" but still understands the business."

One needs to retain a sense of the appropriate balance between Prometheus and Fire Safety Officers:

"[By now you'll need a] Board that offers balance on boring stuff."

"We try to cut the meaningless crap where possible. Some day, we'll probably be required to do more hoop jumping, however, it will be through necessity not design!"

"You can't get dragged too much into process and procedure. Many VCs don't have a clue and fuck this up. Also more junior VCs trying to be kick-ass can amplify this problem."

As time goes by so do your requirements from your Board:

"You should examine the Board more the longer you grow."

"Growing, ones Board gets too comfortable. It's important to think about refreshing it at some point."

When do you change the Board composition? Naturally when you need to but this generally correlates with raises:

"Best way is to set Board composition before a raise."

Although several folks said apparently the opposite (*apparently* as not all raises are from VCs and a tidy-looking Board is a prerequisite for fund-raising in the first place):

"The VC will dictate your Board [structure] if they can."

THE GROWTHCO BOARD

There is no one day when you move from being a ScaleUp ("wow this works let's do more of the same") to a GrowthCo ("now we are on our way to being a BigCo let's tighten all the nuts and bolts"). If, as a "low-res jpeg", ScaleUp Boards need less of a mentoring focus compared to Startups, then GrowthCos compared to ScaleUps may need value-add around "industrialisation" or "operationalising" or "efficiency":

"One NED we added recently is an expert in digitisation. We still have too many processes that are people-constrained and to scale significantly from here these need digitising."

As your focus moves from desperately doing everything you can to spread your fire to building boilers to contain it and industrialise it you need people who have experience in bigger businesses. You start moving away from "the best we can do with the time and resources available" engineering (in all aspects, including sales and marketing as well as Tech) to "top of the shop"/professional engineering.

As part of this evolution the CEO's role at some point undergoes a phase shift and the CEO becomes more strategic, having a COO, or de-facto COO, or even whole hierarchy in place below him to "do the day-to-day stuff".

One aspect of a GrowthCo is that, to a large extent, it has proved its idea and can consistently deliver on that. As a result this, broadly speaking, starts to be the stage when it first becomes possible to think of switching CEO – especially if he is an early stage guy/gal who can't move beyond the "hype plus string and sellotape" model. This succession planning/consideration is another phase shift for the Board when they start to have to act in a more BigCo fashion:

> "People sometimes change, but more often they don't. A CEO who was able to build the product often won't be able to scale up its monetization. That's fine. But you [the Board] need to manage that transition."

> "Generally a CEO can transition across one, two, maybe three of the five stages" – Startup, ScaleUp, profitability, exit, listed."

A final aspect of the Growth Company is the lead-in to pointing one's firm towards the North Star of a "liquidity event":

> "We added a NED from [Prestigious Floated Digital Firm] as he has done it all. He's been through what we would like to do and so knows the journey and what it takes."

THE IPO-READY BOARD: WHEN TWO TRIBES GO TO WAR

> "I have just joined the ranks of a FTSE250 Board. I'm getting to grips with the various worthy souls who tell Boards what to think about governance, diversity, remuneration, etc. etc. The institutional

shareholders don't think these thoughts for themselves, they pay people like ISS to do that and tell them how to vote. Given that the unquoted company often needs to IPO to extract founder value, being structured acceptably to these pseudo-shareholders ensures a wider number of potential real shareholders, so whatever one might think about the accepted norms (and I'm thinking about your delightfully controversial views [re Corporate Governance not exactly being mankind's greatest invention]), there is a cost to being different." [NED via email]

The IPO-ready world is kind of the end of innocence, the end of many paths up the mountain. From now on, you, sadly, have to prepare to enter the world of listed Corporate Governance and The One True Way Of Doing Things Which Must Be Obeyed At All Times. Thus your Board, whatever unique or idiosyncratic path it followed up to now, starts to look like all the others, the Conquest of Abundance.[24] Not just that but it may be a shock to see how quickly the value-add that you so carefully crafted to accelerate your journey drops away:

> "The whole [public company] Board had never been to the company's premises. The NEDs don't add a jot of value at all."

The triumph of process over content enters the equation. This isn't to say that you can't retain some of your Corporate Creativity vibe but it certainly will be ever-more crowded out by the box-ticking. So much so that, as we shall see in the next section some FTSEs have taken to setting up Advisory Boards in order to have a senior forum where they are not filling in the State's dot-to-dot but rather can focus on those oldskool "creativity" and "growth" topics.

The IPO is a super-busy period for the management team:

> "We were working 18-hour days in the months leading up to it."

Part of the preparation is accommodating changing parameters of the Board per se. You need to start adapting to a different world. One key

---

[24] Feyerabend's posthumously published book.

example is around compensation and "independence" (as far back as 1992 Cadbury was proposing that the majority of BigCo NEDs needed to be "independent"). We will examine independence in more detail in our chapter on NEDs but naturally, as always with rules, they are mechanical not substantial:

> "I had to step off a Board due to not passing the independent criteria – the Chairman was unhappy about this but there was nothing he could do. As he said he had found me the most independent of all the Board members."

> "My world is completely nuts. Eg have to have independent non execs but you are not independent if you have more than 3%. So instead I have to get someone who knows the business far less and cares far less."

I spoke to some CEOs who created their IPO-ready Board somewhat in advance of IPO-ing. This can be helpful as long as you don't do it too far in advance (and IPO timings are very subject to market timings and windows). If you do it too far in advance you end up with tight shoes long before you were required to wear them. Often IPO-readiness Board evolution is left quite late in the day (to avoid the tight shoes but also as it never quite made the top of the priorities list):

> "All too many build pre-IPO Boards about ten minutes before the IPO."

> "Most [Techs] do their IPO Board at the last minute."

If it's a rare founder that creates a NewCo and CEOs it all the way to IPO then it's an even rarer founder who continues long after the IPO. The two worlds are so different and it's not just a question of skillset and experience but of desire, interest and preference. Why would someone who dances with the Muses and dines with Prometheus want to spend a large chunk of his time with Fire Prevention Officers?

> "Going public is like a new dimension."

The whole Board changes from a V2 Company Board to a V3 Company Board which are very different beasties:

> "You see phase changes and cultural changes in issues around motivation and compensation, around 'skin in the game' vs 'independent'."

> "NEDs need some skin in the game and for cash-constrained SmallCos options are a great way of squaring the circle. But there is increasingly a regulatory challenge especially re floating."

Making your Board IPO-ready can easily be the start of two tribes going to war. The two tribes are the more SmallCo-orientated Corporate Creativity types: *"we'll survive despite all the mistakes we make (we always have)"* and the more BigCo-orientated Corporate Governance types: *"we have a huge rule book we have to follow and our reputations to protect"*.

To be clear I am not in the slightest taking aim at BigCo NEDs – all the ones I spoke to share and informed my concerns about the direction of travel of BigCo Boards. They are the ones that suffer, not me, and most likely not you either. However, the realpolitik is that in a world of politicians calling for "heads to roll", "Directors to be held more accountable" and there being no legal distinction between an Executive Director (who will know a hell of a lot about what's going on across the company) and a NED (who will not), NEDs have to cover their derrières. In the Corporate Governanced Company the NED is the panacea so if things go wrong select committees know where to aim their missiles:

> "In these circumstances a NED who hasn't got half an eye on generating an audit trail in case things go wrong is potentially risking his whole career when things go wrong."

"Two Tribes" is a war that, even if the SmallCo Directors win some battles in the short term, will only ever go one way as post-IPO there is Only One Way To Do The Board.

I was told (separately) remarkably similar stories by two CEOs with IPO-ready Boards. I'll condense the two case studies into one as they are so similar and to maximise the preservation of anonymity. The condensed story goes like this:

> "In pre-IPO companies with the Two Tribes on the Board (the SmallCo Corporate Creativity tribe and the BigCo Corporate Governance tribe) there is a crisis. The sheisse hits the fan.
>
> The Corporate Governance types shoot first. Their instinctive reaction is to point fingers, get a lawyer to cover their (& the Board's) derrières and find a donkey to pin the tail (blame) on.
>
> The business builders on the other hand say, 'look, things have always been going wrong, they will always go wrong, and they go wrong far less often'. 'We will do what we always have done, work out what the problem was, how to avoid it happening again and no-one will be sacked'. 'Let's fix it, and act in the interests of customers'."

Having abstracted and merged these stories and, having left out the juicy bits for the sake of confidentiality, the resultant tale doesn't sound too surprising. However, back to Boards and emotions, one thing that has been abstracted away is the horror of the founder/CEOs. It is perhaps akin to the difference between being told about an adventure park ride and being on it. In the queue you are like "OK, sure, yeh scary, I get it." But it is very different when you are on the ride and it plunges in freefall and your stomach loops the loop. You might laugh about it with hindsight but at the time it *feels* like the bottom has dropped out of your world – *"what have I let myself in for?"*

How do you address the Two Tribes challenge?

Naturally the essential number-one hire for your pre-IPO Board is a Chairman with plenty of pre- and post-IPO experience who can guide you through this massive phase shift and manage the Two Tribes on the Board. Also when hiring said Chairman remind yourself of the simple realpolitik of power that in listed companies the real power lies with the Chairman – just read the FT front page for long enough and that will be clear. I'm not sure that this is the most comforting thought, but you may well be hiring the person who will fire you:

> "I have a great Chairman. He's wonderful – amazingly supportive, amazingly skilled with the Board. But I am in no doubt that at some

point in the future when we are listed he will no doubt fire me."
[pre-IPO CEO]

We will return to leaving your CEO role in the next section – you
have to step down at *some* point in *some* circs – it's really just a (very
important) question of when and how. You clearly need an open and
trusting relationship with your pre-IPO Chairman while you are the
CEO. Naturally, during the interview process you need penetrating
and pertinent questions. "Succession" is clearly an important topic and
key questions are how many successions he/she has overseen,[25] what
was the process and his/her experience, how would he/she approach
it differently next time, what criteria tipped the balance and how can
this be best handled in your firm? Another question is whether he was
ever pushed out of a Board (it happens, even if BigCo Chairmen play
Boarding with a better hand of cards than SmallCo Chairmen they don't
exactly win all the rounds of every game over their career).

What else can you do after getting an experienced Chairman and
accepting that you will be unlikely to remain the Top Dog in your listed
company forever?

A super-experienced and successful serial-entrepreneur made a
simple but powerful point:

> "Avoid extremes. Try not to have zealots at the extremes of
> the two cultures of NED. Have private company directors who
> understand BigCo land and have BigCo directors who understand
> SmallCo land."

An experienced NED of unlisted and listed:

> "You need folks who can do all that [Corporate Governance] stuff
> but still understand business. For example they know silly rules
> about remuneration committees [some Catch22] but also under-
> stand that somehow you have to make money despite having so
> many rules to follow."

---

[25] "How many CEOs have you knifed then?" might be a phrasing – just perhaps not a
delicate one.

These are great pieces of advice from people who have been on that fairground ride. Naturally such balanced NEDs are indeed rare so you need patience (start fishing well in advance) and some tasty bait. Never easy but one definition of entrepreneur I like is "someone who sources and organises resources". "Obstacle immunity" is one measure of an entrepreneur, another is finding and seducing "resources" into joining your party.

The burdens of being a listed company and crazy "market pressures" for never-ending earnings increases has led many a company to go private again via some buy-in/buy-out/Private Equity deal. IPO-ing certainly isn't the perfect route for every company.

Other founders don't list but prefer to exit via a trade sale which may avert the Two Tribes Board challenge.

One of the sadnesses of founders/CEOs was summed up nicely in the following quote about a well-established business now clearly worth good money:

> "Of course I understand that Angels and other capital providers that have supported me for over a decade want a return on their money and so I have to have a liquidity event at some point as I can't afford to buy them out. On the other hand it's such a pity to have to turn it into a listed Company just to pay them out."

As an Angel investor myself in a SmallCo some twenty-plus years ago I can certainly relate to the tedium of your investment, even if it produces a dividend stream, having, in effect, converted into a low credit rating perpetual floating rate note supporting a lifestyle a CEO is reluctant to forego. We will turn shortly to CEOs' "VC frustration". However VCs in particular, as they are under time-pressure from their funds' finite lives, do provide the highly useful service to small investors of kicking the CEO into providing a liquidity event for all, something many a CEO would not otherwise get round to doing. This resistance is perfectly human – after all it's your baby and you have a kingdom and subjects around you. It can be very comfortable.

If some founders/CEOs need a prod, for others an IPO is a prestigious, "grown-up", often "front page of the FT" thing in itself, a real mark of personal triumph, a lifetime achievement, a gold medal in business. For others the IPO is merely the only/simplest way to enable folks to cash out.

In both cases the alleged "liquidity" as an argument is easy to overstate:

"My [pre-IPO] Chairman [who listed a prestigious business] was telling us that liquidity can definitely be overstated, the actual liquidity (what can be sold without moving the price significantly) can be very poor." [CEO]

ADVISORY BOARDS

"Our Advisory Board meets four times a year and we just sit and listen for three hours. It's great to get back to brainstorming, being creative and listening to great business people who are achieving stuff. Our Main Board doesn't really discuss strategy and creative things – it's got a different purpose." [Post-IPO CEO]

For BigCos "Advisory Boards" are a way of getting back to the future – to more like what Boards used to be like before the Corporate Governance craze hit town. A forum of folks who didn't have half an eye on regulators and Select Committees and who would bring you refreshing and invigorating tales of life in other businesses outside your own four walls:

"An increasing number of organisations are appointing advisory boards.

There are many good reasons for a company to do so. It could be to ensure it receives expert advice on emerging technology or scientific advances, or to gain insight into doing business in diverse global markets. An advisory board may also assist a company to sell its products and services to government customers, or to provide counsel on public relations and reputation management.

Advisory boards are no substitute for statutory boards of directors. Indeed, properly constituted, advisory boards should complement and strengthen the existing board."[26]

---

[26] Odgers Berndtson "The Role of Advisory Boards – Who, What, Why and How?" <undated>

In this sense, compared to the V2 Board, the V3 Board *is de facto splitting* vertically (into what has been called *conformance* and *performance*) not horizontally (Supervisory and Management Boards). This workaround at least ensures that they can get back to having senior executives plus outsiders focusing on *both* creativity and control, albeit at different times in different places.

Whilst the BigCo move to Advisory Boards is pragmatic and ensures a senior forum focusing on – er – the business rather than compliance this has many risks for BigCo NEDs. Not least of which over time they risk becoming ever more pure off-balance-sheet State civil servants. Over time all the juice, all the fun, all the value-add, all the interest, all the creativity gets bled off elsewhere for other people and the BigCo NEDs, who are not having all the fun, get to bear all the legal and regulatory risk.

Sadly, based on what I have heard from such chums over the past decade, BigCo NEDing is already a long way down this path. As time goes by and the Code Vesuvius keeps erupting the ever more robotised role of the BigCo NED will impact the quality and desire of experienced business folk to do it. Mike's Law of entirely foreseeable consequences in action again.

Several of my experienced NED interviewees used the phrase *"compliance robot"*:

> "Listed companies are building compliance robots. They don't really understand the business they understand compliance."
> [Chairman of several AIM-listed companies]

In SmallCo land the general attitude towards "Advisory Boards" was dismissive, in part as the SmallCo Board should be about creativity and how many fora do you need on the same topic?

> "The phrase "Advisory Board" is patently ridiculous, it is not a Board it's a group."

A somewhat cynical angle is:

> "Advisory Boards are not Boards, they are a cheap way of accessing talent in return for a prestigious sounding but meaningless title."

More neutrally:

> "Advisory Boards? A slightly more formalised group of mentors."

> "What is an Advisory Board? The sum of a CEO's mentors."

Only a minority of SmallCos I spoke to had "Advisory Boards" and for many of those the group/"Board" never met as a whole – rather it was a collection of advisers. In some cases the members of the Advisory Board were not publicly known. For those firms where the Advisory Board met (which can be much larger than the Board – I heard figures of over a dozen members) there was a tendency for it to become a talking shop. Which is unsurprising as it has no executive powers or legal purpose/ standing or even joint decision making capability:

> "It is not a Board as it has no say/power over the CEO – he will just pick off one by one to find someone to agree with [his] latest scheme."

Were they to have any authority it was thought this would result in confusion:

> "Real advisory Boards exist cf the House of Lords and then they are a right pain [two fora to be got onside with different priorities etc]."

Naturally we need to note here the very different purposes of matters of State and matters of business. Simplistically the Lords does two things (a) makes its own mind up on policy and (b) provides drafting refinement. This second function is not needed in businesses. The State has massively complex laws where a review by a second chamber is helpful. SmallCos are on the contrary about rapid implementation of strategy and ideas for which greatest efficiency is provided by a unitary high-level structure.

Having said all the above why might *you* decide to have an Advisory Board?

> "Several Tech firms I have known have got some great advisors for very little cost indeed."

Furthermore if, for whatever reason, your Board isn't exactly supportive or creative *and you can't – at least in the short term – fix that problem* then you are in a similar situation to BigCo CEOs. Then having a second forum where you can focus on what is needed is a pragmatic, realpolitik approach to adding this functionality to your company:

> "For a number of the Tech businesses I've been involved with it's really been the advisors – as opposed to Board members – who have given advice and support (particularly where they're investors [Angels])."

It is important not to be too seduced by terminology and theory into excessive antipathy towards the concept. After all as Shakespeare said rather more eloquently it doesn't matter what you call a rose it still smells the same. No-one spoke to me about the value of the advisers in any sense of being a Board rather than a group.

It is important to note that there is a difference between "Board" and "Advisory Board" skillsets:

> "There is being a good adviser versus a good Board member."

The kinds of folks that are best is unsurprising:

> "You need advisers who have been there and done it."

Disgruntled Advisory Board members are not hard to find (which may well be related to the often de minimis compensation and no real power angles):

> "As an adviser they are surfing off your brand."

> "Beware 'Rolodex raping' [strip-mining your contacts then casting you aside]."

5. The CEO/Founder

"A Founder CEO is in a very isolated and lonely place" [VC/CEO]

At this level of resolution of detail I do not draw a distinction – you can read "CEO/Founder" as "prime driver" if you wish – it's just a shorthand in the same way that SmallCo is a shorthand for unlisted Company. When I use "CEO" I mean "CEO/founder(s)"/"prime driver(s)".

The CEO and Founder are generally the same person or, if not, at least in early stage SmallCos very entangled. I did talk to folks/companies where the CEO was, as it were, a "professional"/"hired-hand" rather than a founder as such – my simple mapping onto this chapter is that such a CEO becomes a kind of second-tier founder. So for simplicity let's just consider the founder-CEOs, founder-non-CEOs and non-founder-CEOs together as "multiple founders".

Being a CEO is a complex matter. Not only do you have to have a winning idea and create and run a business to execute your vision (how hard can it be?) but you have all this Board stuff although as I may have mentioned once or twice that *should* be a resource:

"Seek advice from Board members, that's what they are there for."

One of the things that struck me in speaking to some forty SmallCo CEO/founders was the need for emotional stamina. Thus this chapter is more focused on the emotive side of the journey than the prosaic. Loneliness, faith, and hope figure large in honest accounts of CEOs' journeys.

As we have seen culture runs like a stick of rock through the whole enterprise. Part of that culture is how much or how little you are "friends" (and that is definitely a single word that people use to cover different points on a wide spectrum of meanings) with folks on your

Board (some are, some aren't). Another part of the Board culture is truth-telling. As one CEO put it a key moment is when – and *if* – you can stop "selling a line" and "spinning" to the Board and start delivering the unvarnished truth.

A frequent "fingernails on blackboard" experience for CEOs is bean counters on a SmallCo Board. This is not used in the sense of an accountant helpfully telling you that you are about to go bust but of Board members (you invited them on) who focus on noise not signal.

Appropriately we end the chapter with the all-important consideration of when you, the CEO, will step down and whether it will be your decision or the Board's. Ideally it will be mutually agreed – but life isn't always ideal is it?

BEING A CEO/FOUNDER

Although "theoretically" and "actually" in terms of the actual Board meeting, a Chairman chairs, ie "runs", the meeting, the realpolitik as we saw earlier is that the founder/CEO is The Man (/Woman) and needs a clear angle/approach to his Board and how it functions. Here is a nice simple take on this:

> "It's your business not theirs [the Board's] – don't let them run the business."

At some stage in any Company there is a transition and the Board appoint a new CEO as we shall discuss at the end of this chapter. Generally this is a long way down the track as turning an idea into a real business takes time and crazy amounts of effort – no interviewee told me any story of manna falling from heaven into the laps of founders. Some manna comes everyone's way in life, but the majority of every success was due to blood, sweat and, if not tears, then sleepless nights.

The founder's experience is very unique (sic). One reason founders prize former founders on their Board is that they will have had similar experiences and know what it feels like. For those of us who haven't run a marathon we can say that we know, or at least can imagine, what it must be like. But we don't know, we can't really imagine, we haven't run that race. All too many business books make business sound like some dot-to-dot, some paint by numbers. In the big scheme of things all too often omitted is the emotional journey and – to put it bluntly – the sheer irrational nature of dogged persistence, especially when all seems lost.

Some of you may have run this marathon. Others will have spent plenty of time with marathon runners and have a good idea of what it takes. Others may have book experience or no experience. However for all of us I feel it's important that we start our Board roles investigation with the emotional challenges of entrepreneurialism and especially with "irrational" emotions which can literally be the difference between Game Over and success.

I was very fortunate that in my conversations folks were very open. For some it seemed that it was a chance to pour out their feelings for the first time. There is a huge burden on the founder. Peter Thiel, one of the world's great entrepreneurs, has said that young folks come to him and say they want to be an entrepreneur to which he replies they must be mad. It is such a tough journey, he says, that there is only one reason for doing it, otherwise it is best avoided. That reason is that there is an opportunity, some change you wish to see in the world that you are passionate about creating. If this is the case then you become an entrepreneur as it is the only way to make that change happen. Otherwise you would be crazy.

One of the most challenging examples of the internal cognitive dissonance that is required is the need to project confidence when you do not have it yourself. Or to put it bluntly the occasional need to lie – about feelings, mind you, lying about facts is not good (we will turn later in this chapter to "presenting" facts "appropriately" which everyone does in their lives).

An archetypal example of "lying about feelings" is during the strains of fund-raising. There is probably not an entrepreneur alive that hasn't had challenges around this, who hasn't, literally or metaphorically, woken up at four o'clock in the morning, anxious, concerned or feeling that the raise is failing. And of course said entrepreneur needs to come into the office in the morning bright and breezy and projecting confidence. At times like these the only factors keeping him/her going are inner faith or hope. These may feel inadequate for the task of projecting confidence, but projected it must be. No team is motivated by a miserable, pessimistic CEO.

But before faith and hope let's look at loneliness and multiple founders.

THE LONELINESS OF THE LONG DISTANCE CEO

"For a sole founder in particular it can be a very lonely journey"

It is a tough gig being a founder. A US stat I was told was that the average founder has failed four times before.[1] This introduces the need for such folks to have their own support mechanism around them *outside of any individual companies* (which may come and go) to help them pick themselves back up off the floor.

As we shall see, NEDs have differing emphases on "supporting" vs "challenging" CEOs at the Board. However in the early stages of NewCo the emphasis has to be on supporting and spreading the word. It is for this reason that, regulatory credibility apart, BigCo NEDs are generally not sought at an early stage as their experience and skillset is at the Fire Safety Officer end of the spectrum not supporting Promethean acts.

This angle of support is super-important:

"For me my Board/NEDs provide perspective, balance, a sounding board, coach, mentor, stress-relief." [CEO]

"I certainly sought the advice of my NEDs, being a CEO is a lonely job. Has to be a relationship there to be supportive whilst within professional boundaries of course." [CEO]

This support angle can be addressed in different ways. A minority of NEDs see their role as "not providing a nannying-service". I respect all my interviewees all of whose views are based on hard experience. However there is a long long road from NewCo to FTSE and I wouldn't advise starting the journey with only NEDs whose methodology emphasises "challenge". At some point along the journey when you are

---

[1] My guess would be that the relevant stat is smaller in the UK. The US is culturally much more into failure and bankruptcy.

less of an infant and more of a teenager then perhaps more challenge will be helpful.

At some point most(/all?) CEOs find a "challenging" to, at worst, "hostile" Board and at that point if they need support and it does not come from the Board then it can, indeed needs to, come from elsewhere:

> "CEOs start off having NED/Advisor/Mentor – the name doesn't matter, the role does."

More broadly, away from the personal support, there is the question of the depth of relationship with your Board. The rosy scenario is that you have a Board containing *available* folk of great experience, knowledge or connections who can help you grow the company faster:

> "I see my [independents] for coffee every couple of weeks."

MULTIPLE FOUNDERS

> "Maybe it is just my skewed experience but I think there are many early stage companies with a pair of founders that pretty much toss for who gets the CEO label. Sometimes these 'partnerships' last a long time, but I have had the less than joyous task of doing the hatchet job on the half of one pair that didn't rise up with the development of the business." [Chairman]

One simple question which arises, given the toughness of the gig and the loneliness, is whether it is or isn't a better idea to have multiple founders. One of my interviewees quoted a statistic along the lines that something like 60% of the time it is better to have multiple founders. But this is, I feel, to misunderstand that statistics do not apply to one individual, to one event. Statistically if you get married and are in London then the chance of divorce is around 50%. But this is meaningless – it's digital – you either remain married or you divorce. Stats don't matter – it's what *you* think, feel and do that does. With respect to founders some folks are natural loners, some are natural team-players.

This relationship angle is important – it *is* a partnership just in business not romance. It *isn't* a question of "multiple founders are on balance better" or "divorce is less likely outside London" it is a question for not just *you* but also of your circumstances now. Just as you can't get married if you don't have someone to marry you can't have co-founders if you don't have someone to co-found with. In both cases to suddenly go out and try and find someone to marry or someone to co-found with would be an act of madness – for precisely the same reason. That same reason being that both marriage and co-founding are, inter alia, a long and tough journey that only those who have been on it can appreciate. To survive it you and your partner(s) need to have a close bond, trust and a great relationship – all of which take time to build.

Sometimes you might found on your own and sometimes not.[2] I am not even sure what it means that one model is slightly more likely to be successful (especially without sample sizes and error bars). When the odds are around 50% you might as well toss a coin. And although fortune plays a part in all our lives business is not a coin toss. Hard work, persistence and having a great team below you and around you at the Board skew change the odds.

In passing, the Chinese have a concept that three is an unstable number when it comes to people (as it always ends up breaking into two versus one). Some firms I know had three founders, then two. In some two later went to one. However even then there are exceptions – I started my career in a Startup founded by three partners, one however was "sleeping" and merely on the Board rather than having an executive role so asymmetry was there from the start.

FAITH

"There's nothing left but faith." [The Cure]

Creativity is an emotive process, a journey of transforming vast infinite potential into one specific thing, it is the giving birth to something that

---

2   This isn't a stat (lol) but my feeling is that successful serial entrepreneurs may well co-found less than first-timers. It is much easier to embark upon a journey you have done before and then gather any missing resources (of all types) around you on the Board.

never existed before. In my conversations with quite a few folks on this journey, many have got to the stage where there was no rational reason to continue, no rational reason to believe there was a way forwards. All agreed with the lead-in quote that at some point it was *simply* faith that was left – even if it was "irrational" (whatever that might mean, we are talking about the Muses and the Fates – I'm not sure either are rational per se or rather their level of rationality is well above our pay grade).

Noteworthy here is an important occidental/oriental difference re faith. In Western theology faith is something which is kind of self-supporting – if you had evidence, as it were, you wouldn't need faith. By contrast the Sanskrit for faith, *shraddha*, can be translated as "trustful confidence". I have *shraddha* that, were I to get on a bicycle, I would be able to ride it as I have done so many times. Serial entrepreneurs have *shraddha* that they, far more often than not, will sort out seemingly immovable obstacles as they have done so many times before. That kind of rational faith is easier to sustain and is more supportive than "empty faith".

However most entrepreneurs are first-timers and have no confidence based on direct experience. For many it was simply having "faith" at the low point, even if it was "irrational" that enabled them to continue with their journey.

Thus you the founder are not alone if you have this experience – plenty have gone before you. Furthermore, if at some point there is nothing left for you but faith – even empty, irrational faith – then "never surrender" sometimes works. Faith has kept many people going. Goodness knows what the Fates have in store for all of us – don't quit on them. Wait for them to quit on you otherwise you might be walking away at the darkest hour just as the light was about to return.

HOPE

"Mr and Mrs Rimmer were very religious, taking the Bible scriptures at face value. The Hoppists were primarily concerned with a particular verse from the New Testament. St. Paul's first epistle to the Corinthians, chapter 13, verse 13 had been misprinted in a certain edition of the Bible. In their version, the verse read 'And now these three remain: Faith, Hop and Charity. But the greatest of these is Hop'"[3]

Sometimes even faith runs out, but, in an ever-changing universe there is always hope even if charity does not generally exist for founders. The best tale I have heard about hope and its attendant promise that circumstances *do* change is not from business but from a Buddhist Monk. Ajahn Brahm, a former Physics teacher in London, relates[4] a true story told to him by a former colleague, a British soldier in Burma in WW2 who was on patrol in the jungle, young, scared and far from home.

Perimeter scouts came to deliver bad news. A number of Japanese troops were approaching who vastly outnumbered the patrol and had them surrounded. The young soldiers prepared to die and awaited the order to fight their way out – at least if they were all killed they would do their duty and take out enemy soldiers along the way.

However, the Captain did not give this order rather he ordered them to make tea. The soldier thought that, even though this was the British Army, this was no time for tea. However he followed orders and they put a brew on and enjoyed what they believed would be their final drink. Before they had finished their tea however a scout returned and announced that the enemy's movements had left a gap through which they could escape. They all packed up and went through it to safety and the young soldier lived to tell the tale.

But this tale was only part of the story. Several times later in his life this chap had felt surrounded by the enemy – serious illness, terrible difficulties, personal tragedy – when there was seemingly no way forwards, no way out. Without his Burmese experience he would have been tempted to fight his way out, making a bad situation worse and wasting his energy. Instead whenever surrounded he sat down, made tea and stayed attentive to the natural flow of things. When a safe route out appeared he took it.

We need to be careful with hope though and, if a potential lifesaver, it can also be a deceitful mistress – something the Greeks were well

---

3   Red Dwarf "Tongue Tied"
4   Brahm "Who Ordered This Truckload of Dung? Inspiring Stories for Welcoming Life's Difficulties" 2005

aware of. Back in the day Zeus was pissed-off with Prometheus for giving mankind fire. As he couldn't take fire back from mankind he created a jar (not a box) along with a super-hotty totty called Pandora who he sent to Epimetheus – Prometheus' brother. Epimetheus had been warned not to accept gifts from the Gods. You might have thought that his brother being chained to a rock and having his liver pecked out daily might have suggested to Epimetheus that the Titans really were on the losing side. Anyway Pandora was irresistible and Epimetheus ignored the advice. She was also irresistibly curious and one day opened her jar letting out all of the ills of the world which cause all the business challenges we see today. Closing the jar too late she trapped Hope (the Goddess Elpis) inside.

The Ancient Greeks were very suspicious of Hope[5] and favoured planning and rationality:

> "Greek tragedy highlighted the way delusional aspects of Hope generated overconfidence with catastrophic results. The political and military historian Thucydides took up the theme. Desire and hope hunted together, he said, the one encouraging men to take risks, the other persuading them that their luck would hold. 'But both these invisible influences are ruinous, far more powerful than the dangers in full view.' Far better, he said, to find a reason for hope by 'awareness of odds in your favour'. Then 'you do not have to think about it but can fight with every hope of winning'."[6]

The moral of which is take comfort in Elpis when times are tough – she may get you through a dark night. However do not rely on her gifts. There are plenty of longstanding NEDs who can tell you plenty of modern tragedies resulting from CEOs just *hoping* something turns up and "never surrendering".

---

5 "Brill's Companion to Hesiod" 2009 states that the greatest controversy in all of Hesiod (the author of the source text) surrounds the meaning of "Elpis" in this tale. Elpis as a word simply means expectation of either good or bad future – it is double-edged. Whilst Elpis, like Pandora, has a powerfully seductive voice and her comfort and illusion are at times necessary, her fundamental nature like Pandora is "lies" and "swindling".

6 Jones "Glimmers of Hope" Spectator 13/7/19

FRIENDSHIP

There was much divergence of opinion over the nature of the relationship of the CEO with his Board.

A lot of this I felt with hindsight was as a result of how the word "friend" has multiple meanings in English. One person may say they have less than a handful of friends (*qua* Real True Friends). Another may say they have a hundred (using a weaker concept) and in the weakest sense some may have thousands of "friends" on Facebook.

Some interviewees verged on feeling that it was "unprofessional" to have "friends on the Board" whilst others had made friends for life with those on their Board.

Once again there are many paths up the mountain – choose the one for you but just make sure you recruit Board members who are up for the same path, the same culture. Once you are at the top of the mountain and level-up to the world of rules & regs there is probably one about how friendly you are allowed to be and ways to measure that.

However you are not CEO to win popularity prizes. Sometimes you are there to lead and if folks always respect a leader they are not always guaranteed to agree with your choice of route, praise you for it, or enjoy "being led". Glossing over the friends point but emphasising the unpopularity point:

> "The main mistake is when the CEO makes a Board his friends – he needs to be able to be unpopular."

Which brings us nicely onto the next sub-topic.

TRUTH-TELLING

We touched on the truth topic earlier but let's have a closer look. I don't believe anyone I spoke to was dishonest – vice versa I was grateful for the honesty with which folks related various tales, not all to their credit. This was in a private context however where they kindly trusted that my word was my bond. A different context might be making a presentation to the Board or to the regulator when maybe things would be expressed differently.

More broadly, society survives precisely because we don't always pass on a "screendump of everything inside our head" to the other person. Set and setting, "time and place" are something we learn to absorb when young – along with some thoughts being kept entirely private.

One side of the "truth-telling" coin is "factual honesty"; not telling lies is a rather important aspect even if facts often need contextualising appropriately. The other side of the coin is emotional honesty – the screendump of the contents of your heart. Certainly with the team, and to a large extent with the Board, a Founder needs to project his confidence and vision not his fears and doubts. This becomes more important over time. You are not going to survive as a CEO of any scale of company if you are riddled with self-doubt and project weakness.

A nice metric around how well a Board is functioning is how honest a CEO/founder feels he can be with his Board:

> "The good thing is to be open when things are not going well. The disadvantage of VC-backed Boards is that the founder is often trying to sell a story."

> "All too often one sees a mentality of selling 'all's well' to the Board."

This quote is from a founder/CEO of a Company who moved from projecting confidence and vision to being able to share fears and doubts:

> "It's hugely important when a CEO can move from spin to truth-telling. My NEDs won't judge me for it, they will ask questions, listen and advise but don't tell me what to do."

A successful serial entrepreneur chose honesty as one of his Board Secrets Of Success:

> "Telling people the truth is one of the key skills of a good CEO."

Before one has perfected that art, for some the Board has proved to be a useful reason/excuse/pretext. Not ideal perhaps but it is an honest realpolitik nevertheless:

> "I have found that the Board has been a useful buffer for me. Being able to say to staff 'I might agree but the Board...' has made it easier to have difficult conversations." [CEO]

Nor is it just the disposition, inclination or skills of an entrepreneur; as always context matters. A serial entrepreneur gave examples of Boards where he had had to put a spin on things and others where he simply told the truth:

> "I've had Boards where frankly I just agreed with them every quarter for a quiet life. I've had other Boards where I can tell them what is keeping me up at night."

So, back to "set and setting": **it is the mindset of the Board which either produces an environment where they are more likely or more unlikely to hear the unvarnished truth**. The above example is a clear example of why it is not just that a certain person is brutally honest or spins but rather the combination of a certain person in a certain setting. Personality is "conditionally dependent" – ie dependent on conditions. The Board creates an atmosphere that encourages or discourages varnishing of the truth.

Thus truth-telling generally requires a Good Board. There were some I heard of who would see anything confessional, or any sign of weakness, as resembling the irresistible temptation that a limping deer presents to a pack of hyenas.

The same CEO continued:

> "The most important point is to have people on the Board with whom you can be honest.
>
>   It is important to have people on the Board who have fucked up – they will have more empathy. To be honest most people have fucked up at some time in their lives, it's the ones who pretend they haven't you have to watch out for."

Once again we can make the analogy with romantic relationships – an air of honesty and non-judgmentalism will lead folks to be open about their issues and concerns which is the vital first step on the path to addressing them. An atmosphere of always feeling judged or criticised will shut that process down and leave the field tense with Unspoken Issues.[7] Whether business or romance these can end up being fatal to the relationship. You don't want to spend all your time focusing on the negatives but you do need to address and fix holes in the roof and leaks in the pipes.

Overly-critical Board members ironically can initiate a vicious circle. If their focus or manner inhibits the CEO from full honesty then they can tune into this, develop strong suspicions that they are not getting the whole picture, which leads to greater criticism and yet more defensiveness.

Naturally the Board may well not be responsible if a CEO is so economical with the truth that he is simply not saying it. Once again this is inevitably toxic and destructive – in part or in whole:

"Half the truth can still be a lie." [NED]

A further complication of truth-telling these days beyond the logical/ emotional truths and the impact of context on whether those are communicated is the very curious and very recent attempted interjection into Western culture of Japanese concepts of "socially-acceptable" truths – *honne* (what you honestly think or would want to say) and *tatemae* (what you have to say in society). I was talking to one strong-minded founder about some crazy PC/culture wars aspect on which we both agreed, who added:

"However these days I have to go along with all this stuff Mike."

BEAN COUNTER AVERSION

Unsurprisingly a popular annoyance for CEOs was overly critical NEDs. More specifically many CEOs' moans to me were about NEDs/VCs who were overly-focused or overly-invested in targets – KPIs or financial:

---

[7] Czech has a good phrase – "napjatá atmosféra" – literally a "stretched" atmosphere.

"You can model the three types of Board Member as bean counters, who quibble over the tiniest accounting/KPI variation, the PC Corporate Governance crowd – premature in most Startups, and finally 'what a CEO needs'." [CEO]

"What I hate are penny-pinching spreadsheet jockeys. After all, forecasts can be anything – who knows – this is not a mature business like IBM." [CEO]

"I can't stand bean counters who worry about one basis-point whilst not getting the big picture and focusing rather on the sheer noise along the way."

KNOWING WHEN TO STOP

"Know thyself" [inscribed above the Temple of Apollo at Delphi]

Will you jump? Will you be pushed? Will you decide to call it a day?

One of these fates always befalls a CEO. Furthermore it is a rare CEO these days who continues for decades. Besides – and precisely to the point – why would you want to?

In lifestyle businesses with a non-growth, bumbling-along mentality, the CEO effectively has resources around him to support his business lifestyle. If you have no external investors there's nothing wrong with that, if that's what you want then good for you. It is unlikely however that if you have investors they invested simply to support your lifestyle, they are likely to be after a financial return. This generally involves the "growth" word.

Each stage along the growth trajectory is a very different experience for the CEO. At the extremes, NewCo and FTSE CEO-ing are antithetical, but even along the way it is a rare person who will be equally good at each stage. However, more to the point of the Delphic Oracle, it is an even *rarer* person who *enjoys* each stage equally. Some will go the whole way and enjoy/tolerate each of the stages as a kind of pentathlon, a whole bunch of different sports. Most folk gravitate towards, say, creation (NewCo), operationalising (GrowthCo) or process-centric

(ListedCo). Depending on your sector the "profit" thing may become important at different stages. Here too some folks are good at, and enjoy, spending but less so at the more tedious job of squeezing costs.

You know which parts of the journey you enjoyed best, you know what you are good at:

> "The CEO role [in a successful sub-10-year-old business] was becoming more samey every year. I was still enjoying it but others around me were much more interested in operationalising, in finding efficiencies, than I was so [having kept my shares] I decided to stand down and go back to what I really love – creating businesses."

> "It wasn't a question of not enjoying it. I was enjoying it. The important question was 'Am I enjoying it as much as I used to?'"

You know when the fire has gone out, when you no longer have the passion. Some folks don't mind or tolerate this out of "needs must" – every day the trains into London are full of people "just doing a job". But, if you are the founder/CEO that is unlikely to be enough. CEO-ing a growing SmallCo needs passion to provide the drive and ability to keep finding solutions and keep moving forward against all sorts of resistance. Sure no one feels passion every day – we all have rhythms in our lives. But what you don't want to see is the moving average of your enthusiasm and enjoyment heading relentlessly down.

Do you know which stage you enjoy most? Are you the rare "all stages please" entrepreneur? In either case eventually you will step down. If you linger and linger then external capital providers are likely to tighten the ratchet if there is no liquidity event in sight. As we saw previously if you get to the IPO-ready Board stage then you will need a ListedCo Chairman and they arrive wheeling a gallows into your Boardroom, leaving it in the corner until it's needed.

Like many things in life, no matter what the challenge, if you are proactive, rather than reactive or avoidant, challenges are easier to deal with. Sort out your own thoughts on the matter – will you jump, be pushed or step-down?

If the personal reflection is for the sake of your eternal soul, then in terms of the day job you want to be creating a professional company.

You want your creation to be as professional an organisation as you can make it *in all respects* and a Board's succession planning is one of them. You wouldn't want your last thought as you accidentally fall in front of a big red bus to be "darn this is going to screw my company, they won't know what to do" along with realising that your estate you leave to your loved ones will have collapsed in value as a result:

> "I'd discussed this [my stepping-down] with my Board some time back but it was always left for another day. In the end I had to push it but I was very fortunate as the team around me had been in the business from the start and were very well placed to take the business forwards. I am the kind of person you want starting a relay race – my team were ideal for running the next legs."

So sort your own thoughts out and in the day job work with your Board and Chairman as partners at all stages on this. If you don't see them as partners then you are probably in need of the Broken Boards chapter.

After some time most business folk have seen many CEO departures – pushed, jumped and stepped-downs. The chances are that real stepped-downs (as opposed to those who "decided [after a gun was placed to their head] to spend more time with their family") are in a small minority. Tenacity is the ne plus ultra of entrepreneuring. Power, control and prestige are biochemically as well as psychologically addictive. Besides, it takes guts and a supportive domestic situation to be able to exchange a certain tomorrow for an uncertain one:

> "I am very fortunate that my spouse has always been highly supportive. I can imagine that for many spouses the idea of their partner, who is no longer working the crazy Startup hours, giving up the security of a prestigious job with a solid salary for – well nothing certain at all – is a real roadblock. This would especially be true if there are mouths to feed and not enough funds in reserve."

Badly done this CEO transition can leave people feeling bitter for years or even nursing grievances for life. Sometimes you have to fight for yourself, your company, in some Boardroom battle which you may or may not win. The realpolitik is that you do not always plan your ending, sometimes you fight and lose. Most importantly however having personal and professional plans at least maximises the chance of meeting your objective even if nothing is for certain in this realm. **Most importantly don't try and cling on like a limpet forever just for the sake of it or out of habit.**

My first ever ski-instructor was a sagacious old Italian multiples of my age. I recall to this day him saying when we were on a chairlift together "must always enjoy". Well, maybe you can always enjoy up in the mountains. I've found that you are unlikely to enjoy every day in your life. However, I remember the advice, and it is good advice:

> "I've always done things I enjoy. If I wasn't this way I'd just go and join the City and earn ten times as much."

You won't enjoy every day of your career but you should try on balance to enjoy it as much as possible.

So spend your business life predominantly doing the roles/stages you most prefer.

Why not?

6. The Chairman

There is a real art to this appointment. A good Chairman was appreciated as a real asset by every interviewee who had one. A strong Chairman who was respected for his strengths which were needed at the relevant stage. Anything below that would in essence be filling a seat in easy times but prove too weak for the role in hard times. "Pre-Chairman" companies generally picked someone to Chair a given Board meeting – often founders in rotation.

Perhaps more than any other role this seat at the table needs managing over time. You are highly unlikely to get a Chairman with listed experience when you are one man and a dog. Indeed even if you did, unless said Chairman has Startup experience, he might well be the wrong person for that role at that stage. Vice versa one with no experience of listing will not be the right one to take you through that metamorphosis. The CEO/Chairman relationship can be a complex one.

In virtually all the SmallCos I spoke to the Chairman is a NED. So to that extent the next chapter on NEDs also applies – notably "what do we as an executive team lack?", "what *type* of Chairman do we need?" and some points, in particular "get to know them before appointing them", apply in spades.

As you might imagine great Chairman are rare so you, the CEO/founder, need to think through why an experienced Chairman needs all the risk/hassle with your company. As you can imagine the "we are unique" pitch sounds very lame after hearing it for decades and it isn't always a bed of roses being a SmallCo Chairman.

ROLE

"The chairman's role in securing good corporate governance [read as company governance in my terminology] is crucial. Chairmen are primarily responsible for the working of the board, for its balance of membership subject to board and shareholders' approval, for ensuring that all relevant issues are on the agenda, and for ensuring that all directors, executive and non-executive alike, are enabled and encouraged to play their full part in its activities. Chairmen should be able to stand sufficiently back from the day-to-day running of the business to ensure that their boards are in full control of the company's affairs and alert to their obligations to their shareholders."[1]

There are plenty of definitions out there for the formal role of the Chairman. Templates, no matter how worthy, are always cookie-cutter though. Size, stage, phase, type of company, sector, personalities, country will mean that one needs to deviate from any single recipe:

"The role of Chairman and Boards varies per country. In the US some investors don't care about the Board at this stage."

Sometimes founders may resist a Chairman "not yet Josephine":

"If an early stage founder is against having a Chairman we finesse it by using an independent non exec." [VC]

The key point that came up time and again was:

"It's about making sure that the strategic agenda is debated by the right group of people."

Some felt that, especially at an early stage, an important aspect was:

"Sharing of the burden of promoting the company."

---

[1] Cadbury Report 1992

A huge aspect of the Chairman's role is Capital Providers:

> "Increasingly over time the Chairman can take on the role of
> handling the shareholders."

One heartfelt and deeper than it looks on paper comment I liked was:

> "Dealing with issues."

After all, for the experienced Chairman "there is always something"
which rather relates to the observation that "history is just one darn
thing after another":

> "As Chairman you also need to be a chameleon – so many different
> needs/modes."

Timing is everything:

> "The Chairman has to organise when a direction has been to be
> found convergent, not divergent."

Taking this to the max, when the proverbial hits the fan prior experience as a CEO is invaluable:

> "In extremis the Chairman has to step-in and manage the company
> even when their Board has run away from this responsibility."

As always there are many paths up the mountain and the model of Executive
Chairman does exist. The input I had on this was simple and clear:

> "If it works it works."

The model has obvious challenges compared to the more frequent model
(in the UK at least). However let's get back to basics – we are talking,
in general, of a handful of people in a room here. If those people work
well, they work well. It's a bit like football or bridge – you can play a
rare system – but if you win, you win.

THE COMPLEX CHAIRMAN/CEO RELATIONSHIP

The realpolitik of the Boardroom is all about who has control. In terms of CEO and Chairman it will be somewhere along the spectrum of NewCo "CEO fires the Chairman" and FTSE "Chairman fires the CEO".

More complicated models exist. Thus, for example, when you have a Chairman, a non-founder CEO and a founder you have a sort of triangulation vibe going on. Without drilling down into this level of complexity, it's not immensely different from simply having multiple founders on an early Board – there will be differences of opinion and the need to formulate a joint policy.

Let's keep things simple however. Sticking to the simple Chairman and CEO/founder model it is important to notice the complex relationship between the two positions. An experienced Chairman summed this up ranging from the simple power dimension to the need of a Chairman to play on both sides of the net – they are, after all, Chairman of the Board not Chairman of the CEO:

"Chair is hired by CEO as Founder.

Chair can be fired by CEO as Founder.

Chair's role in replacing CEO in instances of sustained underperformance or fallouts around strategy.

Chair's role in holding CEO to account on behalf of shareholders (aggressive VCs in particular).

Chair's role in being coach, mentor and shield to the CEO (from aggressive VCs in particular)."

Reflecting these last two dimensions a CEO responding to the question "what does the founder/CEO need?" said:

"You [the CEO] will need two things from a Chairman (a) pastoral support and (b) tough love."

Perhaps unsurprisingly CEOs had a common perspective on which side of the net they preferred the Chairman to play (although noting that early-stage asymmetry must fade over time as the firm matures and ownership/control becomes more dispersed):

"A Chairman is a human shield especially against capital providers when they misbehave."

"Chair fights your [CEO] corner against investors or bashes you down."

"[When there are] fights amongst capital providers [the Chairman] takes pressure off executives."

This all leads nicely into "neutrality" or "independence" which is an area where experience varies massively and certainly deviates from "textbook" or "one size fits all". Naturally, VCs, or some VCs with certain sizes of stake, are very happy to have the whip hand. In other circumstances, not unsurprisingly the founder(s) is/are very happy to have control. And in between there's a balance where both recognise that a neutral Chairman is an asset. So "your mileage may vary" definitely applies to this issue of "Chairman positioning".

Generally there was a leaning towards neutrality or independence although early in the journey there is this need to act more as a shield for CEOs. The following quotes are all pro-independence of a Chairman and of course Independence Is A Good Thing. However balance these with the "human shield" angle above, the need to protect the founder/ CEO *when the company would not survive their departure*:

"An independent Chairman is very important."

"The Chairman is the impartial role."

"A Chairman is an arbiter, a mediator, who balances stakeholders."

"A 'neutral' [on the Board] is always useful – a professional Chair of Board does that."

In the next chapter on NEDs we will look at independence in greater detail. As always a handful of letters in one apparently simple word conceal a whole world of complexity.

This Chairman-CEO balance can have something of a tipping point along the journey between "CEO fires Chairman" and "Chairman fires CEO". It also comes with a sense of lifestyle change – somewhere along the journey you go from being comfortable on your throne in your own kingdom to having to polish your boots and do some unaccustomed square-bashing as you are held to grown-up standards. As a CEO who had crossed that Rubicon and recently acquired a high-powered Chairman said:

> "Rest assured my new Chair comes with its own challenges, I am having to quickly adjust back to having a boss!"

One day you have a baby and although there are plenty of worries and teething troubles it's all cosy and in your control (acts of God/the Fates to one side). Then in a blink of an eye you find your kid beating you at tennis and you suddenly have to get into proper shape and lose your mid-life paunch. Even then it will be tough to regain your mastery of the situation.

Actually this is a good point at which to raise a topic that none of my too-carefully selected interviewees mentioned. Not all founders want their business to cross that Rubicon. Plenty of SmallCo founders kind of settle at some stage, they would prefer to be cosy rather than grow, and if they still have sufficient control they can ease off the growth path and give up on "growing-up":

> "It's the 'vicarage and Maserati' syndrome [ie if your NewCo yields you a nice Cotswolds house and a nice car, well, that's more than good enough] that means many UK entrepreneurs do not achieve the success of their American counterparts [who are more ambitious and driven to want much more]."

Anyway it's your choice dude. Just be aware that somewhere along the journey there will be a Rubicon, which, when crossed, will be near impossible to retreat across.

APPOINTING A CHAIRMAN

In the early days of NewCo there are many demands on your time, effort and pulling-power:

> "Chairman? Most [Startups/ScaleUps] don't have a decent one."

> "At first you can choose an Angel but the further you go up the curve the more you should spend time finding the right one who can handle the growth curve."

Later on you will appreciate the need for a higher-powered Chairman and thus be prepared to make the investment of your time and potentially head-hunter fees.

In the Tech world coding tests are a key technique for many interviews of developers – after all you are less after someone who can talk well than you are someone who can code well. This is a useful analogy for recruiting Chairmen:

> "Interviewing the potential Chairmen – give them recent difficult strategic situations or challenges you have had and where you/ the Board/the current Chairman didn't necessarily find the right way. We did this and with the Chairman we eventually found, we were super-impressed with his robust answers to various situations which we wouldn't have had the confidence to try on our own."

Your ideal Chairman needs to be something of a shapeshifter, purring along like a Bentley on smooth roads, but equally show no naivety and plenty of realpolitik when the going gets tough and you get assailed by bandits (inside the Company, on the Board or outside the Company).

Do not forget that you are unlikely to be The Greatest Company Ever. So unless you are blessed with good fortune you will find it hard to appoint your Fairy Godmother Chairman:

> "I am getting five Chairman offers a month (as I understand compliance and business) and I'm not that good [MB: excessive modesty no doubt] there are just so few in the market."

"Be realistic, but still aim high."

As with all things time and effort goes a long way:

"We spent six months courting a new Chairman. It was super-time-consuming but the time was very well spent – it was worth it."

TYPES OF CHAIRMEN

What you need in part relates to gaps in your armoury.

"[Different Companies have different] types of desire for Chairman – mentor, figurehead, door opener."

Just as with a good spouse/partner you will ideally get plenty of attributes:

"Our new Chairman brings different skillsets. Air cover and protection. Good Board meetings. Brings perspective on the industry and how we interact with it."

In heavily regulated sectors the Chairman carries more kudos points than a plain NED:

"Our Chairman brought regulatory credibility."

The flip side of this equation is that someone with a good regulatory reputation, all too easy to lose, is risking that reputation on folks who don't have such a good reputation and thus they can be hard to attract.

Extending the idea of different *types* of Chairman this quote, importantly, was from a VC:

"'Chairman as Rolodex' model and/or with BigCo Board or extensive Startup experience to manage factions and to eg deal with VCs when they turn aggressive."

We will return to the VC angle later but one interviewee had an interesting rule of thumb:

> "FS-Chairmen can often accept poor VC term sheets – VC money at poor rates or on poor terms [which in itself can put off later VCs]."

This brings in the whole "horses for courses" angle in the growth phases. Fluency in capital raising – especially the realpolitik thereof – is likely to be important in all Chairmen. However especially in the earlier stages, the Chairman does not have to be Board expert at raises if another NED is. However, the further you go up the growth curve the more likely it is that the type of Chairman you need *has* seen it all before and can deal with demanding actual and potential investors.

To this point of managing the Chairmen along the growth curve:

> "Pretty soon on, try and get a Chairman – someone the CEO looks up to is not a bad thing."

As you progress along the journey the necessity of starting to keep more of an eye on ensuring that your fires don't burn out of control creeps in. This type of risk management has always been an issue but when you have minimal staff and minimal capital it's unlikely (if possible) that your tiny sparks can cause an explosion. The size of potential explosions get larger as your capital, staff and client numbers increase. One of your engineering challenges is to ensure that the probability of explosions goes down faster than the potential size of explosions increases.

This quote is from a CEO of a SmallCo that went through a tradesale, looking back on what their final Chairman had brought to the party:

> "Our [BigCo] Chairman helped formalise things by just the right amount. We had never had a risk matrix which he required. We thought we knew the key risks but the act of formalising it was very helpful. He didn't ask for a list of hundreds of risks as he understood how stretched we were, but just the key handful and what we were doing about them."

This control discipline clearly came at the right stage for that Company and was of the appropriate weight. However premature Board focus on Fire Safety rather than Prometheus can become a real ball and chain.

One of a CEO's important honesty strengths is to admit mistakes. The realpolitik, as I am sure you all know, is that relationships in general don't always turn out the way you had expected:

> "We had to sack our Chairman – he had too much focus on minutes, agenda, bureaucracy and not enough on growing the business."

REQUIREMENTS

There are the usual, obvious, "job description-y" requirements. Don't use too many adjectives however otherwise you will never find anyone:

> "Chairmen need respect, gravitas, relevant skills. Role is very very different in different companies."

> "A Chairman needs to be empathetic."

Naturally folks differ stylistically. You can have two Chairmen who achieve equal results by doing things in opposing styles (eg introverted/extroverted). So it is less of a question of compiling a list of nice words – experienced, diplomatic etc – and more of a question of a match between founder(s)/CEO and the Chairman personally and stylistically.

There is no right Chairman for everyone any more than there is the right spouse for everyone. This analogy carries much weight:

> "You want a Chairman as partner."

Sticking with the partner angle, other emotive aspects are important, at least at the early stage when there needs to be some sparks of passion to help the fires burn:

> "A neutral Chairman?! Unrealistic. At small company stage you need passion."

Beyond the personal connection/relationship there is the important angle that one of the major requirements is to fill gaps in the executive team:

> "We needed gravitas. We got, via investors, three or four suggestions for Chairman. In the end we took an ex-CEO of a major FS incumbent who was also a serial entrepreneur."

One case study that was explained to me was where the CEO had a huge chunk of his personal wealth in his firm:

> "It's best if the Chairman is not a big shareholder as he will then be able to walk away [from a bad deal]."

In this case the CEO related that he had had so much at stake that, when at the last moment they were being screwed over re funding, the Chairman got up and walked out taking the CEO with him. This subsequently led to the capital returning to the table on sensible terms. The CEO said that due to his own personal over-exposure he would never have been able to walk away on his own.

As we saw earlier share options are generally part of the package. Many Chairmen have successful careers behind them and what may appear to be a significant stake to a first-time young founder might well be a round of drinks to the Chairman. All a question of proportion and taste in drinks:

> "You need a Chairman with skin in the game and not an Angel but not overly deeply invested (walk-away-ability)."

Back to "many paths up the mountain", I equally spoke to early stage founders where an Angel had made an excellent Chairman. Again there is a stage/phase thing here. Once you start mixing categories of Capital Provider you need more of an independent Chairman. As SmallCos are not yet entirely living in the tick-box world you can decide what amount of independence is required and what is or isn't a significant stake.

IT'S NOT ALL ROSES BEING A SMALLCO CHAIRMAN

Former CEOs/NEDs who became Chairman often found that the actuality was rather different to their expectations:

> "I was a Chairman a couple of times but I hated it." [serial Founder/ CEO]

> "I don't think I would be Chair again if I had known what it involved."

> "It's a very different thing, in some ways I don't like being more of a referee, I preferred being a player." [Serial CEO/Chairman]

It is also a role that can be a load of hassle. One interviewee, long past the nappy stage with his children, related to me his feelings when approached by a relatively young, naive, if enthusiastic, firm in search of a Chairman:

> "They don't realise how much time I am going to have to spend changing nappies and teaching them the ABC."

It would be something of a mistake for current CEOs to see Chairmanship being for them a kind of post-burnout, semi-retirement promotion/gig that they might do one day when they can't be bothered to do real work any more. Said folks might be better off having a holiday for a year or two and coming back and founding another company. Equally, whatever your prior CV, naturally before you take on your first role as a Chairman make sure you do your face-to-face, realpolitik research to understand the pros and cons of the role and what it really entails. It ain't all roses.

7. NEDs

Non-Executive-Directors are ubiquitous and de rigueur these days but in our myopic times the long view is poorly understood. So we start this chapter with a look at NEDs over the past five centuries. Actually the first four are easy – there was no such thing as a NED. They first appeared in the 19thC in the V2 Company and didn't exactly – er – "command the highest respect". In the late 20thC, almost out of the blue, "independent NEDs" suddenly became the panacea[1] of Listed Corporate Governance, the remedy that cures all known ills. Allegedly.

So far we have used the abbreviation NED to cover a whole host of different terms – external Director, outside Director, independent Director, investment Director and any other such nomenclatures – there have clearly been many concepts of the NED over the past century. The Holy Grail in the V3 Board for a NED is the sacred "independence", which label obviously confers magical powers beyond those of normal men/women. If it did not then such a NED might be "just human" after all and not capable of bandaging the V2 Company wounds sufficiently to staunch its genetically-caused bleeding all over society and the economy. What does "independent" mean according to the Holy Writ of the Corporate Governance Bible? What is the realpolitik, or indeed relevance, of "independence" to the SmallCo Board?

The idea that NEDs "represent shareholders" is widely heard but what can this mean? How can NEDs represent people they have never met?

Back in the day you just needed to be the right sort of chap (and it was almost entirely chaps) to be a NED. Now you can do courses lasting months and get a Diploma in NEDing – or at least NED *qua*

---

[1] Just to keep the Olympian motif going, Panacea was the Goddess of universal remedy.

"compliance robot". Some long-standing BigCo NEDs have by now given up the unequal struggle against robotisation:

> "I like your sense of outrage, I've given up by now. If there's a rule I just ask what it is and do what it says." [listed/unlisted NED]

Next we turn to the theory of NEDing and thence the realpolitik of what NEDs are doing in SmallCos.

Never hire "just a NED" – hire a certain *type* of NED that fills a gap for your Company and your Board. We take a look at nine types of NED – which do you have? Which don't you have that you would like to have? What do you want from your NEDs?

Finally we look at some examples of aligning expectations with your NEDs. The SmallCo Board is not large and it is as important for you as it is for your NED that you are both on the same page with the same expectations.

A BRIEF HISTORY OF NEDS

"NEDs" in the simplest sense are Directors who are not executive Directors, who come to the company rarely and have no place in the day-to-day management of the organisation. Their powers/authority derive from their position on the Board.

The English V1 Company was governed by a legislature, a Court of all the members/owners on top of an executive, a Court of a tiny subset of members/owners who had been committed to do something specific (ie managerial). There was neither any concept nor any possible role for any kind of NED. The very idea would have been incomprehensible and in a sense *against the Company's constitution* (as you had to be a member to gain admittance). What business (ha!) would anyone have being in your Courts who was neither member nor owner?

The first NEDs appeared on V2 Company Boards. Their function in the 19thC was simply to add credibility and help attract funds:

> "It was in the last two decades of the nineteenth century that it became the fashion for many companies to seek a titled person to

sit on the board as a non-executive director, on the basis that this would add tone or lustre, attracting the investors."[2]

As we shall see later in this chapter this type/role of NED still exists today (unsurprisingly as SmallCo is a V2 company). Professional advisers – solicitors and accountants[3] were also amongst the first NEDs (and once again this also exists today in some early SmallCos).

For almost the entire history of NEDs they commanded minimal to negative respect. In the 19[th]C they were known as "guinea-pigs"[4] and were similarly regarded well into the 1980s: "Christmas tree decorations".[5]

Being a NED was less demanding back in the day. If you are a hard-working NED look away now:

"(Coote) got me in as a director of something or other. Very good business for me – nothing to do except go down to the City once or twice a year to one of those hotel places – Cannon Street or Liverpool Street – and sit around a table where they have some very nice new blotting paper. Then Coote or some clever Johnny makes a speech simply bristling with figures, but fortunately you needn't listen to it – and I can tell you, you often get a jolly good lunch out of it."[6]

It is a great irony, and some phenomenal rebrand, that:

"...a role that has traditionally attracted so little respect has now become a cornerstone of best governance practice."[7]

Now the NED is the central feature in the newly developing V3 Company. The independent NED is the panacea for all known Company Governance ills. I raised the question: "If you are the panacea then

---

[2] Slinn Spira "A Jolly Good Lunch: the evolution of the role of the non-executive director in the UK" 2002

[3] In the inter-war years with mergers creating ever-larger companies these faded away to be replaced by a full-time in-house accountant who later turned into the modern CFO.

[4] Websters 2013 "A director (usually one holding a number of directorships) who serves merely or mainly for the fee (in England, often a guinea) paid for attendance." Traders were paid in pounds but Gentlemen in guineas (£1.05).

[5] Tiny Rowland CEO Lonrho.

[6] Agatha Christie "The Seven Dials Mystery" Collins 1929

[7] Spira, Bender "Compare and Contrast: perspectives on board committees" 2004

surely you are being set up as the fall guys?" with an experienced listed/ unlisted NED who replied: "Yes we are."

Every corporate collapse, every study (there have been many[8]) showing that there is zero empirical evidence that they help, is followed by a doubling-down or a redefinition of "independence" by supporters.[9] All of which leads to an ever-more robotised and systematised role for BigCo NEDs who are becoming nigh on off-balance-sheet civil servants, in effect auditing processes and policies according to paint-by-number guides.

How did we get here? How did the NED go from laughing stock or, at best, a good chap who wasn't going to rock your boat, to panacea? How did the NED go from zero to hero?

In any sense remotely similar to how the concept is used today, independent NEDs date from the 1970s with the dawn of Corporate Governance in the US, post the collapse of Penn Central. In the UK the first straw in the wind was the 1973 Watkinson Committee[10] which was the first to suggest that ListedCos should have NEDs on the Board to *monitor* the executives – **a novel concept at the time.** Government white papers in 1973 and 1977 suggested that NEDs could benefit Boardrooms but held back from mandatory recommendations. These white papers led to the Bank of England, along with eight other bodies, leading the 1982 creation of ProNed, an organisation to promote NEDs. **At that time only around half of UK ListedCos had NEDs at all and only one-fifth of those were independent.** The Reagan/Thatcher decades of the 1980s moved the governance focus back to the shareholder during hostile M&A activity and there was something of a pause in the rebranding of NEDs.

This is a first-hand (emailed) report of one of my interviewees experience of UK Plc Boards at the end of the ancien regime:

"I remember the conversation surrounding our selection of the new round of NEDs in the early '90s as being focused on broad business-helpful connections rather than any modern notion of 'effective

---

8   See eg Baum "The Rise of the Independent Director: A Historical and Comparative Perspective" 2016

9   There is a whole industry out there – consultants, academics et al whose livelihoods are intimately tied up with "Corporate Governance" being A Big Thing.

10   Chaired by Cadbury Schweppes Chairman Lord Watkinson. Anyone spotting a Cadbury thread?

challenge' or 'oversight' – and the surprise/shock that arose when some of these individuals had the temerity to question the executives' views re pay. My earlier experience outside FS left some of the same impressions. That said I think the 'avuncular' factor (as in your podcast[11]) was also present and probably listened to (but not necessarily admitted to). From a personal perspective I saw NEDs as people that I had to secure alliances with as they were part of the support structure for seeking to take a principled but unpopular line."

UK BigCo NEDs as we know them today were created by the Cadbury Report in 1992. Cadbury himself chaired ProNed from 1984–95[12] and was thus rather pro (sic) the whole NED thing. Given that the Bank of England had driven the creation of ProNed and the Administrative State is always most careful to pick the *right* Chair for any given report we can assume that the Powers That Be had long before decided that NED-centricity was The Answer They Wanted.[13] In 1994, ProNed, by now unsurprisingly worth rather more, was sold to headhunters Egon Zehnder.

But, vitally, what *role* would a redefined NED play? The CBI in its response made clear its concern over turning NEDs into PC Plods:

"We support the view of the committee that non-executive directors have an important role to play in companies. Perhaps because of its terms of reference, the committee has focused narrowly on their monitoring role. We think this is unfortunate, because it understates the contribution which the non-executives can make to the growth of a business: their different experience brings a fresh eye to problems and the development of strategy. Moreover the concept of the unitary board is based on all directors being

---

[11] I'd referred to the role of NEDs that week. Avuncular as in "arm round the shoulder support/advice".

[12] In governance terms this would appear to be quite some conflict of interest. However even if the Administrative State moves glacially, as we can see, the glacier had been moving, albeit slowly, in this direction for twenty years.

[13] And I guess at the time if you were an important part of the Administrative State and did not understand the history of governance then maybe you might have thought this a useful step yourself, especially if you did not have a remit to repair the genetic flaws in the Company V2.

equally responsible for its actions; its effectiveness depends on members of the board as a whole working together. It is for the board to distribute functions to its members; attempts to reserve tasks to one class of directors will create the danger of opening the way to a two-tier system."[14]

As we saw earlier this has led to an utter phase shift in the V3 Board which is by now almost entirely a "Conformance Board" with Advisory Boards surfacing as "Performance Boards". The V3 Board has, as feared by the CBI, split within itself into "angels and (potential) villains"[15] as it has been described but more fundamentally the Board's role has shifted dramatically towards Corporate Control and away from Corporate Creativity. But are the angels (in the heavenly not investment sense) that much more angelic than the villains? A US study measured this:

"Moreover, and perhaps even more troubling, our data also shows that independent directors themselves are not necessarily immune from the temptations of financial fraud, particularly with the gains to be had from backdating stock options. SOX's reliance on them may simply have transferred oversight responsibilities from compromised executives to compromised and ill-informed board members."[16]

Hmm.

The SmallCo takeaway here is that in V2 Companies the NED position has existed right from the start but only as "NED as someone adding some special sort of value to the Company" not as a warden overseeing inherently untrustworthy individuals. Unlike, however, in the days of Agatha Christie's clever Johnnys, no SmallCo is going to blow good money on someone turning up to just to warm seats and have a good lunch. SmallCos need something far more value-adding

---

[14] CBI "Summary of the CBI Response To The Cadbury Committee Draft Report On The Financial Aspects Of Corporate Governance" July 1992

[15] As per FTSE CEO Corrin in "Accountancy" April 1993

[16] Schipani "Do Independent Directors Curb Financial Fraud? The Evidence and Proposals for Further Reform" 16/4/17

in return and fortunately do not have to worry about the BigCo NED mentality until they get near the pre-IPO "Two Tribes" stage. At which point as we saw ideally they hire NEDS who are not just "compliance robots" but also understand business, Corporate Creativity and the realpolitik of SmallCo land. This hiring task does not get easier as the divide between the two types of NEDing continues to widen.

WHAT IS INDEPENDENCE?

> "An independent director – a part-timer whose contact with the corporation is necessarily limited – is not inherently better suited to further the interests of shareholders than is an inside director. Current rules thus over-rely on independence, transforming an essentially negative quality – lack of ties to the corporation – into an end in itself, and thereby fetishizing independence."[17]

The V1 Company was ruled by its owners, the V2 Company by its management and the V3 Company by folks who neither have ownership nor management ties to the Company and are "independent". That is an unprecedented and most curious historical development. Can you really govern a land that you know little about? Constitutionally it is a very odd thing and as we noted not even colonialism as Governors at least lived in the countries they governed. The best colonial rule was by people who *immersed* themselves in the lands they governed not those who flew in rarely and did not stay long before flying out again.

But what does this fetishised "independence" mean? The author of the lead-in quote adds (my bold):

> "...an independent director is a person on a company's board **who is not dependent on someone or something related to the company.** A comparative analysis, however, quickly shows that no universal definition of independence exists."

---

[17] Rodrigues "The Fetishization of Independence" 2007

Remarkably:

> "Given the ubiquity of the concept in statutes, listing rules, and corporate governance codes, it is surprising how little theoretical consideration has been given to the nature of 'independence'."[18]

Notwithstanding which, leading Corporate Governance advisory firms and prominent Corporate Governance involved organisations (World Bank, OECD), have often assumed that there is one definition based on the US concept of independence (which is not the most-common). Contrary to widespread assumptions of the transplantation of the US definition, Puchniak et al,[19] having reviewed 245 Corporate Governance codes from 87 jurisdictions found that *only a handful ever adopted the US definition.*

Who or *what* are you supposed to be independent of?

Generally as a starter one "what" is being independent of financial exposure to the company other than Directorial fees.

In addition **Sarbanes-Oxley equates independence with not being a close relative of** *management* **but not independent of major** *shareholders*. However in locations with predominantly CCC businesses clearly independence from the large shareholder(s) is highly relevant.

The super-important corporate-wise state of **Delaware's approach is situational** – it is one's independence from each situation – for example transactions – that matters.[20]

The UK initially adopted the US definition but in 2003 amended it to being **independence from both** *management* **and** *significant shareholders*. Most of the world uses a similar definition.

What about independence of creditors, suppliers, or employees? Higgs[21] even stated that in the broadest sense of the word *all* NEDs need to be **independent-minded**:

---

[18] Baum "The Rise of the Independent Director: A Historical and Comparative Perspective" 2017

[19] Puchniak, Baum, Nottage "Independent Directors in Asia – A Historical, Contextual and Comparative Approach" 2017

[20] Ibid.

[21] Higgs "Review of the Role and Effectiveness of Non-Executive Directors" 2003

"…all non-executive directors need to be independent of mind and willing and able to challenge, question and speak up. All non-executive directors, and indeed executive directors, need to be independent in this sense."

Back in the day when 3i was pretty much the only source of VC capital in the UK, they used to apply a criterion of **financial independence** *per se* to NEDs – ie that the NEDs should be financially independent as individuals in their own right.

Although legally, *all* Directors are obliged by law to protect shareholders' interests even Higgs acknowledged that even if this is The Law there is a realpolitik which can be more powerful:

"Although there is a legal duty on all directors to act in the best interests of the company, it has long been recognised that in itself this is insufficient to give full assurance that these potential conflicts will not impair objective board decision-making."

Puchniak et al add that there is a *"surprising absence of empirical evidence"* **around the world that independent directors improve corporate performance or reduce corporate wrongdoing. Baum talks about** *"blind faith"* **in the concept as there is no empirical data to support the value of independence.**[22]

However rules in each territory are always "one size fits all" and Must Be Obeyed At All Times and have nothing to do with *actual as opposed to formulaic* independence. **A further definition of independence is length of time on a given company's Board.** An experienced NED I spoke to was on the Board of an important UK entity of an overseas organisation (whose headquarters were in a country which retains a strong pre-rules-fetishisation business culture). He was relating to me that he had reached his nine years "limit" (beyond which on some regulation or another "by definition" he could no longer "be independent") and thus he had to leave the Board. He tried to explain this to the parent company:

---

[22] Both authors op. cit.

"I explained 'why' time and time again. It made no sense to them. Their comment was 'but you know us well, you know our business well, and you give us great independent advice, you are independent why should you have to leave us?'"

A good question well presented. All of which gets us back to what our ancestors knew and what many cultures around the world still know. Strip any sense of linguistic sexism from the following – none is intended but the slightly archaic language conveys some tone we have utterly lost in becoming robotised. **No amount of rules can substitute for a good chap (/chapess) who is ethical (and does not need to be sent on courses to tell them what ethics are), who is independent-minded, who is strong-willed enough to put forward contrary opinions, who is experienced, and who is wise.**

THE REALPOLITIK OF NED INDEPENDENCE IN SMALLCOS

Having seen that independence is differently defined in different places, and that there is no empirical evidence for its value, let us turn to an assessment of the value of NED independence in SmallCo land.

Although there is (currently) no legal or regulatory need for independent NEDs on SmallCo Boards (tick, tock goes the clock?) the realpolitik and relevance of independence cropped up several times:

"What does 'independent' actually mean? Can this be set by codes of practice or should this be left to the Chairman to ensure?"

"You have to consider the independent NED versus a NED."

What is the realpolitik of independence? Well, let's start with bowling at the middle stump – **I believe that complete independence does not exist, all Directors are, at a minimum, reputationally exposed:**

"Looking back I realise that I thought far too little about personal reputational risk."

In the case studies we saw on the Two Tribes Board it is precisely because NEDs are *reputationally dependent* on the company's reputation/performance that the BigCo NEDs' first reaction is defensive ("attack is the best form of defence"). They need to protect themselves – Board roles come and go (especially given Corporate Governance PC rules around length of Board service) but their career and reputation persists. And that's before we even start to consider those NEDs who are deemed to be "Approved Persons" by the Regulatory State. They are risking that valuable badge as well.

Is the Chairman independent? We have covered this complex topic in the previous chapter. A Chairman clearly isn't independent of the company in a real sense (even if there is some rule that says as long as X, Y, Z he is) as his reputation is intimately tied up with it. See how your career goes if you chair a couple of firms that go bust. Furthermore, as we saw, especially in early SmallCos, whilst playing an important role in managing the whole Board, the realpolitik is that he is ultimately behind the CEO. Even Higgs recommended that over half the Board *excluding the Chairman* should be independent.

What about financial independence? *For many/most experienced businessmen with decades of successful career behind them their reputation matters more to them than a few more quid and a handful of options* which, statistically speaking, are unlikely to turn out to be worth anything given SmallCo failure rates. Notwithstanding which, listed rules focus on the size of the options/etc *in absolute terms*. Yet it is relative terms that determine any sense of financial dependence – what might be Big Beer for you and me in terms of exposure might well be not even a round of drinks for your zillionaire co-NED. Even then relative terms might have to be amended for liquid wealth not total wealth – as with the decline of the landed gentry many were asset rich but cashflow poor.

One interviewee asks:

"Can investors be independent?"

In a particular situation on a particular Board a given investment NED may well sometimes be independent and sometimes not. Investment Directors appointed by VCs, institutions et al are clearly there to represent their organisation. An Angel/angel may well be there being a good "independent" or he may be there purely talking his own book. Only to the left-hemisphere are there permanent and definable attributes like "independence", to the right-hemisphere everything is contextual.

But before we go too far down V3 thinking and focusing on "independence" for its own sake we need to address why one would value it in SmallCo land. After all for millennia there was no such thing – the government of nations and businesses was always something that came from the people/members/owners not some "independent" folks who pop in and out now and then to dispense justice and direction. When "independents" did that in England, be they Romans or Anglo-Saxons or Vikings or Normans, we called it an invasion and fought back.

SmallCo remains a CCC variant of a V2 Company where the Board is comprised of management *and* substantial owners who are committed and have skin in the game – so what is the *relevance* of independence?

I heard of many circumstances where an independent *perspective* was very helpful in mediating between major capital providers and management. In this case a neutral-ish, but more importantly, able and experienced, Chairman is the first port of call. In specific cases another independent NED might well be helpful. In the next section we will consider the value of a NED specifically tasked with representing the interests of the class of shareholders not present at the meeting given the Achilles heel of CCCs.

Having spoken and researched widely, it seems to me that what you want on your SmallCo Board is *generally* not to fret about independence as such although having *someone* who is *independent-minded* (by nature as much as formula/rule) on the Board can be helpful. This doesn't just apply to Boards. When I was Head of Fixed Income Investment at Kleinworts I often consulted a contrarian chap who wasn't in the hierarchy at all and who could be relied on to disagree with me about roughly everything (lol), which at least meant I always had someone put a compelling and opposing case to mine which was helpful. This would be a bit extreme for Boards but vice versa groupthink can be a real problem. A little later we shall have a quote by Warren Buffet on this matter; all too often what is fingered as "lack of ethics" is actually groupthink and a lack of substantive disagreement even if formulaic independence exists.

Overall you want the best value-adding NEDs you can find on your Board "independent" or not – business experience matters far more than box-ticking. I mentioned chaps/chapesses before but another vocabulary is a not-so-frequently-used word these days – "character" – you really *do* want NEDs of good character. In East Asian businesses for example, **any consideration of the independence of outside directors is, to this day, less important than their character and business ability and commitment to the "House".**[23]

CAN NEDS REALLY REPRESENT SHAREHOLDERS?

If you are a NED do you "represent shareholders"? If so how do you do it? Do you meet them? Email them? Conduct a Twitter poll? Or, as a member of the Boarding classes, are you granted clarity in your patrician/paternalistic wisdom? Do you instinctively "know" what is best for the masses?

I assume it's none of the above – we will turn to what I believe a NED actually does in the next section.

But first let's examine this very important angle of "representing shareholders" which is commonplace language and cropped up in some interviews.

It is certainly far more curious than it immediately appears. It's repeated like a mantra without much consideration of the meaning thereof. At one level this is somewhat in the mind of a NED – after all they do try and do that. It's certainly The Official Party Line, legal duties and all that. But at another level it is misguided. How can a NED represent people they have never met or communicated with?

As we see all too often with governments *elected officials voted in on manifesto-ed commitments* have a great problem in representing the electorate (or increasingly paying any attention to their own manifesto). How much more impossible must it be for unelected, or elected but no-manifesto/unknown, folks to represent people they have never met.

---

[23] The granular level of Japanese society was the House – *"ie"* – which covered both family and merchant "houses". Property was owned by the House not by the individuals.

What shareholders want *varies* and you can't possibly know what they want. **As we shall see one of the biggest stresses on company Boards comes from different capital providers wanting different things.**

Any notion of NEDs as representing shareholders is perhaps true only in three narrow cases.

ONE. It is axiomatic in Concentrated Control Companies that Investment NEDs (representing the firm/fund which provides the capital) do represent a shareholder whose needs they know as it is themselves.

TWO. Naturally we can assume shareholders are against ludicrous excesses or obvious fraudulence of management. Thus if you are a NED on my Board you might reasonably assume that my shareholders do not want me to use half of the recent raise on a marble statue of myself to adorn reception. So you can definitely represent them in those trivial cases. However what would you know as to whether shareholders as a whole, or as a majority, want, or are happy, with me expanding into business line X? You can't do that as you don't know what they would say – in a sense we are talking about representative governance at best. In practice I don't even think it is that as whenever I've seen some AGM voting form, I next to never recognise a name on it let alone anything about said name.

THREE. **There is one highly important case in which an independent NED can represent *some* shareholders. This is the case of protecting the interests of minority, small shareholders as a class.** The archetypal governance problem in BigCo is that management may make merry at the expense of distant, know-next-to-nothing owners. The archetypal governance problem in CCCs is that large shareholders – which often means founder(s)/CEO *and* VC(s) – make merry at the expense of the distant, know-next-to-nothing small investors. Crowdfunding investors often receive B shares – which frankly might as well come with a subtitle that says "please don't screw me, I know you can now that I have B shares but please don't".

This is an utterly non-trivial concern:

> "I guess the protection of the little guy from the VC is hard – you need a sound founder (eg me). A lot of people act like dicks, for sure." [CEO/founder]

Like all the people I interviewed this CEO was a very ethical individual. But the realpolitik is that many are not. There are plenty of bad actors in all sizes of company and SmallCos are not inherently virtuous.

The problematic issue of minority shareholders in CCCs is massively amplified by the State – its legislation and regulation. The law/regulation *could quite easily* say (as it used to) "one class of share only". The FCA *could quite easily* ban crowdfunding sites from raising alphabet shares.

Ideally a SmallCo is not *just* "making money" but trying to add some value to the world and doing so ethically. An important part of those ethics is surely trying to treat your equity holders equitably even if the State has created rules that mean this is not mandatory.

One suggestion that has merit for virtuous SmallCos would be to consider having an independent NED who is responsible for being the voice of the small investor at the Board table. He/she can't know what small investors think – but at least someone has a formal role to speak up for the little guy and he can quite reasonably assume that neither Janet nor John want to be ripped off by a tyranny of the majority. Having a NED who is independent of management (I am not sure that *realpolitikally* this is always that easy for the SmallCo Chairman) and major shareholders has merit in these circumstances.

However not to be too utopian here in a world of realpolitik, said NED might not always ensure equality – a pragmatic case being a company that needs a raise to survive yet the raise comes on poor terms. In this case the small investor would lose out but at least his shares won't go to zero. The CEO/founder quoted above, reflecting the pressures on the founder/CEO and the value of support added:

"But it's hard to act like the good guy. Advisers also help."

LEARNING TO BE A NED

When I started my career oldskool NEDing was the only way. This was a cosy club – CEO of BigCo A would be a NED on BigCo B whose CEO would sit on BigCo C and so forth. No one told anyone how to Be A NED, however, everyone knew the convention "don't rock the boat". Furthermore, being Directors meant that at least they knew how Boards operated.

Now the pendulum has swung from one extreme to the other. In the days of a rules & regs paradise it takes training to learn to be a good "compliance robot". If you have a spare six grand and some time on your hands you can even do the FT's Diploma in Being A Non-Executive Director. One of my interviewees had done one of the long courses:

> "It was spectacularly dull, a hell of a lot of dry reading of the most boring material you could ever imagine."

None of these courses can teach wisdom, judgement, experience, EQ,[24] or provide industry-wide savoir-faire or contacts. What SmallCos really want from their NEDs is added-value, predominantly on the Corporate Creativity side of the equation with an "appropriate amount" of Corporate Control. SmallCos need well-connected, experienced businessmen/women who can help them grow their business and make it stronger over time. Your best training for that is not a course and some textbooks but rather decades spent in the University of Life's business department.

However before I appear to diss all training the realpolitik side of the coin is only one side. One the other side lie Directors' legal responsibilities. At a bare minimum Directors – whether executive or non-executive – need to know what these are – especially around insolvency. Getting bored for the length of at least a half-day course may have some merit. One obvious case may be for Angels and the like who drift onto a SmallCo Board as a result of a chunky investment but may not have had any Board experience. Another is former Boarders of a BigCo subsidiary Board where there are plenty of folks around to dot the i's and cross the t's for them and keep them out of jail.

This knowing your legal onions is doubly important on so-called "authorised institutions" and the like (in FS, insurance) where in Far Side cartoon terms you have an even larger target painted on your derrière and the regulator definitely knows where you live.

---

[24] Emotional Quotient, cf IQ.

THE THEORY OF NEDING

And now Buffet's quote on, inter alia, groupthink that I promised you:

> "Over a span of 40 years I have been on 19 public-company boards
> (excluding Berkshire's) and have interacted with perhaps 250 direc-
> tors. Most of them were 'independent' as defined by today's rules.
> But the great majority of these directors lacked at least one of the
> three qualities I value. As a result, their contribution to shareholder
> well-being was minimal at best and, too often, negative. These
> people, decent and intelligent though they were, simply did not
> know enough about business and/or care enough about sharehold-
> ers to question foolish acquisitions or egregious compensation. My
> own behavior, I must ruefully add, frequently fell short as well: Too
> often I was silent when management made proposals that I judged
> to be counter to the interests of shareholders. In those cases, colle-
> giality trumped independence."[25]

If the Sage of Omaha considers himself not always worthy, let alone
having seen plenty of good folk who aren't up to being this Holy
Panacea, maybe it's trickier than it looks. Maybe the reality is different
from the job description in codes, codes and codes?

It would require übermensch to fulfil all these codified tasks
and, like Atlas, to carry the corporate world on their shoulders. As the
FT noted:

> "Non-executive director: a task for which no one is qualified.
>
> The list of attributes required of a non-executive director is
> so long, precise and contradictory that there cannot be a single
> board member in the world who fully fits the bill. They need to be:
> supportive, intelligent, interesting, well-rounded and mature, funny,
> entrepreneurial, steady, objective yet passionate, independent,
> curious, challenging, and more. They also need to have a financial
> background and real business experience, a strong moral compass,
> and be first class all-rounders with specific industry skills."[26]

---

[25] Warren Buffett quoted in Monks Minow "Corporate Governance" 2006
[26] FT "Non-executive director: a task for which no one is qualified" 10/4/13

What does the IoD (Institute of Directors) say NEDing is? Its summary is relatively in-line with what SmallCo NEDs told me:

> "Essentially the non-executive director's (NED) role is to provide a creative contribution to the Board by providing independent oversight and constructive challenge to the executive directors."[27]

It does omit the key mentoring/support role so necessary especially for first-time entrepreneurs. It then proceeds to cover the What You Should Do stuff. I read it twice and it was all too much to stick in my mind. Even though it's at a high level it's not the kind of stuff that you could have in your head sauntering along to a Board meeting. It's much more like the kind of content you last saw when you were doing exam revision the night before, trying to memorise a ton of Important Points to regurgitate onto an exam paper the next day and then promptly forget forever more.

Let's pick a shorter summary from Investopedia:

> "1. A non-executive director is a member of a company's board of directors who is not part of the executive team.
>
> 2. A non-executive director typically does not engage in the day-to-day management of the organization but is involved in policymaking and planning exercises.
>
> 3. A non-executive directors' responsibilities include the monitoring of the executive directors and acting in the interest of the company stakeholders."[28]

Point 1 is clearly trivially true – trivially in so far as it just defines the term. The first half of 2 is pretty much the same as 1. The second half of 2 is very vague – policymaking and planning exercises? That could mean anything and is not well matched to SmallCo world. Let's be generous and say this means "help the company grow".

The first half of 3 reflects the reframing of the NED as Fire Safety Officer left in charge of potential pyromaniacs. However in BigCo this

---

[27] IOD "What is the role of the Non-Executive Director?"

[28] www.investopedia.com/terms/n/non-executive-director.asp

can only be at the super-super-super-highest level. As to acting in the interest of the company's stakeholders we discussed this earlier. If you are a NED good luck mate taking into consideration:

> "Creditors, directors, employees, government (and its agencies), owners (shareholders), suppliers, unions, and the community from which the business draws its resources."[29]

To quote myself earlier:

> "There is a real tow-truck problem here. The more extraneous content that the non-profit-making, non-entrepreneurial, bureaucratic State chucks in the truck that a company must tow, the slower the company will go as ever more of its resources go into non-profit-making activity and the less profit the company makes."

This core function – you know "business" and "profit" – is especially important in SmallCo. Established BigCos are generally making pretty chunky profits and one can have theological differences of opinion as to how much else they should or shouldn't be required to do or to tow. However in SmallCo land we are often busy not going under for the third time or struggling to wean ourselves off addictive capital raises rather than ushering in a New Age.

THE REALPOLITIK OF NEDING

So when they are not memorising a long list of Must Dos and considering saving the whale what do NEDs *actually* do in the world of realpolitik?

The obvious realpolitik is ultimately NEDs have to "look after number one".

We must never forget that if you are on a Board that trades when it is insolvent you are in Big Trouble. Limited liability drops away and you can be disqualified from being a Director. This is definitely Not Good!

---

[29] Wiki: Stakeholder (corporate)

Realpolitik does not mean you are too cool for school and the Law doesn't apply to you – it applies to us all. Realpolitik is rather, once one has followed the Law, then what? What happens in the real world of flesh and blood, fear and greed? What have experienced Boarders found that helps and what hinders the creation of a successful business?

Emphasis added:

> "As a director you are protected from the consequence of a failed company by the veil of incorporation, PROVIDED that you acted reasonably, responsibly and within the law. Failure to do so could make directors personally liable for the company's debt...
>
> **If the company is insolvent and if the Board of the company continues to trade whilst it is insolvent, the directors of the company may become personally liable to contribute to the company's assets and help meet the deficit to unsecured creditors if the company's financial position is made worse by the directors continuing to trade, instead of putting the company immediately into liquidation.**
>
> In other words that veil of incorporation can be lifted and the directors protection removed. Then you may face wrongful trading accusations and possibly even directors disqualification."[30]

One of my interviewees related the following tale. He was on a Board where both the management and VC were heavily exposed. Costs had been overrunning and a product was taking too long to develop. A familiar scenario. He raised concerns about cashflow and liquidity and the need to take independent advice on this. The rest of the Board felt he was being over-cautious and, having invested heavily in the business already, were intent on doubling-down. He made his concerns clear and stepped off the Board. Eight months later it went bankrupt.

All Directors have the same legal risk – however NEDs have just a fraction of the insight that executives have into what is *really* going on in the company. As many companies run into hundreds of thousands of employees, the realpolitik of this is that if you are a NED of such a company there is simply no way you *can* actually be "responsible" for that – no matter what laws and regulators say. **All you can do is make**

---

[30] www.companyrescue.co.uk "Trading Whilst Insolvent – A Worried Director's Guide"

sure you have an audit trail to show You Did The Right Thing As Far As You Could. Thus the listed NED's *real* first base is to cover themselves.

I found this myself when a couple of years ago, perchance I found myself on the shortlist for NED-ing on a very large organisation. Crowd-sourcing advice from my BigCo NED chums, the piece of personal advice they *all* gave me was "make sure everything you say is in the minutes". Derrière-covering. Some annotate pdfs with their views, to have an audit trail years down the track about "what they thought".

A SmallCo Chairman interviewee had been on some hotshot two-day course on Boards which included a lot of BigCo Boarders:

> "I was astonished that they thought the most helpful advice of the two days was to have your minutes at the end of the agenda (as otherwise much of the meeting can disappear in endless changes while folks make sure stuff they said was on the record)."

BigCo NEDs are not irrational people – if you were risking your whole reputation (and potentially assets) on the behaviour of zillions of people around the world you have never met in a company that you rarely go to in a political climate of tub-thumping about "holding Directors accountable" what would you do?[31]

It's a prime example that bureaucrats create bureaucratic rules which in turn convert otherwise normal people into bureaucrats. The Invasion of the Body Snatchers.

This impacts SmallCo land well before the "two tribes" stage. I recall some time ago being asked my advice by a NED chum, an "Approved Person" in the eyes of the FCA, who had been approached to be a NED by a Fintech in the early years of the revolution. What did I think of this Fintech? My reply was that said Fintech was very blue-chip as Fintechs go. However he decided not to proceed. After all, God forbid that you are on some SmallCo which blows up and part of the collateral damage becomes that The Unelected Who Must Be Obeyed decide that you are no longer an "Approved Person". Times have changed since and some "SmallCos" now have hundreds of millions in capital which ain't so small. However the purpose of the anecdote is

---

31 Don't judge a man until you have walked a mile in his moccasins. Then when you judge him you'll be a mile away and you'll also have his shoes.

simply to highlight the reality of what goes through a NED's mind in a hyper-regulated world.

If there is a problem on an FS Board where you fall under the Senior Managers Regime there are provisions that mean that you remain on risk *long after you have left*.[32] At which point you may or may not be adequately covered by the company's or your PII (professional indemnity insurance). This is nightmare territory.

Indeed it was put to me that Companies where the Board needs to be Approved in one way shape or form are actually a **different type of Company** – put crudely it is far easier to end up in the clink. To a certain degree as related to me by a few anxious founders it unrolls limited liability quite some way. If we were making a more detailed typology of companies one could call them V2A and V3A. **It *is* a qualitatively different gig being on such Boards, the Companies *do* have a different Governance context.** Caveat Director.

That NEDs look after themselves is not that surprising, rather it is the lengths to which they have to go to do so in the 21stC that is surprising. Agatha Christie's NED we quoted earlier didn't bother in the slightest with managing his own liabilities arising from the then sinecure. The realpolitik is that everyone on the Board has to look after themselves. NEDs do. Founder(s)/CEO(s) are trying to get what they want. Major capital providers on the Board are representing themselves. Angels/angels represent themselves and so forth.

Having first looked after Number One NEDs are also all *in very different ways* trying to "make the Company better". The following quote ties this in with the question of whether, in practice, NEDs actually "represent shareholders":

> "I've never thought of myself as 'representing shareholders' but as representing the company itself – in private companies there are often shareholder NEDs. Whilst a nebulous legal thing, doing the best for the company, not the staff, not the regulator, but trying to hold management to account in making the company ethically and sustainably successful would be my definition of my role.

---

[32] There was even an attempt to "reverse the burden of proof" in these – ie you are guilty unless you can prove you are innocent. This did not make it into the rules/law.

It's a funny thing but after a while as an NED you develop an affection (the 'duty of care') for the business itself – management and shareholders and even auditors these days come and go." [unlisted/listed NED]

So it seems to me that, in summary, SmallCo NEDs do their best, after having considered their own interests and to use their talents and experience, to "preserve order and increase prosperity" within the company.

NINE TYPES OF NED

Let's dive back into some quotes:

"Where is the value-add? Intros? Mentoring? Raise capital with you?"

The most important advice is don't just hire "a NED" As Boards Have Them:

"Don't just put anyone on the Board – people see it as a status symbol."

The most important aspect is to build a balanced team on the Board:

"On our Board we have too many with too similar perspectives" [CEO/founder]

You really should never be thinking of "a NED". Rather you need to know where your gaps are in the company and on the Board and look for a certain *type* of NED.

When you go shopping to make a certain meal for which you already have some of the ingredients, you don't ask the shop for "food". Rather you buy the chicken and saffron that you might be lacking.

A Tech/growth Board head-hunter gave an interesting taxonomy of the three main types of NED…

The **Trophy NED** (which as we saw dates back to the 19thC):

"Equals big PR gain re credibility re appointment; a marketing tool."

The **Practical NED**:

> "Specialists/experts, hands-on, 'not just there to flick through the papers'."

The **"NED on the side"**:

> "Someone with more important things to do eg current CEOs."

Integrating interviewees' comments on NEDs we can expand this categorisation and identify nine types of NED:

1) Trophy NEDs

> "NEDs can generate trust with your users, credibility."

Although caveat emptor:

> "Industry oldies may not be the right people."

> "I am fed up of hearing stories of long ago which just don't apply in the digital world."

2) Rolodex NEDs

> "NEDs can help you network – open doors & help you pitch."

This can be dangerous for the NED. One spoke to me about *"rolodex stripping"*. After his rolodex was thoroughly mined for useful contacts he was thanked for his services and told he would be no longer required. Caveat NED.

3) Skills NEDs

> "They [NEDs] can also help with negotiation – not just the price. We [CEO/team] were focused on price but we didn't focus as much on the T&Cs/SLA. Our NEDs helped us expand our focus."

> "Fund-raising rounds are a difficult process, [NEDs helped with]

how to pitch the nitty gritty, experience with due diligence processes (ours took nine months)."

"Sales and marketing is a discipline as complex as engineering, but somehow everyone seems to think they have an automatic expertise in the former. An experienced NED helped us with getting a structure in place to get proper insights on the sales and marketing environment."

4) Sector Experience NEDs

"NEDs? In FS it's all about the wider [eco-] system and players. This is far more complex than it appears and we couldn't have understood it anywhere as near as well without our NEDs."

"VCs often lack external expertise and one needs to bring it in separately."

5) Entrepreneurial NEDs

Those who have done part, or all, of the journey of creating and spreading fire:

"For me the most important aspect is business building rather than FS – I don't need domain expertise."

6) Angel and VC NEDs

See the next chapter on Capital Providers. Angels may have money but may not have Board experience and if they do it may have been in a BigCo subsidiary. VCs probably have more Board experience than you. Which brings its own challenges.

7) Control NEDs

We can split control into three broad categories – Financial, Risk (business risks) and Compliance (regulatory risks):

a) Financial Control

The larger your Company grows the more important this role is. However it's there right from the start *and you never know when you might be bitten.* One Startup I knew grew from nothing to over a hundred people and was listed on AIM with a valuation that touched nine figures. That was good going and made a lot of people a lot of money. On paper. It was completely undone by a fraud in one of its overseas offices.

What you need naturally depends on your stage:

> "If you are not a numbers person find a numbers person but NB the difference between a CFO and Chief Accountant/bean counter."

To make a simple caricature of the difference being described here, a bean counter, when profits are down, might suggest cutting marketing "costs". A CFO who understands business might suggest raising more capital and doubling marketing "expenditure".

One simple 19thC, almost pre-formal Board line-up, approach was related to me:

> "At first we just had an accountant to join us [founders] on the Board. At least we knew the accounts added up and some basic control questions were asked."

b) Risk Control

Risk in the sense I am using it here is the totality of *business* risks. I heard a tendency on some Boards to lump this in with compliance. Having been a Global Head of Risk when the field was being created and thus having thought about it from first principles I would suggest being *very* careful with lumping them together. There is one simple reason above all other for separating these roles. Business risk folk are experts (hopefully) in the *world* and what goes wrong in it. On the other hand – and nothing to their detriment – compliance folk are experts at dealing with *rules*. These two different categories are antithetical and there is next to no-one who can do them equally well.

FS is a prime example (but not the only one) where "Risk" must be a Board matter:

> "Fintechs are far behind mainstream FS and generally don't have a Risk guy on the Board. It's essential once you get beyond a

certain size and as you know it's highly technical, you need prior experience."

More generally though business risk is a major element is all businesses and hence for all Boards. In some businesses operational risk can be an important subset of business risk for the Board. In other businesses other categories of risk (Tech risk?) might need a specifically experienced NED on the Board.

From the Board's perspective they must absolutely understand the major types of risk in any given business. They must, at a bare minimum, know where explosions are likely to occur.

c) Compliance Control

Given the recent fetish of the State to regulate by minutiae and for "regulators" to be executive, legislature, judge and jury, "Compliance" – ie conforming to laws and regs – is an important business function. Depending on the nature of your SmallCo and its industry Compliance may need representing at Board level. However:

> "Breeding good businessmen who understand compliance is very very hard."

You must be careful that you don't get the dreaded Compliance Robot NED:

> "When you get to the pre-IPO stage you need them but before that avoid the BigCo Corporate Governance compliance robot types."

> "Too many [BigCo NEDs] are becoming governance robots."

> "You have to contrast compliance robots with experienced and well-connected businessmen."

> "It is getting very sad, I am seeing experienced, wise, trustworthy businessmen increasingly reduced to 'pre-programmed behaviour'."
> [Chairman of listed/unlisteds]

There are two more categorises of NED that cropped up in my conversations. In a way these are desirable attributes of *any* NED. However realpolitik tales suggest that they have something of the nature of approaching categories in their own right. In any corporate or personal crisis, *in principle,* plenty of folks should man the pumps although all too often *in practice* only one or two heroes emerge.

8) "THE DEALING WITH ISSUES" NED
Although, in principle, experienced people per se should be equally good at this, in line with the expression *"you know who your friends are when the chips are down"*, you find out who is good in a crisis when there is a crisis. Certainly "dealing with issues" was a frequent benefit that founders/CEOs related to me as a benefit of having NEDs on the Board. It might just be a little tricky to tell this before the chips are down although naturally interviews should include some sense of prior experience when all hell breaks loose.

9) "THE FAR-SEEING NED"

"The wily old fox who can see trouble coming a mile-off is invaluable."

"Nose-to-the-grindstone, stretched management teams all too often do not see approaching crises."

"[One of our Board] was adamant that we should avoid this new line of business. None of the rest of us got it at the time but a year or two later we were bloody glad we had avoided it."

ALIGNING EXPECTATIONS

Your Board needs to balance two opposing factors. We can call them centrifugal and centripetal force. You need independent-minded people of varying backgrounds and experience (real diversity). However you also need to create unity amongst them – you want a team of talents not a bunch of individuals. Too much individuality and you don't have a team. Too much "team" and you have groupthink.

Centripetal force has to be provided by you and/or your Chairman. It is important to create a harmonious culture and to have your Board aligned with that and with a common purpose and understanding. They are not joining *a* Board they are joining *your* Board. What is it that distinguishes *your* Board?

As your Board will change over time, the most important expectation that you can set to help you manage the changing needs of your Board over time is the **"Tour of Duty" concept.** Set expectations right from the interview process that the Tour of Duty is until you get VC funds, or for a couple of rounds, or for two or three years, or until you have to create an "IPO-ready" Board or whatever will ensure that expectations are aligned:

> "How to manage NEDs? Proactively – set expectations up front over the process and expected timescale."

Doing so will reduce the "cluttered Board" phenomenon which arises if a CEO is too gentle in moving NEDs off the Board or the opposite phenomenon where folks who have made a great contribution "suddenly", to their shock, "get kicked off the Board" "out of the blue" when they felt they were doing a great job. You want ambassadors for your brand not embittered ex-colleagues.

Some NEDs may leave of their own volition/professionalism:

> "[On the rotation of Directors] People only want to hear your view for so long." [NED]

> "A NED of skill and integrity does not become stale or go native when their ninth anniversary dawns. They leave when they know instinctively that they are no longer achieving anything."

Others may cling on like a limpet as they like coming to your Board. Too many first-time entrepreneurs took people onto the Board but as they grew had real challenges with growing company Boards. It's not that easy to kick a super-helpful Angel off your Board as some hotshot VC is about to take his place. Or to do so if the company has outgrown their phase of expertise. Tour of Duty is your tool to avoid unnecessary challenges or friction and to help you manage your changing Board over time.

One oft-repeated recommendation from firms that had got to the point where they could pick and choose (rather than just taking a brace of available Angels) was the necessity of getting to know potential NEDs beforehand. This way mutual understanding and role expectations can become aligned. One interview simply isn't enough to admit someone to your small coracle which is bobbing around in the stormy seas:

"Build relationships with Board members before they join."

SmallCo Boards vary enormously. In the NED dating process leading to you appointing a NED/you joining as a NED it's important to ensure you are on the same *stylistic* page. Compare and contrast:

"I [a CEO] want all my NEDs to contribute at every meeting."

"I don't speak often but when I do I have something important to say." [NED]

"I don't talk all the time, I might not make a contribution in many meetings but when I do it counts." [an experienced Angel/NED]

You pays your money and you takes your choice. Vice versa they need to know what you expect:

"They need to know what they are talking about re firm's core IP. Passion and familiarity."

An important question you will need to consider is the bait for your NED fishing trip – "What's In It For Your NED?"

This is an interesting question that deserves detailed consideration. As a CEO you need to decide what you want from your Board and what portfolio of NEDs you need. Unless you have a clear reason to pitch to the potential NED why your Board and Company is super-interesting/attractive you will tend to end up with those with time on their hands who quite like popping into a warm office and drinking some tea. As in all hirings both the hirer and the "hiree" need to make a sale. For the best of anything demand outweighs supply. BigCo NEDs may well see you, not as the wonderful opportunity you see yourselves as, but as being a risk to their entire career:

> "Given the number of these new Tech companies which are likely to fail, I would imagine that a lot of people won't actually want to be directors given the legal and reputational risks that might come with being a director, especially one operating in a regulated field." [Listed/unlisted NED]

Good NEDs will always have options and most likely are busy right now (unless you can catch them post-rotation with a slot in their portfolio to fill). Most "professional NEDs" are hardly poor and are unlikely to turn up *just* for relatively trivial changes in their NAV. Most folk are not as amazed by your firm/baby as you are.[33]

Given the pressures on the modern NED you will also need to provide some measure of credibility that you have appropriate controls in place and are not about to be slapdash, drive off a cliff etc. As we have seen there are all scales of career damage that can befall NEDs in dying companies and in SmallCo land failure rates are high.

Naturally, finding and aligning with NEDs before they join your Board takes time – for both sides. I was told a number of tales where to hook first class NEDs involved a long courtship and multiple rejections before finally closing the deal.

---

[33] I have received thousands of emails from firms wishing to be on the London Fintech Podcast. The most common self-misperception is that they or their firm are truly exceptional. It may be necessary to think that in order to put in all the hard work and overcome obstacles. But by definition there are few exceptional firms.

8. Capital Providers

"Can't live with them, can't live without them?"

So there you are, minding your own business (sic) when one day you decide that some more dough would help. At which point, in all likelihood, you've addicted yourself to a drug and with the highs come the lows. One shot will not be enough and will leave you wanting ever more.

In this context, and back to the days of Timothy Leary and LSD, the "set and setting" makes a huge difference. What your mindset was and is and the circumstances in which you start this part of the journey are key to what you will experience.

A thirty-year VC emphasised to me that it is what the founder thought *long before* they decided to raise capital that makes all the difference. Indeed one can go back as far as what they thought on day one. Some first-time founders are muddling through, learning as they go. Some first-time founders have been scared off by what they have heard, some prior-experience founders have had a bad "marriage" and resolve to never "get married" again (at least to the same type of partner). **Others, especially serial-entrepreneurs, know that they will need to raise big money along the way in order to realise their vision and *start creating on day one with that in mind.*** You can imagine how *they* experience "capital raising" compared to those who just started a NewCo, scrimped and saved, borrowed here, borrowed there, got some mates to invest and then one day decided they need to do a proper "capital raising".

Capital is often viewed as having one function:

"Capital is just the fuel for a still-in-construction vehicle."

However it has a dual function. It acts as both *fuel* for your rocket ship as well as providing you with spending power to *upgrade your rocket ship* as it is in-flight. You end up going faster in a vehicle that can go ever-faster. But, for too many Tech companies, the time spent in the gravity-well of making losses is far longer than expected and escape velocity can be some way off. Starting an addiction is always easier than ending it and certainly ending it is always far harder than you imagine at the start.

This drug-fuelled lifestyle has two aspects.

First, there is the generally painful roller-coaster of seemingly sempiternal funding rounds, a zillion pitches, due diligence et al. On rare occasions you are so hot that you have Capital Providers lining up outside your door but most of the time these are mid-raise dreams and you wake up in the morning and fall out of bed with a bump. Stories of capital raising being easy are seemingly in the media only:

> "I'm a pleasant and amiable chap in the rare periods between funding rounds."

Secondly, the whole Board thing suddenly becomes something else. Curiously, folks who give you capital want to check what you do with it. Suddenly there are people on the Board who, rather annoyingly, often act like independent human beings with their own thoughts, hopes, fears and desires which may be rather different from yours. Furthermore, and even more annoyingly, they start acting like people who actually own a large chunk of your creation.

For any SmallCo on a growth track this is a challenging process and one where an experienced Chairman becomes an important ally, resource and asset. In Fintech, which has been on fast-forward in recent years, the whole process has been very much accelerated and, on average, an annual raise is the ritual.

For serial entrepreneurs who have proved themselves there is definitely an "it gets easier" vibe. You have more experience, you have a better network, you have more trust, you know what you are doing, you have more wins under your belt and importantly *you know what VCs want and what buttons to press and which to avoid.* This comment was from an experienced serial entrepreneur:

"Ideally we are looking to raise money for five years to allow sufficient time to solve challenges without the annual raise distraction/BS/constraints."

Capital-raising is very contextual to the country, amount of investable capital floating around in it, the structure of the investing industry and general attitudes towards SmallCo investing:

"It's better to be in the US – they throw money at you versus in the UK focus on holding you accountable." [CEO]

We start the chapter by looking at the very different roles that founders/management and funders play around the Boardroom table (what is it with furniture anyway?[1]). This is followed by a quick dip into the multiplicity of types of Capital Provider and longer dips into VCs and Institutional Investors.

All these types of capital provider can inevitably come into conflict, which highlights *the* most important aspect of capital raising – how much or how little control over your business you give away.

Finally, we round off the chapter with some simple guidelines for the inexperienced capital raiser to bear in mind when dealing with professional investors.

---

[1] "Furniture and Company Governance – the Everlasting Connection": 16thC/17thC Chartered Companies had Courts. Courts were later renamed Boards from OE/ME bord "a plank, flat surface" which was extended to include "table" ... Hence also above board "honest, open" (and modern "under the table" – "dishonest"). A further extension is to "table where council is held" (1570s), then transferred to "leadership council, persons having the management of some public or private concern" (1610s), as in board of directors (1712). [all definitions www.etymonline.com] The words Boarder, Boarding (eg as in schools) and Full or Half-Board (in hotels) come from this use of Board as a table – "daily meals provided at a place of lodging" (late 14thC). Our ancestors must have had a proto-IKEA thing going on with furniture-centrism as we also see a shift in language from Governor to the Chairman or more recently Chair: "1650s, "occupier of a chair of authority," from chair + man. Ca. 1730 "member of a corporate body chosen to preside at meetings". Chairwoman in this sense first attested 1699. More recently furniture crept somewhat oxymoronically back in with "Board table". We still say someone has a "seat on the Board" – which is odd as it really ought to be "seat at the Board" [that's enough furniture. Ed.].

WHERE YOU STAND DEPENDS ON WHERE YOU SIT

"Sadly there isn't as much humility as you would want to see in the
PE/VC industry." [PE/VC/Angel/CEO]

We need to look at Mile's Law *"where you stand depends on where you
sit"*. If you quit businessing and take up acting how do you play the
various roles in a Boardroom drama?

I recall for example one interviewee being completely astonished
by the idea that I was going to speak to head-hunters as part of this
project: *"why on earth would you want to do that?"* I replied along the
lines of wanting to get a 360-degree perspective to no avail, his attitude
remained one of incomprehension. In the end, as it transpired, one of
my best conversations was with a high-growth Board head-hunter with
plenty of experience over a decade or so and acute insight into the roles
and requirements of Tech Boards.

Eric Berne's "Games People Play" fits in well here. Or Shakespeare's
"all the world's a stage". There are various "games", various "roles"
that are being played out at Board meetings along with folks' differing
personalities. The human predilection is to abstract from the specific
to the (or rather "an imagined") general. One or two bad experiences
with, say, one or two individuals who are head-hunters, and it's all too
easy to generalise to the category "Head-Hunters" although there will
be no one who has met all head-hunters.

As a result of roles and aims being very different in this Board game
(ha!) quite often I encountered "siloed" perspectives. As all interviewees were talking honestly off the record – all these views were fine and
dandy and the realpolitik. However most were a view of the world
predominantly experienced from one "seat" around the Board table.
The world may, and generally will, look quite different from one seat
to another. This is clear even at the simplest literal level – behind you I
see a window, behind me you see a picture on a wall. No-one is wrong,
just different perspectives, different takes on a much larger reality that
neither of us is experiencing.

This in itself brings in an important point about the necessity of
reducing this silo-isation:

"Talented entrepreneurs and VCs [as a proxy for Capital Providers in general] speak outside the Boardroom about eg M&A, key hires and so forth."

This is important to remember. Some folks do it consciously, some do it when they are not busy and as in all relationships some forget now and then.

Meeting informally naturally enables the possibility of interacting as *human beings* **rather than as** *roles*, **as** *fellow actors* **rather than some-times** *antagonistic characters* **in a play.**

One of my earliest lessons in this was when, some thirty years ago, I visited for the first time the NATO provident (ie pension) fund whose money we managed. The very charming French Chairman took me out to dinner the night before at a very Eurochic restaurant and we had a very nice and open conversation about a whole range of things. The following day at the meeting of the committee it was as if I was meeting a totally different person who had never met me before.

A common source of Board frustration is Capital Providers – can't live with them, can't grow without them. I will use "VCs" here in this section in two contexts – first as a proxy for capital providers per se and secondly, as in terms of tales told to me, moans about VCs outweighed all others.

Vice versa it won't surprise you that VCs have plenty of tales of woeful CEOs who promise much, deliver little and generally cause chaos.

Opposing critiques from CEOs about VCs are frequent. One common CEO complaint was over-promising and under-delivering around how much expertise and practical support the VC will bring to the party. Another was around bean-counting and a third around "being difficult". A common frustration on both sides of the relation-ship is attention/focus:

"The magpie CEO is especially annoying [the latest shiny thing is always the shiniest]." [VC]

"As we raised more and larger sums our first VC lapsed into follow-on investment only and lost interest." [CEO]

There are many important asymmetries in the CEO and VC "games" that we need to be conscious of.

The **first** is emotive. There was definitely a significant difference in emotive tone when talking to CEOs about VCs compared to VCs about CEOs. For the founder/CEO SmallCo is their baby, and in most cases their only baby, that is at stake. For the VC it's just another investment in their portfolio many/most of which they expect to go bust anyway (hoping that one or two make it big and generate the fund's returns):

> "If a VC backs 15 businesses they need 2 to be successful, 2 to return the money and they don't care if the rest are write-offs." [VC]

As a result of this massive difference in emotive attachment there appeared to be far more "anti-VC" sentiment from CEOs than from VCs about CEOs (where the tone was more of world-weariness, "it goes with the territory").

A **second** asymmetry is that one side needs money and the other has it. Thus, in almost all cases, founders/CEOs are supplicants to the VCs when they are pitching for a new raise (unless their SmallCo is super-hot in which case supplicatory roles reverse). Naturally this produces plenty of war stories about stupid or frustrating questions, answers, rejections:

> "After a long process the [VCs] investment committee turned us down as their spreadsheet jockey said we would only ever be worth £0.5bn."

A **third** asymmetry is around control. We shall return to this topic but a consequence of funding rounds is that founders are slowly losing control and VCs (as a whole) slowly gaining it.

A **fourth** asymmetry is aims. The VC will be investing money from a fund with a certain lifetime (typically five years investing and five years disinvesting) and will need to realise cash over that lifetime – ideally with a super-duper return. This brings a lot of arbitrary time pressure unrelated to the actual business's cycle. A CEO may have many aims, many desires and no such arbitrary "line in the sand".

The **fifth** asymmetry only occurred to me when doing a podcast with a Private Equity/VC turned CEO. For most CEOs, Board meetings are a small part of their day job. They might have been on no, or very few, companies Boards beforehand and their average week, or even month, might go by without a Board meeting at all. On the other hand VCs' two main tasks are fund-raising (rarely) and Board meetings (frequently). As a result, in a sense, VCs are "professional" Board-ers whereas often CEOs are "amateur" Board-ers. As a result VCs are often more experienced and more skilled at the Board game.

A **sixth** asymmetry can be age:

> "It is a weird situation where you get twenty-somethings telling forty-somethings what they should be doing." [VC]

Moving on from asymmetries, it is important to note that the VC market is in some sense "broken" – or perhaps more politely "ripe for disruption". The genre classic article on this topic is by former VC Diane Mulcahy in the Harvard Business Review: "*Venture Capitalists Get Paid Well to Lose Money*". In the greatest Tech boom ever, she writes, VC returns have been poor and incentives are misaligned. Her four critiques are:

> – VCs aren't paid to generate great returns (average fees are around 2% pa)
>
> – VCs are paid very well when they underperform (fee-stream locked-in for around a decade)
>
> – VCs barely invest in their own funds (~VCs 1%, investors 99%. "It's an interesting split, considering that, to hear VCs tell it in a pitch meeting, there is no better place to invest your money than in their fund... In fact, many VCs don't even invest in their fund from their personal assets, instead contributing their investment via their share of the management fees.")
>
> – VC industry has failed to innovate

To this last point, why would they when it's so cushy. Ironic however as some VCs present themselves as experts at innovation.

In the UK the listed VC investment trust Augmentum Fintech plc is an innovative structure and, as a closed-end fund, potentially can provide longer-term more "patient" capital than time-limited traditional funds. Time will tell.

Overall there are huge asymmetries in the "game" and VCs themselves acknowledge the challenges their industry faces. In terms of the weight of relative comments in this chapter, bear in mind that, as well as the above asymmetries, the majority of my interviewees were founder/CEOs with VCs a minority. So baked into the quote set is more quotes from one side of the table. However, as VCs are equally aware, a SmallCo is almost always about the founder(s) and team – so their concerns are paramount for quite some time. One should not naively assume that there would be total symmetry if I had spoken to equal numbers of CEOs and VCs. Thus for example the following quote comes from a *VC* when I asked him what one piece of advice he would give a nephew about to start a NewCo:

> "The most important thing you can have on the Board is someone that understands VCs so that when [NB not "if"…] your VC has a tantrum they will know how to handle it."

Finally, there is also this minor matter that if someone buys 25% of your business, well they now own 25% of your business. You may have given birth to this baby but it is no longer solely your baby. In extremis the founder/CEO may be moved out of his seat by the Board. This might even be in the best interests of the company. You might be great at starting fires but less good at scaling and controlling them. CEOs aren't always right and VCs aren't always wrong. Ultimately it is a relationship – both sides do pick each other after a dating process (and if you had to "take what's going" maybe you should have gone to the gym more in the first place). Just as hearing folks whine about their romantic partners elicits a certain degree of sympathy it also inevitably returns to the fact that both sides chose each other.

TYPES OF CAPITAL PROVIDER

"Good Capital Providers are consistent, engaged, ideally market/
domain experts (insights, networking, recruitment), champion your

business and do everything they can within their power to make it a success." [VC/Angel/CEO]

There are many avenues for fund-raising – key ones being "Friends and Family", Private individuals (notably crowdfunding or Angels), specialist firms (VCs which contain different sub-species), family offices, institutions in general (especially around strategic partnerships), corporate VCs (a cross between institutions and VCs), pension funds that invest directly, Private Equity, stockmarket investors and no doubt several more. These can also combine in weird and wonderful ways – one of my interviewees was an Angel that has a VC co-invest, another model is an Angel that has the crowd co-invest.[2]

The capital-raising industry and journalists (all too often merely reformatting press releases) like to wrap things up in terms and jargon. Seed capital, rounds A, B, C, development capital, venture capital, investment capital, growth capital, strategic capital and such like are used so widely and in so many different contexts that it can make the head spin.

But, from the perspective of the realpolitik of the Board, a simple schema of NewCo's raises will suffice.

Many firms start "as is" – a couple of you working for nowt. You may or may not be wrapped within a company structure while you flesh out your original plans. In the modern world a company costs next to nothing to form, gives you the ability if you fail to have other people pick up the tab and companies can literally start with very small sums of money indeed and keep going with the founder(s) forgoing their salary and funding a small wage-bill.[3]

After not very long you may raise money from "friends and family" a category which includes former colleagues.

After that you might raise money from "the crowd" via a **crowdfunding** site. Naturally this is an art in itself – the essence being that your enthusiasm and "unique" idea thrown in front of a bunch of folk who don't know you is almost certainly doomed to failure. Those most successful at crowdfunding have some evidence of traction and business already and a warmed-up tribe of followers. Then crowdfunding is

---

[2] Syndicate Room's model.

[3] I heard tales of credit cards being used – that seemed crazy to me given the interest rates.

firstly an administrative conduit and only secondly a way of drawing-in folks you don't know into a pitch that *already* has real momentum.

An interesting observation on this phase relating to the Board and to the "CCC governance concern" – protecting the small investor – was:

> "Apart from us next to no Fintech that raises from 'the crowd' has one of them on their Board. It's great to appoint a Board member from the crowd. There tend to be lots of qualified people in the crowd, and they are great at keeping you accountable and to represent the crowd."

A major category (which almost all founders had tapped) is **Angels** – generally friendly folk you uncover via your network with a few quid to invest and an interest in your sector. Maybe your first NED is an Angel who represents the interests of the Angels and external small shareholders as a class.

As mentioned earlier there are **Angels** and **angels**. The former have plenty of SmallCo Board skills and bring a lot to the party as well as money. There were one or two Angels I heard about whose CEOs could not have praised more highly for their dedication to the business and support of the CEO:

> "[X, an Angel] puts in an enormous amount of unpaid work for this company."

Vice versa it is a simple error for the unwary and inexperienced to mistake someone having time and money for someone who will add value to your Board:

> "Indeed, it can be somewhat troubling at times to see early-retired big company executives hawking themselves round as potential non-execs of small businesses, whether under the guise of so-called 'business angels' or as would-be institutional-nominees, or simply as bog standard non execs counting in their own right. Whilst obviously some of these people are extremely competent and valuable, regrettably others can sometimes do more harm than good."[4]

---

4   Smithson "The Role of the Non-Executive Director in the Small to Medium Sized Businesses" 2004

Some founders had to accept someone on the Board in the early days simply as they needed their money and a Board seat was a condition for providing it. However someone who has bunged you some dough having made it big in, say, MegaBank, may have no relevant skills whatsoever in the SmallCo world – an angel with a small "a":

> "There's investing and there's having the right skills and experience to serve the Board."

Where Angels/angels on the Board don't work out it is simplest to see this under the guise of the "mismanagement of NEDs" that we discussed earlier. No relevant skills in terms of filling your SmallCos skills gap, no Tour of Duty concept from the outset and they subsequently out-stay their welcome:

> "Most Fintechs have Angel/angel investors on the Board first – but then later there is pressure to reduce the numbers and it's difficult as they have been there since the beginning."

Indeed you might be better off having a non-capital provider NED with relevant skills joining the Board and as well as their other value-adds, specifically representing the external small investors.

One repeated pattern was that, even if the Angel/angel capital got you so far, they may then start holding the Company back rather than accepting that their stakes need to be diluted in order for the firm to progress, and possibly leave the Board and hand-over to VCs. This quote is very much in line with the earlier longer quote about the development and growth of SmallCo – clearly NEDing gives several NEDs flashbacks to parenthood:

> "You can see it like bringing up children. Friends and family at the nappy stage. As an Angel you help them through junior school and teach them how to tie their shoelaces and turn up on time. But you have to accept that one day they will leave and go to senior school and at that point you have to let go. Your job is to get them into a good senior school."

The next fund-raising stage is generally **VCs** – although some founders I spoke to swore that they would never take VC money given its "challenges". Alternatives/additions can be **institutional funds** – pension funds, institutions of all sorts, family offices et al were all mentioned. We will cover both VCs and institutions in the next sections as they are important topics for SmallCos growing fast and consuming capital rapidly. Unless you know oligarchs you are unlikely to be raising tens of millions from private individuals.

The IPO and stockmarket listing is both a liquidity event (ie chance for investors to cash out) as well as an opportunity to raise new funds.

At the top of the shop, if only as they can buy whole companies from the stockmarket are **Private Equity** firms. The principal difference between PE and VC firms other than scale is that generally PE buy secondary (ie already issued) shares and VC primary (newly issued for this purpose) shares.

There is also a huge gap in mentality with PE firms acting far more as owners for whom you work:

> "We [PE firm] changed about 70% of all the C-suite executives across our portfolio firms and changed CEOs around 1 in 2 to 1 in 3 businesses."

VCs

> "Ultimately no VC is a founders friend." [VC]

In terms of this realpolitik map of the territory VC land might perhaps be compared a region containing plenty of tropical fruit, albeit sometimes difficult to get into. Once there as well as the ripe fruit there are also attendant tropical dangers such as snakes and crocodiles so one needs to tread carefully and cross rivers cautiously.

Perhaps unsurprisingly given the relationship "challenges" and frictions as above there are CEOs who were adamant that they will never raise Venture Capital (the following four quotes are naturally from different folk):

> "We'll do anything to avoid the VC route."

"Turned down VC money as we didn't want all the problems."

"We never had VCs so never had the problems others have had."

"No VCs so not that bad re conflicts between shareholders."

In the Fintech revolution/bubble the narrative at the start (perhaps 2014 was when it really hit the mainstream) was "on the basis of just a PowerPoint you can raise millions for your idea". Plenty were seduced by the availability of "millions" only to later realise the implications of this. Several years later and the "word on the street" had spread about the realpolitik:

"The last 6mts have seen more and more try to avoid VCs who try and manage and control."

Those who went the VC route were realistic about where VC strengths lie in reality:

"In reality many VCs have never ran a business nor can they really make the introductions they promise, hard to believe they can really deliver."

"Very few VC know how to run sales, Tech teams and so forth (re added value)."

"80% VCs have never run a business or built a product."

"Most VCs skills/focus are at best strategic, or finance."

"These are people who have never run, let alone created, a business themselves telling me how to run mine."

"VCs have one and only one reason to invest – to exit with a multiple of their investment." [VC]

Of all capital providers VCs perhaps – due to their funds' finite lifespans generally bring the most time pressure as we can see by looking at the BVCA "Model Subscription & Shareholders' Agreement":

> "12.1 It is the parties' intention to effect a Sale or IPO as soon as practicable and in any event within [five] years of the Completion Date.
>
> 12.3 If a Sale or IPO is not achieved by the [fifth] anniversary of Completion then the Company shall if required by an Investor Majority at the Company's expense appoint a professional adviser (to be agreed with the prior sanction of an Investor Director Consent) to report on exit opportunities and strategy and copies of such reports shall be made available to the Investors (at the Company's cost)."

The other thing to note is the complexity of these SSAs – this model (ie standard starting place before one adds special conditions) is 66 pages long.

Although VCs are under pressure to get a "realisation" (ie cash in return for their pieces of paper), as one experienced VC indicated:

> "Often VCs miss the opportunity to sell their stake and rarely sell too early due to unrealistic return expectations. A prime example of this was in the dot com bubble where very good offers were rejected."

One important realpolitik item is that a VC *firm* never turns up on your Board but an *individual* does. Whilst this is "obvious" some underestimated the importance of this point. Some had done due diligence on the potential funding *firm* but not on the *individual* who would ultimately sit on their Board:

> "Especially more junior VCs [on the Board] just use KPIs to beat up the CEO."

There is also the angle that in a world whose metric is ultimately "financial returns" it is important to remember that VCs are neither charities nor churches but profit-maximisers. Some are more ruthless than others:

"One VC invested in several companies [in a given sub-sector] and then deliberately underfunded most of them to reduce competition for his favoured investment."

There is no limit to ruthlessness:

"Over a long and vital funding round I ended up with one [US] VC who had done the due diligence. A few days before the close on the agreed terms, long after others had walked away [and of course hadn't done the due diligence] they tried to screw us on the price slashing it for no reason other than because they could. I walked away from this but eventually the business never recovered and it foundered."

So trust in Allah but always tie up your camel. This is where good lawyers and experience on the Board are invaluable. Recall the VC's "advice to a nephew" to ensure you have someone on the Board who really understands how VCs can behave.

Your mentality is important:

"One of my best NEDs has said to me on many occasions before a challenging Board meeting with difficult VCs 'repeat after me "it's only money, it's only money" [that VCs provide]. Then he makes me do it again. And then again. Surprisingly it has always made a big difference and I've been able to approach the meeting with far more detachment."

It is important to note that any "power asymmetry" may be significantly less than it appears:

"For VCs changing the CEO is the nuclear button."

"For VCs, more often than not, there isn't a CEO succession for the firm which leads to a successful exit."

It is important not to paint an overly bleak picture. Comments were not always negative, and quite a few had a good working relationship.

but other than warm expressions of lurv there weren't many *specific* praises. This is perhaps not unsurprising as the realpolitik is that, for experienced CEOs, the chief VC "value-add" *is* money and once that's in the bank most of the added-value has been delivered. One specific positive was:

> "Sometimes VCs are better as faster decision making, less govern-ance more interested in outcome."

So I heard happy tales if perhaps the majority of tales I heard were over difficulties in relationships with VCs. But what kind of relation-ship is it?

> "It is a relationship but not a marriage. That is unless it's a marriage where the bride is first bought and then later sold!"

It is important to note the third category of relationship challenge – a relationship growing too cold rather than too heated. This tends to correlate perhaps with success, if a company keeps growing then just as with Angels, your early VCs may not have deep enough pockets to keep your rocket ship accelerating:

> "The challenge with making the VC/CEO relationship work can be to ensure that the VC remains engaged" [VC/CEO]

Naturally the greatest challenges were for first-time founders who were new to the territory. Forewarned is forearmed.

If the governance problem with CCCs is that major capital provid-ers may often disservice the small investor, the other side of this coin is that they may often provide a service to the small investor. **Even if CEOs don't always "appreciate" VC pressure, small shareholders can defi-nitely miss out if it isn't there. In many a purely small-investor backed SmallCo the CEO can come to treat equity investment as a de facto perpetual zero-interest loan with no need to exit "just right now".**

INSTITUTIONAL INVESTORS

In an infinitely complex world everything has subtypes. "Institutional capital" is itself a combination of many subtypes of entity with differing investment goals. Let's sketch a few major types.

There is the Corporate VC, whose mentality might well be very similar to an independent VC, especially if there are formal LLP funds with return targets in the background. However other Corporate VCs may provide more "patient", "evergreen" capital if they are investing using the firm's balance sheet in which case they may well be "less VC-like" and more like a plain-vanilla institutional capital provider.

There are Family Offices, Asset Managers and Pension Funds which are such diverse sectors that it is hard to generalise.

There is the Strategic Investing Institution which wishes to place a stake on a new conduit/angle/entrant where they don't have the time/energy/bandwidth/knowhow to readily grow organically in that area.

There is a Strategic Partnering Institution where the motivation is more about mutual-business creation and creating a tighter bond.

No doubt there are many other types of motivation – the main point here being that "institutional capital" per se doesn't, in itself, mean as much as one might think. However there is no reason to make this complex. As in all dating with a view to a longer term relationship the key question is "so what are you in this for?" The important question to understand is "*why* are they investing?" This trumps any categorisation based on "type" of institutional investor. Dependent on that motivation you will get a different experience/behaviour on your Board.

The rosy scenario is that you get "more patient capital" and investors who are more interested in the long-term growth of your business than they are on a "Liquidity Event within n years".

In some circumstances your new institutional friends come with some real fringe-benefits especially with more strategic investors. Far larger organisations' footprints, in a sector of importance to you, can be immensely valuable. An intangible fringe benefit not to be overlooked with strategic partners is that this could be opening a door to a trade sale if that is what you might desire.

As always there are risks to manage. One business I spoke to had taken an investment and partnered with a global MegaCo with the principal motivation for the SmallCo being a significant inflow of new business and for MegaCo exposure to the new digital world. As to the risks for SmallCo:

> "Yes there is a risk that we might just become a de facto "division" of theirs but the opportunity is too good to miss."

This clearly is great news in terms of P&L but it may well mean that, in effect, your landing lights are on and there is an airstrip that you are aiming for/being aimed at. This is fine as long as it's what you want – it's your business, your motivation and desires that are important in choosing airstrips and the length of your flight.

Other strategic partnerships I was told about lacked any sense of an "endgame" and were very much focused on the "journey". If your strategic partner isn't about to become the source of the majority of your business flows then the "basically you are becoming part of them" concern is far less significant.

In others a natural question arose about getting into bed with a ten-ton gorilla. How comfortable is that?

Interestingly (although based on a relatively small sample size) I didn't receive any of the concerns that I expected re bullying or control – quite the opposite:

> "We were pleasantly surprised. Rather than have excessive control they were quite the opposite. For accounting reasons they need to avoid any sense of control to avoid consolidating our accounts into theirs. As a result they were keen to have clear distance on this matter."

As with the "VC losing interest" challenge in the prior section, challenges in such circumstances can be more around remaining significant to your gorilla (who probably has a zillionth of a percent of his capital invested in you and a zillion times more clients).

Overall my experience of interviewees experiences of institutional investors was that the *potential* benefits of institutional investment are real and, at a minimum, it is an avenue you should not neglect to consider or investigate. It isn't just "friends and family", "Angels", "VCs", Float. Think, and look, outside of those boxes.

CONFLICT BETWEEN CAPITAL PROVIDERS

"Fights among capital providers will occur."

If the prior sections largely related to challenges between the founders and those who take large stakes in their business there is another important area of potential/likely conflict – multiple capital providers pulling in different directions:

"Providers of capital must be aligned with the agenda."

Reasonable men(/women) can differ, let alone unreasonable men(/women). Capital providers will have different expectations of their role, entry prices, desired returns on their capital and the timescale over which this will happen. As mentioned earlier one of the first occurrences of conflicts between capital providers can be the Angel to VC phase shift:

"Our Angels ended up getting in the way and holding us back."

This is perhaps the first time you might meet the **"tidy up your cap table"** challenge. A "capitalisation table" lists all your raises and owners of various equity and equity-related securities and options and tweaks thereto. Tidying it up is less about changing its fonts and alignments and more about dealing with legacy shareholder issues. As a CEO/founder explained by email:

> "Early stage shareholders don't always have aligned interests (eg they often can't follow on, so are reticent about new capital coming in that could drown them out). Even if they're aligned, too many shareholders is a pain in the butt as it creates a lot of noise and distraction (every shareholder has a pet subject and pet peeve).
>
> Very importantly, in the desperate early days you may take on things like convertible loans, which are problematic to unpick (but unpick them you must). On the same note, each round usually involves giving away some special lead investor rights, and ultimately those must be negotiated away to attract future capital."

Another explained his experience:

> "At our last raise, I had a horrendous time unpicking some early rounds (alongside consolidating my early investors into a single Board director representation), but very glad I endured it. Once it's done your life is easier (eg smaller Board), but – most importantly – you're a lot more investable in the future as you have less 'hair', as they say in the [ie Silicon] valley."

It is not always possible to "do the obvious" and keep your cap table tidy along the way:

> "Of my many Startup fuck-ups along the way, a messy cap table feels largely unavoidable in retrospect as it was decisions taken at the time in order to survive." [founder/CEO]

Naturally you try and keep your Board as simple and as clean as possible – if only for practical considerations about numbers (take one look at a full UK Cabinet[5] and I defy anyone with experience of any form of meeting not to roll their eyes). However conflicts on the Board will arise and managing these inevitable conflicts is where a great Chairman adds real value. As mentioned earlier at best he provides a human shield for the CEO from difficulties with Capital Providers. If the CEO is waking up at four o'clock in the morning then it is better that he is worrying about challenges within the actual business rather than between those with part-ownership certificates.

There have been some notable examples recently of Fintechs raising large sums of money and ending up with many many VCs on the Board. One prominent SmallCo did a raise and ended up with several VCs on the Board at the time of some of my interviews, there was complete unanimity as to what this would entail:

> "What a nightmare it will be on [X's] Board at some point."

The subsequent word on the street confirmed this.

---

[5] More furniture eh? Obviously some deep-seated (groan) British connection between furniture and governance at both State and Company levels.

Returning to asymmetries as the principal most driving conflict there are three further asymmetries when multiple VCs invest in a firm. The first is the price(/round) at which they bought. The second is the time pressure/deadlines from the fund whose capital they are investing. These can be complicated by a potential third factor – the needs of the VC firm itself not the fund. A fund approaching its wind-up date will be aiming to realise its investment with a liquidity event (*pace* leeway/ extensions and other such devices). However depending on the firm's need to *raise* other funds it might wish to show some realised gains in existing funds which will lead to pressure perhaps well ahead of the fund's end date objectives.

In terms of the number of perspectives on the Board:

"The third VC on a Board doesn't add a new perspective."

Ultimately all of the many stories I heard about conflicts between capital providers hinged on four plot elements.

The differing players' motivations.

Boarders' personalities.

How well the Chairman manages these.

And last but not least – control.

CONTROL

"And she turned around and took me by the hand and said, I've lost control again. And how I'll never know just why or understand, she said I've lost control again." [Joy Division]

In "stamp-collecting" countless Boardroom challenges, issues and how to fix them there was a steady drumbeat underlying all of them.

It's All About Control.

If you have control you can fix anything on the Board – after all, ultimately you can sack the lot, including yourself and hire a new Board and even new CEO.

I don't believe anyone has ever done a raise without looking at how much of their company they are "giving away" in return for what sum of money. Equally I don't believe there is anyone who doesn't try to minimise the amount they give away and maximise the amount they raise. So it may seem trite advice to talk about maximising control.

However by analogy with life, one mistake here, one bad decision there, one "I had no choice", one oversight over some minutiae, some unforeseen changes in circumstances and before you know it you are in the gutter. Over the years small mistakes can compound. In just the same way perfectly sensible folk may found a company and years and rounds later find themselves in circumstances they wished they were not in.

In the context of raises, other than for "friends and family" perhaps, it is rarely a simple question of £x for y% of the company. As we saw, the VC's art/sorcery is built around complex terms and conditions, provisions, voting rights, warrants, options and such like. Which – as I have heard – often carry implications that were insufficiently appreciated at the time. Unenvisaged or unlikely circumstances occur all the time – it's why structured investments in FS blow up with predictable regularity and why Lucas made a fortune.[6] Naturally when you are desperate, taking funds at any price/terms might be the only way to stay alive.

If the VCs have armouries of sorcery then the experienced entre-preneurs have skill in the art of fund-raising. If you don't it is a prime example of where you need someone with relevant experience on the Board holding your hand and if necessary, as per an earlier tale, making you walk away *especially* when you feel you cannot.

The main divergence within my sample group was how successfully the negotiations around the terms and conditions of the raise had been conducted. This was the one single factor more than any other which correlated with how happy a time they were having with their Board.

At worst (for the CEO/founder) the VC gets plenty of bang for his buck – votes, power, control, rinky-dinks.

A good par for the course is bang pari passu with buck.

A better than par score is to take VC funds, but give away less than pro rata control – investments with no Board seat or simply an "observer" seat (ie non-voting and not a formal/legal member).

---

6   At the time of the contract for the first Star Wars film, merchandising rights were seen as being of little importance and so Lucas easily managed to negotiate owning them. He turned things round, the film took off and something one party had regarded as worthless became worth megabucks.

The hole-in-one (again from the founder(s) perspective) is funds and no control. It's simply the model of "look we are going places we are offering an investment return only but no voting rights". Like a hole-in-one on the golf course this is easier said than done but I did hear of several examples.

If this sounds a little unreal then recall that some of the hottest Tech, founder-centric, CCCs are the biggest in the world right now. **Google, Facebook and Amazon did not get where they are today by Page/Brin, Zuckerberg or Bezos losing control at an early or even later stage.**

VC sorcery, and countering it, are part of the dark arts of capital raising. Like many arts one of the secrets is "doing the basics well". There are plenty of devices around all of this but the rosiest outcomes were associated with offsetting VC sorcery in particular via the simplest of devices:

"We insisted on having only one class of share."

"We made sure we had A shares only."

"One class of share ensured a level playing field and no clever tricks."

The underlying aspect of all dark arts is power. If you do the simple things and your power is weak you will not succeed. Do the simple things with strong power and you will succeed. Power comes more from how well you have created, built and managed the company as well as how experienced your Board is. The simplest metaphor about "power" is if you think back to your sixth form days – which boys/girls had the greatest pulling power over the opposite sex? Which of them knew how to use it? That's the kind of power I mean. It really helps to be hot property. A supermodel gets better offers than Miss Jean Brodie. Metaphorically-speaking that power, allied to knowing that one has it, and how to use it, *is* the secret of better-than-par raises.

I may have mentioned that it's all about control:

"It's all about control – we always maintained strict control and investors are, by and large, not on the Board."

"Our VCs bought in for the [potential] economic gain and were kept off the Board."

"X [prestigious pension fund] invested in us but got no information rights or voting rights."

"We [mainly Angel-funded] do have a VC but they are not on the Board."

There are many dimensions to raises which relate to more subtle aspects of control:

"Occasionally I have to say to my VCs 'are you here to run the business or invest in it?' Their skill isn't managing. The boundary determined at raises needs negotiating along those lines."

A further, more nuanced, aspect of control is "influence on Board composition".

VCs sometimes see the merits in an independent NED on the Board but may also actively fight against or block this in order to retain their control/influence in an undiluted fashion. This can clearly be to the detriment of the Company at large as it undermines the fundamental core concept of the turbocharging SmallCo Board being a balanced portfolio of added-values:

"We wanted greater diversity [in the old-fashioned sense – ie substantial (experience/skillset)] on the Board but our VCs stopped us as they want to maximise and not dilute their power/influence."

"Most VCs average age 35–40 think they are masters of the universe and hence don't see the need for a neutral/outside NED."

"We wanted to appoint an independent Chairman but our VCs blocked it."

As always beware of generalising:

"I have seen Board strengthening led by a VC especially if there are two or three [VC firms] on the Board."

And understand the roles in the play:

"You are so right about power and control. Naturally VCs have Board seats or Observer seats to try to bring value. However the most important reason is to offset the information asymmetry – the entrepreneurs have it all but the investor has far less. For the VC the most important point is to access enough information and to widen their due diligence **in order to enable them to decide whether to invest in the next round.** If they are the lead-investor in particular it is important to the company as investing or not investing in the next round sends a huge signal to the market." [VC]

SUMMARY OF VC MANAGEMENT

It is the many asymmetries in roles, aims, desires and constraints between founders/CEOs and Capital Providers that lead to friction and challenges.

This is particularly the case with VCs who are the main conduit for fund-raising for growth SmallCos and who are professional investors with plenty of experience and expertise in getting their way.

Ultimately no one forces the founder to take VC money – it is your choice. Equally one should not be scared away from potentially transformative fund-raising by the need to manage the risks inherent in the situation. Some firms liked their VCs, some had nightmares and some bumbled along in the middle.

My hope is that now you have a better map of the jungle and can sharpen your machete before you enter it and know what to look out for when you are in it.

If you decide to go the VC route then six key items to pack for your expedition would appear to be:

ONE: an experienced Chairman to manage the relationships.

Two: failing that, as per the VC's advice I quoted earlier, have a NED who is used to VC tantrums and knows what to do.

Three: a good legal eagle to advise and ensure decent terms and conditions.

Four: an experienced fund-raiser/negotiator who has seen it all before.

Five: do your due diligence on your potential partner firm *and* individual:

> **"All VCs are not the same, all partners in one firm are not the same. Some are more resistant to firm pressures (around marketing driving realisations). Some view investments like apples to buy and sell. Some view themselves as partners in a journey."** [VC]

> "Seek references on capital providers from both their investment successes and their failures; get a feel from their online blogs, social media etc."

Six: a realistic understanding *on both sides* of desires, aims, targets, constraints, timescales etc. VCs have their own job to do. Like two circles on a Venn diagram there is *some* overlap but the centres of the circles are in different places *outside the overlap* and:

> "Ultimately no VC is the founder's friend."

9. Fixing Broken Boards

"My Board Meetings are shit" [CEO]

The rosy scenario is that your Board (the one you created or allowed to "happen") really supports you and your company and is an engine of growth, problem solving and advice along with checking that the accounts add up, you are not heating gasoline on a naked flame and that you are not sending hate mail to the regulators.

But as you, along with the CEO quoted above, may have noticed – life ain't always perfect. Business being a subset of life conforms to exactly the same principle.

What if your Board is not a headache tablet but a headache (a **Warped Board?**) or even worse (definitely the full **Broken Board**)? What if it is just a **Stale Board?**

> **"The best answer to what to do with a broken Board is not to let it break in the first place."** [serial entrepreneur]

If a well-constituted and functioning Board is a real asset to both the company and the CEO the reverse is also true:

> "I had a period when I really dreaded going to my Board meetings." [CEO]

Governance failure is a topic that stretches across all societies at all levels across all time. However, as with life, once one has grasped a few of the basic ways that things can go wrong, one generally has enough tools to cope with unexpected situations. In this chapter, I have distilled the many tales I heard down into nine key scenarios. Understanding these will give you a feel for the Broken Board topic overall.

Starting with the least painful level there is a Stale Board – neither warped nor broken but:

"It's routine, dull."

If you realise that your meetings are simply too routine then at the simplest level you can just shake the agenda up and, say, periodically have a specialist topic on the agenda. The key elements of business are infrastructure, product/service, marketing, sales and client contact. There is no reason that in companies of the appropriate size these can't be dived into once a year – if only for educating the Board and some brainstorming.

At a more fundamental level, as with an aberrant golf swing, go back to basics – revisit your Whys, Whats, Whos, Hows, Whens, Wheres and How Much for your Board and re-plan accordingly. **A shakeup in those Q&As will help you reform and re-form a Board and move it on from a sense of stuckness.** Naturally this might/should also have an invigorating impact on you the CEO as well as your Company. It's not "set and forget" man. Work out where you want to be and set sail in that direction. You may be far from there right now, but if you are sailing in the right direction you are always getting nearer.

Turning to the nine Broken Board scenarios…

ONE. "The fish rots from the head down" – you need the right Chairman and at *some* point maybe even a new CEO.

TWO. As emphasised at the outset a key error is to start a SmallCo as a mini-BigCo. Keep it simple at the start. Keep it Corporate Creativity centred. Have some appropriate Corporate Control of course but do not confuse the necessary control function of all Boards with the V3's Corporate Governance manuals.

THREE. If over-control is one way of deforming your Board the opposite is clearly a slapdash "control, risk and regulation are the least of our problems" Board – hell-bent on growth at all costs. Putting sensible internal controls to one side, driving a coach and horses through regulations and laws will, at some point, require a lot of fixing as we have seen in many high profile fast growth Techs. "Grow fast and break things" sounds like fun to the adolescent mind but when you are a little older you find that it takes a hell of a lot of time and energy to put things back together again.

FOUR. We then move on to the uncultured Board.

FIVE. Achieving a balanced Board is an art and the unbalanced Board can definitely present problems.

SIX. The waterline that divides matters reserved for the Board from stuff management can just get on and do is a very key parameter. Boards can take too much on themselves or too little. In the former case they gum up the works, in the latter they will not add value commensurate with their cost or potential.

SEVEN. All of us fix a burst pipe at home but most of us leave dripping taps for a while – and sometimes too long – this is another key Board challenge.

EIGHT. If you are unfortunate you all end up hating each other – or at least you are all pulling in different directions. At which point it's obvious that, as per management guru Dolly Parton's advice, you need a D.i.v.o.r.c.e.

NINE. If it comes down to a battle – and often it does – some people really are determined to win. On your Board it may be you or it may be someone else.

May you avoid all of these situations or if you find yourself in them may what you have read give you the motivation and possibility of fixing your Board.

Finally, in order not to end on a negative note we wrap up with reflecting that we are living in one of the greatest times ever to be an entrepreneur. No matter how tough the competition it's never been easier to set sail.

Centuries ago in London when the first companies were being born the first "beta" of their products/services generally led to significant of the "first-movers" being killed. Whatever problems your SmallCo has they are bound to be that bad. So we wrap-up the narrative with an examination of some of the challenges of England's greatest ever Startup over half a millennium ago.

THE 'FISH ROTS FROM THE HEAD DOWN' BOARD

Whatever your Board challenge your Chairman is likely to be the first port of call – after all apart from "it [the Board] is his job" he really should have vastly more experience of Boards than you. As a founder/CEO in a sense you'd like to delegate a lot of the Board functioning to the Chairman in the same way you'd like to delegate Marketing to a CMO. You want to retain involvement in input in both but you would really rather someone more experienced and better at it than you did all the heavy lifting and gripped both topics.

However if the Chairman is, or becomes, part of the problem then you need to start with him:

> "If your Board meetings are bad change the Chairman, get better people on the Board. It's vital [over the longer term] to get it right."

If in a BigCo the Chairman is the *capo di tutto cappi* in a SmallCo, as we have noted, the founder/CEO is the actual head and heart for quite some time. All VCs will have examples of where a CEO was good as, say, a "first stage rocket booster" but then needed replacing with a "second stage" and so forth. Succession planning is one of *the* most important topics that a Board must be on top of.

More subtle than replacing the CEO/founder is the CEO/founder's morale and drive. Nothing gets anywhere without a founder's oomph and drive. The sheer grind can – and will – drain these reserves. In the modern world plenty of folk do not take enough holiday – or if they do it's not real downtime away from the phone and email. Even though with plenty of adrenalin and youth this can be survivable for quite some lengths of time, everyone's well needs refilling/refreshing at some point.

There are morale-boosting or morale-sapping things that a Board can do. One morale-sapping SmallCo Board mindset is that of "if the

CEO wants a friend he should get a dog", if he has issues then he should resign and go see a shrink. I caricature (slightly) but if that is "100" on a scale of 1–100 then there are Boards strung out all along the spectrum. Experienced SmallCo Board members will know in their bones that you need your creators to feel not just challenge:

> "Generally a Board should be holding management accountable."

...but also the lurv. Being Atlas and carrying the world on your shoulders is a lonely and difficult task. All of us have ups and downs and rhythms in life. Less experienced or more BigCo-focused NEDs can underestimate this aspect of caring for Atlas. One quote on the role of the Board is quite true:

> "To hold the company accountable and look after its interests as a whole."

However one must recall that the earlier stage the Startup the more that SmallCo utterly depends on the CEO:

> "If I walk there isn't a company ... the founder is the business."

If the CEO or team are demoralised, or even tired, or just lacking spring in their step the Board Needs To Address This as, after all:

> "The Board is responsible for the company as a whole."

Naive insistence on wanting tough cookies who never need lurv will simply produce CEOs who lie or spin to you on bad days. Not only that but one day they may well just "crack" apparently "out of the blue" and then you have a "sudden" crisis on your hands. Far better to keep your eye on a pressure gauge than merely have a red light which one day flashes "broken".

One key morale-impacting issue at all stages of development is compensation:

> "One of the most important aspects of the Board which can be easily neglected is putting in place mechanisms to ensure the management

team are happy – compensation/incentives and defending those to
the shareholders." [slightly disgruntled sounding CEO]

As we noted earlier, an ad hoc, souk-like bartering approach to compensation can lead to unnecessary irritation and ultimately demoralisation.

In summary, any company needs a good Chairman – it is only inexperienced and new founders that I spoke to who didn't get this. In SmallCo this is one of the most important hires for the founder/CEO.

Naturally SmallCo is nothing without a motivated and great CEO. Given the centrality of this position, before sharpening your knives when he pops out of a Board meeting to go to the bathroom, have a conversation about what the rest of you are already doing to make this situation better or worse.

And if you are the founder you are going to be a super rara avis if you really can – and more importantly want to – go all the way from founding NewCo to being a FTSE100 CEO. Better to have some idea up-front of your own vision of when you step aside than to return one day from the bathroom and find that others have thought this through on your behalf in your absence.

THE 'MINI BIGCO' BOARD

"Our Chairman had to go. He was too focused on the processes, formalities and paperwork of the Board and not enough on growing the business."

As repeatedly emphasised, a SmallCo is absolutely not a small BigCo. A SmallCo Board needs to focus on creation and growth. A BigCo Board needs to focus on control and is increasingly burdened with a whole raft of state-imposed "must-do"s, sub-committees and a million other "triumph of process over content" features.

Most founders/CEOs do not fall into the trap of building a mini-BigCo Board – if only as they simply did not have the time for it. However quite a few had an *implicit* concept of the Board which did not encompass two very different, indeed near-antithetical, paradigms – SmallCo and BigCo – but rather "just one" which, given asymmetric media coverage, will be the BigCo version – V3 in my terminology. Of course you can crib anything you like from it but once again recall that "Corporate Governance" as we know it is "designed"[1] for the governance problem of a diverse and remote set of shareholders whose concern is ensuring that management don't make merry. The governance problem of SmallCos, which are generally Closely Controlled Companies, is not control of management (see the name for the clue) but rather not screwing the small shareholder – a quite different challenge.

Mistakes in this direction generally followed a similar pattern where a CEO:

"Tries to get things [on the Board] right from the start."

A good plan but what "right" *is* varies as you grow. A BigCo or Corporate Governance inspired vision of "right" will massively over-emphasise structure, process and control. This gets compounded over time by ending-up with, say, a VC who is far from cuddly, very keen on their control of the agenda and far more into "challenging" (aka "giving a good kicking") than spreading peace and love or adding fuel to the fire:

"I cocked-up. Too much Corporate Governance – burdensome, inhibiting rather than promoting creativity."

"There are too many [Governance] robots around."

Like many problems in life the best solution is to avoid the mistake in the first place.

I should note however the many paths up the mountain motif once again. I came across one interviewee who had started "Corporate Control heavy" and succeeded. This chap was a serial entrepreneur, getting into FS for the first time (and hence had a desire for strong controls from day one). As a successful serial entrepreneur he was perhaps like an accomplished poet who could write poetry in iambic

---

[1] I actually doubt that word but let's keep it simple. More accurate perhaps might be "emerged as a tactical/political State-BigCo collusive response to issues such as excess MegaCo collapses, executive pay etc". After emerging it has continued to grow – always in the direction of bureaucracy. I'm not even sure Cadbury, were he alive today, would support the current Byzantine complexity.

hexameters if necessary. Most first-time founders are still struggling to write poetry let alone to fit it into a rigid metre.

THE 'CONTROL, RISK & REGULATION IS THE LEAST OF OUR PROBLEMS' BOARD

"An earlier company of mine [that ended up being sold] was much simpler – no non-execs, no external shareholders, and in particular very unregulated." [serial CEO/founder]

Naturally if one can focus too much on control issues one can also, especially in challenging or highly regulated industries, focus too little on them:

"Generally Fintech can have an anti-establishment vibe and doesn't really get it." [serial FS-CEO]

"It" in this context stands for a whole raft of things. In many Techs you can release your minimum viable product, make mistakes and move on. But good luck with that in FS if your App loses your clients' money. In insurance woe betide you if, like Uber, you decide to drive a coach and horses through any regulations. Similarly strict protocols apply in many industries these days – Biotech being a prime example – you can't rush your latest drug to market regardless.

In major Fintech sectors getting regulatory approval has been a painful and time consuming process.[2] However how much "risk & regs" are embedded/rooted at Board level varies:

"We have risk & reg reporting to the Chairman, but few do." [CEO]

More generally:

"Few Fintechs have an experienced Risk guy [NED] on the Board responsible for these areas." [CEO]

---

2   Especially bearing in mind that some firms were not much more than a couple of dozen people, the year or two it took/takes to get regulatory approval is astonishing.

"Fintechs by and large don't have an independent non-executive risk director on the Board."

On the generic journey from Corporate Creativity to Corporate Control, highly regulated/risky businesses have to start much earlier:

"The key word is Fintech – very different from the traditional Startup man/dog/garage."

"Corporate Governance [used in the sense of Corporate Control]. Have to do that. Regulation – have to do it. Learn how to deal with it."

"There are rare examples who start early – for example sub-committees of the Board with reporting lines to the Board or Chairman. 'Checks and balances' and so forth."

There's an important lesson here:

"You either fix before or after."

"You can tell who has Corporate Governance [used in the sense of Corporate Control] from day one (a traditional Startup wouldn't bother). For those that don't the danger is that the whole culture then comes from that lack of CorpGov and is very hard to change once you are as far down the track as X [which was subsequently pilloried for playing it 'fast and loose']."

"Regulation? I [CEO] read the FCA handbook ten times – you can't palm it off, you absolutely need to live and breathe it."

Nor should non-Fintechs think they are off scot-free in the early-days:

"Controls is a super-wide topic well beyond FS of course. They apply to your dealings with suppliers/customers/investors." [experienced NED]

So (motherhood and apple pie bit) make sure you have the appropriate controls for your stage/industry. Not too few, not too many. Also while, as I have emphasised the following angle...

> "Listed companies are building compliance robots. They don't really understand business at all they understand compliance."

...the opposite also applies – you don't want a Board composed entirely of swashbucklers.

THE UNCULTURED BOARD

> "My hot tip? Mentor the Board – ensure that everyone is on the same page." [Experienced CEO/entrepreneur]

Only in the later stages of growth with an IPO in mind does the whole There Is Only One True Path For Your Board thing start impacting your poetry. Before that you have freedom. Use it while it lasts! Have a clear vision of the type of Board culture you are trying to create.

If your fairy Godmother appeared now and offered three wishes for your Board what would they be?

What culture do you want? What is its point *for you*? What is the Board's purpose in *your* company? And so forth. What works for one company may not work for another. I've laid out a map for you but you have to decide your route that you wish to take within it.

Many drift along without any explicit consideration of Board Culture just "having a Board". Others simply do what their lawyer told them to do. If so – or any variant on these – one day you might wake up and realise you have an uncultured Board. Or perhaps more precisely implicitly multicultural – not just in terms of roles – Chairman, Angel, VC etc – but in terms of your Boarders' mentality, attitudes, perspectives, models, implicit understandings of what a Board is. This whole project started precisely as I realised that many *Boarders* conceive of the Board in many ways.

Although naturally there was much commonality amongst responses to simple questions I did not interview two folks who I thought had identical perspectives. We all have our quirks, our emphases, our lack of interests:

> "Luke, you're going to find that many of the truths we cling to depend greatly on our own point of view." [Obi-Wan Kenobi]

Having created your vision you should not *assume* that just because folks are experienced with "Boards" that they know what *you* are aiming at. We discussed earlier, in the context of the Board's role in "challenging", that words may be defined in dictionaries but their usage varies enormously. Thus even if you, the founder/CEO, were to come up with some fine words to describe your desired Board culture this is only half the battle of getting your whole Board encultured – you might have to explain what you really mean.

Back to the lead-in quote about Board mentoring. This is clearly the Full Monty and might sound a bit rich in an early stage company. However at some point you need to ask yourself the question of whether a football team, even one comprised entirely of superstars, *that was never coached as a team* would play optimally.

So be cultured!

Be a culture-maker not a culture-taker.

THE UNBALANCED BOARD

As we saw when looking at the "Who?" question about Boards one needs a breadth of experience and skillset. In the absence of this we end up with unbalanced Boards.

> "[Re Board composition] too many with too similar perspectives."

> "There is too much 'grey hair', oldFS on my Board. I am fed-up of hearing irrelevant stories of decades ago which, post-digital, no longer apply."

Why might one end up with unbalanced Boards?

ONE. The key cause of unbalanced Boards is not managing the Board – whether through lack of knowing that one has to or simply lack of time and focus. The following quote speaks to one of the headaches of this approach:

> "It's egos, isn't it? What happens with bad Boards is when five angels invest and the founder knows fuck all and invites them all. Then when a professional investor turns up they are all competing."

Assuming that you have absorbed the combined wisdom herein of millennia of Board service and are managing things proactively then how could you still end up with unbalanced Boards?

TWO. The gene pool of experienced NEDs is very small in any given sector and achieving a balanced Board may well be easier said than done:

> "You have to remember that Fintech is a very small pool. Those with Fintech Board experience are a super-tiny pool."

So it's not easy as supply is low in some niches. However identifying and seducing the right people into joining *at all levels of your company* is a (the?) core skillset of the entrepreneur.

THREE. Especially in the listed world, but also in larger SmallCos who have the budgets for proper searches, it's commonplace to blame the head-hunters:

> "It's easy money for them [head-hunters], they just recommend the same old names time and time again and that's a cheap business model to run."

> "Lack of real diversity in the shortlist – headhunters are not imaginative."

Lack of imagination may or may not be the problem. In the BigCo world there are clear disincentives for head-hunters to produce anything other than the "same old, same old". I spoke to a senior Big4 partner who said that he was often asked personally for "out of the box candidates" for PLC Boards and had suggested many excellent ones. None of whom was ever appointed. I have heard similar remarks from head-hunters – there is not much point in putting time and effort into producing "out of the box" candidates for a market that, *fearful of what the regulator might think* ("no one gets sacked for buying IBM") only ever buys "in the box".

Four. With the reach of regulators growing daily – *there is no counter-vailing force* – increasingly the State is stepping in to the process. The FCA's "Approved Persons" criterion – a hugely Orwellian phrase – are increasingly applying in Fintech:

> "An 'approved person' is an individual who we approve to do one or more activities – what we call 'controlled functions' – for an authorised firm." [FCA website]

I recall a well-written article about Tom Blomfield's challenges in being "approved" as CEO of Monzo when they were applying for a banking licence. A conversation which presumably went along the lines of "Who are you?", "The CEO of Monzo", "No you are not", "Yes I am", "No you are not as you don't fit the bill for a bank CEO", "But that's the whole point..." A lesser entrepreneur might have rolled over and given up.

Like much in the modern world this is sold on a kind of "health and safety" basis – you wouldn't want wrong 'uns on Boards, would you, and naturally Nanny Knows Best. Nanny also has her political slant and is increasingly "woke", which as we noted leads to focusing on characteristics a baby had at birth rather than what it learned in the subsequent decades.

Five. Regulators are a prime example of Power. At first in NewCo you have all the power and left to your own devices you can do what you want for better or for worse. *Some* founders – generally the less experienced whose concept of a Board is that it's an unnecessary pain in the derrière – cynically construct their Board:

"The cynical answer to 'who to have on the Board?' is for the most impressive-sounding people you can find who will ask the least questions once a month." [Angel/VC]

"Optics are really important due to the regulator. Get some folk who look good but won't get in your way too much."

Once external capital is represented on the Board, "it" will have its own ideas which may also be more about cynically maximising its control than doing the best for the company:

"One round of finance providers provides the NEDs anyway."

"We wanted to have a more diverse [in the real sense of thought/perspective/experience] Board but the VC stopped us."

The example of an excessively VC-controlled company is ultimately an example of where you lost control anyway so "it's not really your Board any more". Putting to one side the challenge of fixing (from your perspective) the power/control/balance issue the simplest workaround in these circumstances is to have an Advisory Board which can focus on Corporate Creativity and issues where you need input that you are not getting from your Board.

Ultimately one day the sheisse will hit the fan. It always does. And then you may find that you haven't accumulated enough balanced wisdom and support around you and the karma of cynicism – or its cousin, benign neglect – will fruit.

THE 'WATERLINE IN THE WRONG PLACE' BOARD

"It's vital to get the Matters Reserved For The Board right. You don't want to be getting a sign-off every time you buy a postage stamp. Equally, to have any real meaning the Board needs to have the ultimate sign-off on important issues."

I once spoke to an investment bank CEO whose executive committee meetings lasted for six hours and even then often didn't complete the agenda.

Now, this is one thing in a MegaCo – after all the vast majority of business is transacted many organogram levels below such a committee. But in a Startup it would be fatal – you need the CEO and team out there banging the rocks together and adding kindling to the sparks not stuck in meetings for hours on end. Over time the CEO's role evolves and he/she becomes more strategic in focus, leaving the day-to-day fire-fighting and running of the company to a COO/the team.

At one level this waterline is "obvious", "basic", "common sense" stuff:

"You must get the dividing line drawn appropriately. What the Board needs to approve. What management can do on its own without needing approval."

"Matters reserved for the Board? Capital structure, budget, over £75k signed off by the Board – about a dozen things in the investment articles."

"Too much of founders' time can be spent managing upwards [Board/shareholders]."

However, as individuals or groups, do we always get the basics right? Of course not and I doubt there are many of us who haven't sat through some committee at some point that went into too many marginal points and missed, or avoided, the salient.

Returning to personal dictionaries even if you define the waterline apparently clearly different people will interpret the words differently. One clear example was that when I drilled into more specific examples there was a kind of quantum blurriness about where strategy ends and where tactics begin. Is expanding into a new area a tactic or a strategy? To me it could be both or either.

A cross-cultural example of key words meaning different things to different people is the process leading to the handover of Hong Kong from the British to the Chinese. A "Heads of Agreement"[3] had been

---

[3]   The 1984 Sino-British Joint Declaration (the handover was in 1997).

signed. Notwithstanding which there was much friction in the whole process.[4] No doubt inevitable, but one crucial drafting point was around something like the nature of consultations along the way. According to an interesting article, the British had taken the relevant word to mean "big picture" consultations and the Chinese "detailed" consultations. This difference of interpretation had taken a long time to come to light. You can imagine the frustration along the way.

The net takeaways on this are…

ONE. Have the waterline in the right place – duh!

TWO. Be wary of terms that you might think are unambiguous but which others may not.

THREE. Evolve this over time in the light of what works and as the company grows.

FOUR. Have a human being in the Chair who, rather than simply parroting the Memorandum and Articles of Association, will use wisdom and sense on a meeting-to-meeting basis. The waterline varies with the seasons and tides – the Board needs to be responsive not mechanical. In an innovative company you don't want to slip into being a kind of 1950s Board:

> "If you have an agile culture in the biz you need an agile culture in the Board. Ours is too Old Financey."

THE 'DRIPPING TAP' BOARD

"I guess it [a Crisis] wasn't totally out of the blue."

If you come home from work one day and your kitchen is flooded it's a nightmare and you call an emergency plumber right away. A huge crisis leads to immediate action – not always the right action but at least action.

---

4   Nor, as we are seeing in 2019, is the deal enforceable.

But let's say your tap drips slightly. It's annoying but you have other more pressing things to deal with. Sounds familiar? Over time the tap drips more and more and is more annoying but there never is a sudden catastrophe sufficient to necessitate having to take immediate action.

This applies to the maintenance of all structures in our ephemeral world. You can "save money" on the upkeep of your house and in the short term you will have more money in your pocket. However one day some "accident" will "suddenly" and "unluckily" befall your house. However you created the conditions for it to happen.

In my decades in FS I saw countless examples of where some folks, some departments, some organisations could only get their act together when the kitchen finally flooded. This applies at all governance levels – Britain and WW2 is one of countless examples at the State level of exactly the same phenomenon. The tap drips more and more and for many psychological reasons, even when it's nigh on gushing, there are always folks who are avoidant and in denial or recommend inadequate "solutions" – let's just try tightening the tap again.

In almost all the tales of a "crisis" I heard in my interviews it wasn't actually a totally unanticipated "bolt from the blue", a meteorite suddenly crashing through the roof that was the "cause". Rather it was one dripping tap or another.

It would be unrealistic and sanctimonious to give advice of "stay ahead of the curve". Not because that's bad advice – far from it – it's great advice. But in the crazy world of a fast-growing SmallCo there are too many curves to be able to stay ahead of all of them all of the time. The reality is that you prioritise the limited organisational bandwidth on the most important taps at any given time. As we heard earlier a simple risk matrix is a start – you could have a "three key risks for each of these main areas and what we are doing about it" matrix even in a SmallCo.

Culturally one wants to have a non-avoidant Board which appreciates that the many calls on the team's time mean that one cannot fix every drip one day later. The solution is perhaps to attach realistic timescales for individual issues to be resolved within or at least return to the Board.

There are always matching pairs of cultural challenges on the Board. If one is the inability to focus on dripping taps and resolve them over pertinent timescales, the other is to overly-obsess about one tap:

"One of our NEDs has really got his teeth into a certain bone, won't let go and it's causing no end of problems."

Flooded kitchens are always best avoided wherever possible. Fix those taps!

THE 'WE NEED A DIVORCE' BOARD

"There have been plenty of fights on the Board."

What do you do when you know this ain't working for you? When the heat and the friction just ain't worth it no more?

As per one of the eight essences of the SmallCo Board, folks who haven't been on Boards are likely to underestimate the degree of passion. This earlier quote was from a gentle man:

> "I am not in the slightest bit violent but the nearest I have ever come to punching someone in the face was at a Board meeting."

Let's sit briefly in all the seats around the Boardroom table.

Starting with NEDs, it is important to appreciate their relative powerlessness – this abbreviated tale is a combination of two similar case studies I heard:

> "The CEO was being economical with the truth [at the Board] on material matters and was running the company as his own personal medieval fiefdom. Having consulted with lawyers I was surprised at my powerlessness. As the CEO and his buddies could command a majority at an AGM/EGM there was no way forwards. I conscientiously put my points and motion to an EGM. The CEO bloc voted en masse, I came off the Board and the business subsequently went nowhere."

As a rule I was impressed with how conscientious the NEDs that I spoke to were about their job. Maybe that was partly my sample – folks I respect – or maybe it is partly the simple fact that most people get out of bed most days and try to do the best they can and those who are selected as NEDs (outside the "cynically constructed" Board) are conscientious:

> "There's a dilemma here. If you hold your position but it is clear you are making no progress with it over time and indeed only aggravating the Board what do you do? The problem individually is that there is no "dissenting opinion" on a Board which is collegiately responsible for all decisions.[5] If, in your opinion, the ship is heading onto the rocks and you care about your reputation there is little short of resigning in important disputes. The trouble is this often leaves a viewpoint unrepresented."

Let's sit in the Chair. I can think of examples I have seen where the "wily old fox" type of Chairman has smelt trouble over the horizon and stepped down ahead of its arrival. I can think of others who, in their package negotiations, ensured that it would be costly to remove them and were quite happy to take a decent cheque to quit a room where opinions are divided and one faction wants to move on unopposed. Other more naive Chairmen (and here I am thinking of listed examples so "not entirely naive" by any means) stay and fight conscientiously for the right thing and are destroyed either by the situation or by paid PRs whispering to the press.

If you are a Chairman and don't match the above vertices of a triangle but lie somewhere within then your position is just like a standard NED only with greater responsibility for resolving the situation and more personal reputational risk. In SmallCo land – although this is rarely said and almost never the vibe – the Chairman is a hired hand – even if generally/often a prestigious hired hand.

Investment Directors – NEDs representing major capital providers – are often on one side of this divorce. Maybe the CEO is doing their head in, maybe they are doing the CEO's head in – in a sense if the situation can't be resolved then it doesn't matter "who started it".

---

[5] In the V1 Company, at the Court of Proprietors dissenting opinions and their owners were recorded. At the Court of Committees dissenting opinions, but not their owners, were recorded. In the V3 Company, as we have seen, an audit trail for NEDs is changing this dynamic.

Which leaves us with the founder/CEO "whose company it is" or at least "whose baby it was". As discussed, if you have the power then you can sack the lot. Vice versa if "they" have the power they can sack you. Both extremes are simple even if not a bunch of laughs. In between lies a lot of realpolitik. In the next section we cover the angles of street fighting – where the desire to win at all costs is predominant. This is not exactly MBA stuff, but, in realpolitik land all folks will at some point fight and all that differs is how experienced at fighting they are and how far they are prepared to go.

For the moment though let's stick with above Board (ha!) approaches.

At the simplest it's all about voting power. Voting power is highly correlated with being a major capital provider and/or good negotiator. So if things are going badly with your capital provider "all" you need to do is swap your current capital provider for a new one.

This is easier said than done – swapping capital providers is an infrequent activity at best. This is in part as the secondary market for VC stakes is nascent. There are some routes for tidying up your "cap table" and ridding yourself of possibly lesser pesky varmints. One notable example being "Balderton Capital Liquidity I", a $145m fund to:

> "Purchase equity directly from early shareholders including angel investors, existing or former employees and founders."

Dealing with divorce is always a tricky matter needing the best advice – you really need a good Board/Chairman/NED or adviser/bank/corporate finance house to guide you in your specific situation. The below are presented to whet the palate rather than satiate it.

The simplest route is:

> "Dilute them." [a super-successful serial entrepreneur]

Individual VCs are generally capital-limited and as we heard earlier can lose interest (and certainly influence) if you are in a position to do ever-larger raises. Naturally beware swapping the "single VC is a pain" for "multiple warring VCs are an even bigger pain".

Another clear route to divorcing capital providers is the "liquidity event" – the most common form of which (if your NewCo has progressed this far) is the IPO, the listing on a Stock Exchange. After all, despite PR puff, your VC is not in it primarily to save the planet/whales/society but to make money.

Another route for divorce is a trade sale. Again, depending on how (in crude terms) the power balance lies you do a deal or someone sells you. In the former case it can be good news – a kind of payday and maturation of your business at the same time. Institutional/strategic investing partners can have laid this ground years earlier.

Earlier I quoted a VC who had emphasised that the ground for the "trip" is laid down at the outset. In terms of your options if you need a divorce it is easier if your partner is less greedy. This is a case study from the same VC:

> "We [a more patient, less greedy type of capital provider] had invested in [X]. The business grew very rapidly and even paid us dividends. They enjoyed the business as it was and did not want to list or have a trade sale. They bought us out at 3x with which, given our [parameters/nature] we were happy. This would not have worked if their capital provider had been a more typical higher-return-requiring type of VC."

Another example I was given was an example where it was not VCs who were the pesky varmints but an institutional partner/capital provider. In this case an MBO was the way for SmallCo (not so small actually) to buy the institution out.

Another play is the Private Equity firm. This is a different world altogether, earn-outs and such-like to one side you are likely to become a servant not a master:

> "Compared to VCs who are used to sharing control Private Equity houses are definitely owners. If you are the CEO and your face doesn't fit you are out that day. End of."

The final divorce case was a fascinating one. A divorce that doesn't relate to capital providers for a *listed* company. Do you recall me mentioning the point that the liquidity offered by an IPO and a listing can be easily over-estimated?

"A relatively small listed company I was on [as a NED] had a problem as it became illiquid. The quote was purely nominal. It was decided to do a buy-back which was completed successfully. Here the independent NEDs were particularly useful as it was us who decided the price at which this was done."

SOMEONE IS GOING TO LOSE AND IT'S NOT ME

"I have found that in the end people will screw you if they can."

A while ago I learned a certain type of qigong in Asia from a Chinese master. There was an intensity about him that went beyond his martial arts background. The thing that sticks in my mind is a comment made by one of his senior students that, if a cage of monkeys were thrown in the river and his master was one of those monkeys, he would be the one monkey that escaped.

In Thailand there is a "forest tradition" of monks – back to basics, super-hardcore, keeping well clear of city temples and politics. In the 1960s, after serving in the US peace corps, Robert Jackman ordained and became Bhikku Sumedho. For the first year he stayed in a hut on his own – enduring months during which he had literally gone mad. He then moved to Isaan, the north-eastern province which was dirt poor in those days, and started learning under renowned meditation master Ajahn Chah[6] despite not speaking Thai and being the only westerner there. One story of someone visiting him recounted how Sumedho was sitting upright in the lotus position and smiling. The visitor asked him how he was doing. "Terrible" came the reply – at the time Sumedho had both malaria *and* cholera. Subsequently, much against his own inclinations, he ended up founding many influential monasteries around the world and he is now the longest-serving western Buddhist monk. An insider's comment as to how he survived conditions that no-one else could was the simple "he had guts".

James Cracknell is a multiple Olympic and world rowing champion. Rowers have the antithetical body shape for running long distances,

---

6   Getting on for a million people went to his funeral.

notwithstanding which at 6ft 3ins and 92kg and despite having a broken bone in his foot[7] he came twelfth in the 2008 Marathon des Sables (over 150 miles across the Sahara carrying all your kit). Less than a decade ago he suffered a horrific cycling accident which left him in a coma for a week, brain injured, after which he had to learn to walk and to read and write all over again, suffering long-term mood swings and personality changes. In 2019 as well as studying for a masters degree he became, at 46, the oldest man to compete in the Boat Race (he and his crew won).

The point of these stories is that some people triumph over circumstances despite everything thrown at them. This is the most essential point of this section.

Business is one specific aspect of life but in some ways no different from all the others. Even if the *techniques* used in qigong, meditation, rowing and business vary it is not the techniques that matter but the drive to succeed, the will to win.

It would be wrong at this point to utter banal clichés about "winners never quit and quitters never win". Sun Tzu would never have written that – you need to pick your battles. Especially in business sometimes walking away *is* the right thing. Seth Godin tells the tale of a friend of his father who never quit on his business for his whole life – but nor did he ever succeed. Walking away and taking his fishing rod elsewhere would have been a far better idea.

I recall some thirty years ago a COO chum of mine making a visit in a very first-world country to follow-up on a bad debt that his bankers had been rather dilatory over dealing with. After a "rather scary" conversation with the "gentleman" about repaying the loan he decided that discretion was the better part of valour and that writing the debt off was definitely best all-round.

After the fall of the iron-curtain a chum bought a property in one of the former republics of Yugoslavia. A year or so into renovating it he arrived in the village one day to be told he did not own that property but another, rather inferior, one. Protesting this did not get him anywhere and it was suggested that the safest course of action would be to accept the new state of affairs.

---

7   marathondessables.co.uk/race-history

Another chap I know had land and a business in – well let's just say a former part of the British Empire. One day the local heavies and politicians turned up, took both and built a housing development on the site. He now has a business in the UK:

> "You guys didn't get everything right when you ruled us but you are too self-critical. You are actually very straight. Now I don't have to fear anyone just turning up and taking my business."

Although the UK is "pretty straight" compared to other countries there is a spectrum of behaviour from dealing with trustworthy monks to dealing with gangsters who will stop at nothing. I thought the lead-in quote to this section rather shocking when I heard it but the more folks I spoke to the more that *"trust in Allah but tie up your camel"* came to mind along with *"be prepared for a fight with the bloke who comes to nick your camel"*.

Freedom from physical violence is hopefully the rule – I am glad to say I didn't hear any tale of actual violence on UK Boards – although I heard "I wanted to" and "I was quite prepared to". However this does not mean freedom from reputational violence – indeed the hottest stories that even the respectable financial media always love are the battles for power and control in BigCo Boardrooms.

Weaponisation of the media is no new thing – even if modern PR companies, as with the deepest 20[th]C roots of Corporate Governance, owe rather more to 1930s Germany than is generally acknowledged. Reputational violence per se is ancient and the truth does not need to stand in the way. I recall the first time when I saw things "happen to appear" on the front page of the FT, where I knew the inside-track. Naturally said-things were quite untrue and clearly put there by one-side of an ongoing power struggle.

A current example surrounds App Bank Revolut which featured in the press a lot in early 2019 with all of the angles/leaks/narratives negative. On the one hand, they were a firm that prioritised rapid growth rather than dotting all i's and crossing all t's and definitely bent if not broke things. On the other, it has been a highly-personalised campaign against the CEO – the word I hear on the street is that it is orchestrated "Black PR". It may not be kosher to hire heavies with baseball bats in polite business circles but it appears to be meat and potatoes to hire PR firms to get certain "messages" into the media.

At a more subtle level, like real violence, reputational violence can just be threatened to have an impact – messages not only don't need to be true they don't even actually need to be released. Imagine a major shareholder making a reasonable but below true value offer to buy a chunky stake from an individual shareholder. This would likely be rejected. However what if the major shareholder suggested that it would be unfortunate if the media and regulators received "unhelpful" tales relating to the individual? After all you can spend a long time trying to clear yourself of false accusations and besides some mud always sticks. Lacking any proof if the suggestion is oral where do you go? Not good! Bad! But these things happen as I heard.

Getting screwed-over can be perfectly above Board given all the rinky-dinks that exist in Company Law. A very public tale is how Zuckerberg screwed his co-founder of TheFacebook.com – the subject of the film "The Social Network". We mentioned the dilution via no pre-emption rights angle earlier. Here is a snip from a Business Insider article discussing how Zuckerberg could cut his co-founder out of the company:

> "In an IM exchange with Parker after a meeting with Peter Thiel, who would soon become Facebook's first outside investor, Mark and Sean discussed the Saverin [the co-founder] problem. Zuckerberg hinted at a hardball solution, one based on some "dirty tricks" used by Peter Thiel. Thiel had learned these tricks, Parker said, from one of the most legendary venture capitalists in the Valley, Michael Moritz of Sequoia...
>
> Parker: Peter [Thiel] tried some dirty tricks. All that shit he does is like classic Moritz shit... Zuckerberg: Well, now I learned it from him and I'll do it to Eduardo.[8]"

Nor does that just happen in the US. This happens in the UK – FanDuel is a good example of what can happen to a SmallCo (albeit once again there is a US connection – culture is so important in business). This

---

[8] Business Insider "How Mark Zuckerberg booted his co-founder out of the company" 15/5/12

beats the usual CCC governance weakness of screwing the little guy by screwing the founders as well:

> "The founders of Scottish Tech star FanDuel are suing its majority shareholders for $120 million after receiving no return on their investments following its sale to Paddy Power Betfair, claiming the merger undervalued the company.
>
> FanDuel, a fantasy gaming specialist focused on US sports, merged with the gambling giant in a $465m deal announced in May.
>
> But the deal, which has seen Paddy Power Betfair shareholders take 60% of the merged company, and FanDuel investors 40%, resulted in no return for the five founders in the Edinburgh business, as well as around 500 ordinary shareholders."[9]

The article continues with the all-so-clever legal rinky-dinks that two US Private Equity Houses used to screw the founders. By now even if you have no personal experience at founding and growing a company you should have got the idea that it's hard, very hard, to succeed. What about succeeding to the point where the business ends up being sold for half a billion dollars *and you get nothing...?*

A year later this is still ongoing – and talking of rinky-dinks:

> "The original dispute arose after Fanduel's main private equity backers Shamrock Capital Advisers and Kohlberg Kravis Roberts (KKR) exercised their majority shareholder drag-along rights to exclude all ordinary shareholders from the Paddy Power Betfair deal.
>
> Drag-along rights are supposed to be used to force minority shareholders to participate in a sale on the same terms as majority shareholders. However, due to a number of clauses that had been added to the company's articles of association over the preceding few years, KKR and Shamrock were able to force the sale while claiming the $465m valuation placed on Fanduel was insufficient to pay out on any ordinary shares."[10]

---

9 Herald Scotland "FanDuel founders sue company for $120m" 16/8/18
10 Herald Scotland "Harper Macleod takes forward $120m share fight for Fanduel founders" 21/8/19

In a well-governed world stripping away all the misusable rinky-dinks would lead to far less of this behaviour. However while we wait for a well-governed world watch your camel especially when dealing with firms who think ethical behaviour is defined as anything that they can get away with.

If getting nothing for working 24x7 for years is the top of the shop in terms of being screwed I heard other tales of founders being screwed to a lesser but still significant extent.

Vulture Capitalism is a well-known phrase but a less known phrase is Roadkill Capitalism. In the former you pick over the bones of something already dead, in the latter you hit it first with your car to kill it and then throw it in your trunk. Of course you are not supposed to run things over but who knows whether you accidentally hit that pheasant or swerved into it?

One public UK Fintech demise is an example where most folks only have a "media-derived" view. Insiders I spoke to told me tales of undoubted roadkill capitalism although a smaller number had more of a vulture capitalism slant (or at least "it shouldn't have run into the road"). The essence of the story is that a Fintech "became bankrupt" and "was bought from administration" by its major shareholder.

All tough stuff guaranteed to spoil your whole day and even leave you a tad grumpy the next. But in a book focusing on the realpolitik of Boards it is important to acknowledge that these scenarios exist.

There are many books on this topic of street-fighting in business. On the grandest scale we have the likes of "Barbarians at the Gates", the archetypal story of the shenanigans, dirty tricks and betrayals surrounding the takeover battle for RJR Nabisco. Unsurprisingly this is not just something that happens in BigCo land – it's just higher profile there.

So back to the stories of meditation and rowing. What you do when someone is trying to screw you is a question of guts and desire which manifest themselves in terms of how much of a fight you are up for. This is of course tempered by where you ethically draw the line over "techniques" and pragmatics about how much you are prepared to trade-off price versus a quiet life.

For sure "being a nice guy" in these circumstances is unlikely to win the day but equally spending the rest of your life on a chain gang for murder will severely reduce your business opportunities going forwards.

Almost by definition if you are in these circumstances something went badly wrong. As a serial entrepreneur replied when I asked him about this:

> "What to do when you are in the gutter [in business]? Well, like in life you should just avoid getting there in the first place, it is often too late when you are that down and out."

How do you get out of a tight spot?

If you have made it this far through the book with all other remedies failing then one suspects the following divorce route hasn't worked, as after all for the professional capital providers it is return that is their aim.

> "Get someone else to buy them out – institution or Private Equity firm."

Upping the stakes, one suggestion I received was the walkout – implied, threatened or actual. If you as a team are still required and if you are about to get nowt or far below fair value then your actual leverage is higher than your legal leverage. Neither an IPO nor a trade sale will go that well without a management team.

Recall the quotes earlier re *actual* power asymmetry as opposed to *apparent* power asymmetry:

> "For VCs changing the CEO is the nuclear button."

> "With VC more often than not there isn't a CEO succession which leads to a successful exit."

Downing tools might appear to be a mutually assured destruction scenario but such a threat is leverage to achieve a more "win-win" proposition.

PR firms run defensive or offensive campaigns. Putting helpful stories in the media is a long-established technique. Whether this can specifically help you with a tricky shareholder is less clear. After all, you and said shareholder are in the same boat.

Further up the scale, a stronger approach which builds on the fact that it is a person, not a "firm" sitting on your Board is:

"In the case of a VC unfairly squeezing your balls make it personal."

One set of tales I heard where a *lot* of money was at stake involved the use of private detectives to uncover "interesting" facts about individuals which the individual really wouldn't wish to come to light. Conversations with the relevant folks who were being difficult had always led to a more "win-win" outcome.

Back to the lead-in quote of this section. In life I hope everyone does not screw you. The subset of life that is business does however involve signing contracts with folks who themselves are often judged almost entirely on the financial returns they achieve. From their perspective it is just a game and if you sign a deal you sign a deal. If the consequence of that is they win and you don't then, from a purely legalistic, "neoliberal" perspective they are "not to blame".

However I do retain the optimistic perspective that in small and less cut-throat markets (and there are few large VCs for example in individual sectors in the UK), generally VCs do need to retain a decent reputation and hence do have a motivation not to wring the chicken's neck so much that it becomes a talking point all around the market. As a (reputable) VC said to me their need to maintain a reputation is a realpolitik restraint on how far they will actually go.

However if some day someone does try and screw you, you have been warned.

To wrap up this street fighting section on a historical note and offer some final practical advice for Board members, I mentioned earlier that I hadn't heard a tale of actual violence on Boards. However I have. It was a little while ago though.

In the late 18thC there was a long-running saga involving Board conflict between the EIC's Governor General in India, Warren Hastings, and a State appointee to a newly-formed "Board of Control",[11] Sir Philip Francis. This was a classic example where Board frictions arise from personality differences compounding two Board members coming from two very different positions trying to achieve very different ends in the same forum.

---

[11] On which the State had a majority. It overrode, in India, the EIC's Court of Proprietors and Court of Committees.

Hastings, against massive government pressure, was trying to keep the company primarily a trading company. After the de facto World War Zero (the Seven Years War, fought on five continents) and against a backdrop of a crumbling Moghul Empire, the EIC had got dragged into territorial acquisition. Hastings wanted to draw the line, take no more territory, and focus again on trading (as the EIC had done solely for six generations):

> "No other Governor General or Viceroy would last anything like as long as Hastings and no other would approach his profound understanding of India or his affection for its peoples… even today his reputation rests on the two seemingly irreconcilable assertions that he was both the architect of British India and the one ruler of British India to whom the creation of such an entity was anathema."[12]

However the British State had other ideas, especially after the loss of the thirteen colonies in North America. Francis was the State's representative on the Board in Calcutta on which the State had given itself a majority. Mutual reputational destruction had been continuing apace.

Tensions grew so high that it was decided to resolve matters with a duel. This took place in a Calcutta Avenue which still exists today (Duel Avenue) at 05:30 in the morning. There was much faffing about over location, rules and what the time was (?!). Francis had never discharged a pistol and Hastings only once or twice. They turned, walked fourteen paces, fired and Francis fell, shot in the chest.

Francis was injured not killed and was fixed up and sent off back to England where he schemed and plotted relentlessly until, eight years later, in 1788 he finally persuaded parliamentarian Edmund Burke to impeach Hastings (on grounds unrelated to the duel) in a parliamentary show trial that lasted for seven years.

I'm sure (cough) that this had nothing to do with William Burke being a relative of both Francis and Edmund Burke (who he called cousin but was actually more distantly related) nor Edmund Burke

---

12 Keay "The Honourable Company: A History of the English East India Company" 1991

having lost his lifetime savings in the "Bengal Bubble".[13] Nor was it anything to do, I am sure (ahem), with Edmund Burke being fed information by the Rajah of Tangore who was indebted to the EIC and its employees. Nor was it to do in the slightest with the State's desire to crush the EIC management and re-purpose the EIC going forwards as a sock-puppet for the State's new ambition to gain a new empire in the east having lost one in the west.

Eventually Hastings was acquitted of all charges. He said that the trial was a worse punishment than pleading guilty in the first place would have been and had cost him a small fortune. This was all part of the UK State's de facto takeover.[14] Hastings was the last Governor General appointed from within the company and before long Parliament sent Governor Generals who did their bidding and conquered the subcontinent.

So the moral of the story for you 21stC Board folks?

A non-executive Chairman (Hastings, as Governor, was in our terms Executive Chairman which was the model in the past) is important in refereeing Board conflict between two people playing two different roles and your Chairman should hopefully prevent duels.

But the real moral of the story here, my final practical advice, is that if your Chairman does not manage to prevent a duel, take twelve paces not fourteen if you are using 18thC pistols. When it comes to a power struggle winging your opponent just outrages them rather than finishes them off.

In extremis in the tales of Board Room rumbles I have quoted and many I have not there is always someone who takes just twelve paces – it is either you or your opponent.

---

[13] Wiki: *"By 1769, the East India Company stock was trading at £284... By 1784, the stock had declined to £122, a fall of 55%, and a series of bailout measures and increasing control by the crown led to the demise of the company."* In passing there was a lot going on but a major contributor to all this had been the State demanding an extra £400k pa from the EIC. "State Roadkill"?

[14] Formally the Government did not take over the EIC until 1874 – which leads to them being "blamed" to this day for the conquest of India – something that even Marx spotted was quite false. In practice via this Board of Control the State had taken over the command of the EIC in India in 1784 and used them as an imperial agency.

CHEER UP IT COULD BE WORSE

Let us not end with considerations of rough and tumble but with some perspective and the overwhelmingly good news. After all we know that terrible things happen in the world every day – but knowing that they do is important to understanding that we need to keep ourselves safe.

Wrapping up with the Big Picture, despite the mainstream media and social media spreading unrelenting negativity we live in an amazingly prosperous world compared to all our ancestors. To recycle a quote from earlier:

> "In the last quarter century alone more than 1.25 billion people escaped extreme poverty... In 1820, only 60 million people didn't live in extreme poverty. In 2015, 6.6 billion did not."[15]

Not only are most of us far less likely to be in poverty than our ancestors we are far less likely to be at war. My generation must be the first, or one of very few, in this country that never had to go to war or be conscripted. Our material comforts were unimaginable even a few decades ago. I happened to be reading an autobiographical account of the training of a WW2 pilot[16] recently. In training they died left right and centre. This airman in training had to fly the Master I, a death-trap,[17] to somewhere an hour away. This plane had already had engine problems but it was lightly fixed and he had to fly "regardless".[18] It duly caught fire en route and, too low to bail out, he had to make a forced landing in smoke and flames at an airstrip that fortunately hove into view. He was rescued and put up for the night. The next day before being sent home (in another Master I which had come to collect him) he was presented with an egg *"a by now rare and much prized commodity"*. He cosseted this egg for the whole journey but on getting out at his home air base he

---

[15] www.HumanProgress.org

[16] Neydler "Young Man – You'll Never Die" 2005

[17] It was cooled by glycol which leaked and when it did was inflammable (!). The plane was also near impossible to pull out of a spin which it was prone to, which "feature" even killed instructors.

[18] Apparently this had an important usage in the RAF.

broke it and had to fight back the tears.[19] An egg – something you and I never think twice about.

Turning to business it is super-competitive now but that is nothing new. If you were an entrepreneur four centuries ago in London you would have been super-busy – there was a boom in trading companies. But to wrap up and cheer you up that in business as in life "we've never had it so good" let's look at how tough that market was – and not just the market but even being a company.

The first long-distance trading Company was the snappily-entitled *"The mystery and companie of Merchants adventurers for the discoverie of regions, dominions, islands and places unknown"* (later known as the Muscovy Company). Its Chartered monopoly was worthy of its own Far Side cartoon – the *north-eastwards* route from England to China and the Spice Islands. Unlucky! It raised £6k,[20] from a syndicate of two hundred, bought three ships and headed off. The expedition didn't go entirely well and not that long into the journey two-thirds of the ships perished and their sailors froze to death.

Not only was business "tough" but the very concept of the Company was in severe jeopardy. Companies were very controversial (changes from Guilds to Companies created more losers than winners) and The Company came very close to being snuffed out at birth (a 1604 bill in Parliament would have abolished them all). The Spanish Company took the brunt of the counter-attack when Parliament abolished it in 1606. In the 1600s the Muscovy Company gave up the unequal struggle to be a Chartered Company and converted back to being a Guild.[21] The important Levant Company, formed by the first corporate merger,[22]

---

[19] It wasn't so much the overall stress – their lives were filled with that. It was disappointment over the egg. Food rationing did not come to an end in Britain until 1954 – eight years after it ended in America and four years after it ended in Germany.

[20] Before long they had spent £10k. Cost overruns are nothing new. There was no walking away from your debts in those days and shareholders had to cough up regardless.

[21] Interlopers (independent merchants who just ignored the Charter/monopoly), continuous attention and attacks (especially from Parliament which was to haunt the joint-stock companies), the greater challenge of managing your overseas agents as a company, and the per-voyage funding model at the time (which meant after successful voyages fundraising was easy, but also vice versa) meant that the first experiment was over.

[22] In 1581 the Turkey Company was formed for trade with the Ottoman Empire (silks, partially-finished luxuries). In 1592 the Venice Company (formed 1583) and Turkey Company were, after complex negotiations over terms (sound familiar?), merged into the Levant Company (the Levant being the collective name for the countries at the east end of the Mediterranean).

also converted back into being a Guild. Those three Companies represented almost *all* of England's long-distance overseas trade at the time. So whatever your problems today no-one is threatening to abolish you and your business format.[23]

All of these problems and more would haunt England's greatest ever Startup, the EIC. Let's look at their "entrepreneurial challenges" four centuries ago. Compare them to your challenges today and see who has/ had it easier. The EIC founders took one year to get permission from Elizabeth I to even be able to form their company in the first place. Its first voyage was delayed by its Governor suddenly being locked up in the Tower of London. It started, and lived for *twenty* years, in a couple of spare rooms in its Governor's house. Two-thirds of its crew died on route on its first voyage. Its second voyage was delayed by plague. It failed in its original aim to trade spices with the East Indies and also failed after a decade of trading in Japan, Siam and Malaya. Having bought/been granted a sole franchise on Asian trade in 1618 James I granted a second, ultra vires, to a friend and when the EIC protested he demanded they compensate his friend for his supposed loss and demanded a £20k loan on top. In 1623 Charles I pulled a similar trick. After high initial profits its 16th C financial position was generally parlous. Its HQ was a mere 400 metres away from the source of the Great Fire of London which destroyed the homes of 70,000 of the City's 80,000 inhabitants.[24] It took *fifteen years* of grovelling and supplication to get a full trading licence from the Moghul Emperor.

It had to keep the English monarchy onside, which was tough enough (I guess to be fair to you, you may have to keep the modern equivalent "the regulator" [etymology from Rex King?] onside]. Before you know it the monarchy was abolished in favour of a republic who didn't exactly like any of the old regime. Cromwell did not renew their charter and they put themselves up for sale for a derisory amount which no one bought [after the ensuing free-for-all chaos in Asian trading Cromwell reversed his decision four years later which led to the first creation of a "permanent joint stock" English Company]. In 1698

---

[23] Although your format is being a little distorted by the gravitational impact of the Corporate Governance black hole.

[24] An official threw the firefighters a hatful of gold coins just short of East India House saving the day for them. The City (which back in the day was centred on doing real stuff not abstract FS-y stuff) has always appreciated the role of incentives.

Parliament, now flexing its muscles, copied earlier monarchical tricks and granted a charter to yet another Startup EIC (the two merged in 1708). Parliament hauled two EIC Governor Generals in India in front of them for show-trials.

The EIC's original business model was to export England's only real commodity – wool – to hot climates. Aargh! This wasn't exactly a "great business model" and instead the EIC ended up exporting so much silver (in an era when a country's store of precious metals was a measure of its wealth) that it was blamed for causing recession (and contrary to modern narratives the corresponding importation of silver into India caused inflation where they traded). They had to invent the concept of balance of payments to try and get over this problem but that didn't help either as their trade looked bad for the country on that basis too. East India House, its London HQ, was attacked by domestic wool growers angry at being displaced by the importation of foreign cloth.

How are you doing in comparison so far? Your challenges not so bad as theirs?

Its competitors were no light touch. The European market leader against which it competed – Portugal – had a one hundred years' lead and ran "a vast protection racket" (you had to pay the Portuguese for protection from – er – the Portuguese) requiring licences for operating in the Indian Ocean. Its biggest competitor, the Dutch VOC, had ten times the capital, was not averse to massacring natives to get its way[25] and in 1623 captured ten EIC sailors and tortured them to death. In the face of this, other than the odd skirmish with European competitors at sea, they renounced violence[26] (a policy well ahead of its time which lasted for generations) and resolutely stuck to business (they were known as the Honourable Company for a reason even if current presentations are awry):

---

[25] 14,000 of the 15,000 inhabitants on the key Banda spice islands were killed. Jan Coen, two-time governor of the Dutch East Indies and founder of Batavia (Jakarta), wrote in 1614: *"Your Honours ought to know by experience that trade in Asia should be conducted and maintained under the protection and with the aid of your own weapons, and that those weapons must be wielded with the profits gained by the trade. So, we cannot carry on trade without war, nor war without trade."*

[26] Sir Thomas Roe, English Ambassador to India, in a letter to EIC HQ in 1616: *"Let this be received as a rule – that if you will profit, seek it at sea, and in quiet trade; for without controversies, it is an error to affect garrisons and land wars in India."*

"There is no sense of superiority. No sense for the first 130yrs of the EIC of any Imperial project. This is very much trade not conquest."[27]

Despite all these obstacles – far far worse than anything a 21stC Startup will face – they succeeded in rising to become the powerhouse of the City (ahead of the Royal Exchange and a much more junior Bank of England), the most important and certainly most seminal company in the world, created modern techniques like leasing infrastructure and the London money markets and in the end saw all their competitors go bankrupt. Talk about "never surrender"!

The EIC pioneered "corporate art". They built huge docks in London's Docklands and created one of the world's greatest civil services. They had their own alms house for poor sailors. They led the way in market research – what fashions were in and out and what to order for the next season. They had their own virtual currency centuries before Bitcoin.[28] Not only that, but eventually in India they created a far more successful and long-lasting (to this day) single currency zone than the EU has (or will I'd venture to say).

Did you know that some two million sailors are believed to have died from scurvy in the Age of Exploration? That in the 18thC the British Navy lost more sailors to scurvy than to enemy action and that it continued into the 20thC with it even being deemed to have been a factor in the 1915 Gallipoli disaster? Maybe you did. But you may not have known that all of this could have been avoided. Centuries of suffering could have been avoided. In 1614 the EIC's surgeon-general published "The Surgion's Mate" a guide for ships' surgeons in which he included the cure for scurvy – eating oranges, lemons, limes and tamarinds, a cure which had been known about for some time.

Even the US was heavily impacted by the EIC. The US flag is based on the EIC flag.[29] It was EIC tea on an EIC ship that was dumped into Boston Harbour in 1773. In the early days the EIC held the minuscule spice island of Run (2 miles by 1/2 mile) which was later swapped with

---

[27] Bowen "Making Money, Making Empires: The Case of the East India Company" YouTube 2014

[28] They accounted in the "common rupee". A currency that was virtual – it didn't exist.

[29] The EIC flag has horizontal red and white stripes with at first the cross of St George in the top left and later the Union Jack in the same spot.

the Dutch for "New Amsterdam", better known today as New York.[30] And to give but one more connection, the founder of Yale made his money from having been the EIC's President of Madras in 1687.[31]

Furthermore, contrary to general opinion it even advanced Indian culture. India's first Prime Minister, Nehru (a graduate of Trinity College, Cambridge, and member of the Inner Temple), writing in 1946 whilst imprisoned by the British (so hardly at his most well-disposed) acknowledged:

> "To [Sir William Oriental] Jones [an East India Company man], and to the many other European scholars, India owes a deep debt of gratitude for the rediscovery of her past literature."[32]

This is not an anomalous comment.[33]

You also have the EIC to thank that you are in a Company now – it was the first to avoid the chop and first to make being a trading Company a success. In 1600 when it was formed there were no "Boards", no "Directors", no "Chairmen", no permanent capital, an uncertain relationship between Shareholders and Management, no Stock Exchanges, no accounting texts, no company law and no a hell of a lot more. But over its nigh on three centuries of existence these all evolved along with the EIC. Give the distances it traversed (round trips to Asia took well over a year and relied on seasonal trade (sic) winds), its operations required refining all the necessary elements we use in global business today (including information technology – in which they were market leaders – they just used "writers" rather than computers to capture and process it all).

---

[30] At the time this wasn't as mad as it sounds. The tiny Banda islands (of which Run was a part) were the only source of the super-valuable nutmeg which you could sell for 320x the original purchase price in Europe. By taking Run the Dutch completed its monopoly.

[31] He was born in Boston (and so English in those times) in 1649. Elihu Yale joined the East India Company in 1671, became President of Madras 1687 but was dismissed in 1692 for repeatedly flouting EIC rules re illegal profiteering.

[32] Nehru "The Discovery of India" 1946

[33] "The father of the Indian Renaissance", a sufficiently important chap to have been celebrated in his own Google doodle, Ram Mohan Roy (1774–1833): *"Besides security from foreign invaders and internal plunderers, let us ask ourselves whether we could have rescued ourselves from stigma of female murder (burning of widows) but for the English? Whether we could have otherwise obtained the power of equalising ourselves with the rulers of the country in regard not only to civil but to criminal jurisprudence?"*

And to put all the above tales into perspective those were the struggles of England's *most successful* Startup ever. There never has been an easy ride to business success.

It is a wonderful time to be in SmallCo. Yes there are obstacles – but they are generally not lethal unlike in the past – and, like weight training in the gym, lifting them will make you stronger. By following your predecessors' advice contained herein on how to lift those weights safely I trust that you will be far more likely to succeed and grow stronger.

Anyway, next time you feel it's a bit tough being a SmallCo, recall the first century or so of the EIC's life. You are better off now. Far better off. Far far better off. And like them if you persist all sorts of weird, wonderful and unexpected things might come to you.

Epilogue

"Freedom is never more than one generation away from extinction. We didn't pass it to our children in the bloodstream. It must be fought for, protected, and handed on for them to do the same." Ronald Reagan[1]

RABBIT HOLES

"The struggle of man against power is the struggle of memory against forgetting."[2]

Having related to you the highlights of nigh on a hundred Boarders' stories and stories about the Boardroom before we were born, now the hurly burly's done let's reflect on stories as such. In this epilogue we'll sit back, do help yourself to a glass of port, and have some stories about stories. They are at the core of your life, your family's, your business's, your Board's and society. Stories really matter. Stories, as we shall see, are the building blocks of your world and mine. Healthy stories, healthy worlds, polluted stories, polluted worlds – literally and metaphorically.

Strange things happen when you spend too long down rabbit holes rather cut-off from society. Writing over a third of a million words, most of which I didn't use (aaargh), was one of them. Gaining far too much mass was another. Zillions of atoms have turned up when

---

[1] One of my favourite tales from the podcast is from the guest on LFP060 who, along with some others, was having dinner with the Reagans in the Sherlock Holmes Pub in Baker Street. As one does. It was part of a book tour and Ronnie and Nancy's last trip to London. During the meal there was considerable consternation amongst the special agents as the Reagans had disappeared. Upstairs there was a small museum of Holmes and Watson figures and Ronnie and Nancy were found sitting there dressed in the costumes :-D Who says you can't have fun no matter how old or how senior you have been?

[2] Kundera "The Book of Laughter and Forgetting" 1978

I was distracted[3] and have taken up residence. It's going to take quite some persistence to persuade them to going back to leading more independent lives.

An even less expected side-effect was watching Kate Bush's Wuthering Heights video[4] (red dress version) off and on, for a week or so. Which was strange. Both the video itself and me watching it after not seeing it for decades. Exploring dead-ends in rabbit holes gets tedious but that isn't an explanation as to why this one hooked me. I guess part of it, to the prior point, may have been the recollection that almost everyone young was skinny in the 1970s. This of course was due to no moral superiority but rather it was all prior to this fatal (sic) advice that "fat is bad for you". It may be but it turns out that sugar is far worse – diabetes is estimated to affect nearly half a billion people worldwide. As well as being correlated with weight it is highly correlated with sugar intake. Anyway, back to La Bush, now, like me, rather larger than forty years ago, her whippet-like figure reminded me of a young lady I espied from a school oriel many moons ago. At the time the amateurishness of the video[5] didn't leap out – everything was amateurish back then (which actually was more relaxing in a way). Along with the ethereal voice, a song which remains unique, she did convey a sense of being completely nuts as well as being a super-hotty totty, these last two conflicting factors causing great confusion and conflict in the teenage male brain. In the end fear over-ruled attraction but like many of life's calculations it was of no practical import.

Veering away from an analysis of *how* she conveyed those tones, where I have more of a clue now than then, an even more bizarre outcome from the rabbit-holing was, for the first time in my life, appreciating Confucianism. Which is very odd for someone who is a natural Taoist. Although Confucianism is rule-bound to an extreme extent, which is not my cup of tea – it is one religion/philosophy/way of life that does not travel (you do rather have to be born into it to tolerate

---

[3] Lack of attention, which means one's single attention was focused elsewhere, is of course a reason for things going wrong at all levels from body to business.

[4] Best YouTube comment: *"Daddy, the strange gypsy lady is dancing in the yard again…"*

[5] Another good YouTube comment: *"This video cost 12 pounds to make. It would have been 9 pounds, but the director incurred a late fee for the videocamera ;)"*

living it) – it does place high importance on ancestor worship. Ancestor worship? How could I worship them, most of my ancestors died before I was born so I never met them?

And besides, worship? I thought we were supposed to diss our ancestors these days. What did those folks know?

One thing all/many/most original/pre-modern societies around the world knew was that if you diss your ancestors all hell breaks loose and ancestor worship was seen as essential. We have chosen the opposite and, just as the ancients would have predicted, the Gods are punishing us – the ground beneath our societies is shaking, the walls are crumbling and cultural revolution is underway.

We might not believe in ancient Gods these days but we do understand code bases. All CTOs with huge systems to maintain have a healthy respect for their ancestors and a reverence for the code. They don't junk core subroutines and rewrite them in a completely different way without expecting the ground beneath their systems to shake, the walls to crumble and revolution from their users.

ANCESTOR WORSHIP

"It is lack of confidence, more than anything else, that kills a civilisation. We can destroy ourselves by cynicism and disillusion, just as effectively as by bombs."[6]

Before we kick off with "six things Mike never appreciated before about ancestor-worship" let us not be as literal-minded as I was in the past. I have no idea, for example, whether my ancestors were involved in the first English companies, or opposed them or knew nothing of them. The vast majority of our ancestors alive then would have known nothing of these new-fangled experiments. Taking an average generation cycle of 25 years (probably too high back in the day) we would all have over 130,000 ancestors alive in 1600 when the EIC was formed. Wouldn't it be cool if one could see where they all lived at the time as a mass of tiny pinpricks of red light on a globe?

---

[6]   Kenneth Clark "Civilisation, Episode 13 – Heroic Materialism" 1969

Curiously, in passing, family trees and common sense deceive us as we have had twice as many female ancestors as male. Which is odd – I know biology is old-hat now but how can my ancestors have had two mothers? On average?[7]

Let us turn to the six benefits of ancestor worship that occurred to me when leaving the rabbit hole.

FIRST let's deal with the "worship" word – an English word/concept. **Venerate** is perhaps a more appropriate translation although for our purposes let's just use the simpler phrase "respect your ancestors" as the flavour. An ancestral shrine in a Confucian home or Chinese temple is used as a ritual focus to pay respects and offer thanks. A ritual is a systematic *practice*. At an esoteric level whether this has any impact on any ancestors in some other realm, as many original people around the world believe (including Confucians "looking after your ancestors" is a big concern), need not trouble us. At a practical level, the realpolitik is that a regular practice is something that will change you. Practice stretching and you will be looser than before (even if not perfect). Practice *humility* (bowing) and *gratitude* and you will end up more humble and more grateful than before. Humility is sorely lacking in much of occidental culture right now – it is the essential antidote to the egomania and the general narcissistic ego-inflation[8] that is nigh on de rigueur (most everyone on social media seems to think they know the truth of everything). Gratitude has repeatedly been proven to be *the*

---

7   We are deceived as we assume that at any layer in the family tree all entries are unique (as opposed to the same name cropping up in several places (/beds)). This "twice as many female ancestors" is well-established and measured by research into Y chromosomes (passed solely down the male line) and mitochondrial DNA (passed solely down the female line). *"Men and women differed in their participation in reproduction, the researchers report. More men than women get squeezed out of the mating game. As a result, twice as many women as men passed their genes to the next generation"* Science Daily "Genes Expose Secrets Of Sex On The Side" 21/9/04. If you are a bloke you are lucky to be living today: Pacific Standard "8,000 Years Ago, 17 Women Reproduced for Every One Man" 17/3/17

8   Christopher Lasch wrote "The Culture of Narcissism: American Life in an Age of Diminishing Expectations" in 1979 in which he said American society had normalised pathological narcissism. It has spread rather further by now (just look at all the me-me-me posts on LinkedIn). It's very unhealthy though (Houellebecq "Atomised" qv) as most people know they are a bit rubbish (and the rest really are narcissistic). Peter Thiel is good on this point in the business world: having to act out a lie (that you are super-great, know everything etc) is damaging for one's soul and mental health. Our ancestors knew this of course, in the same way they knew that untrammelled greed is bad per se and certainly does not make a "good" economic system.

most impactful thing you can do for your well-being. Gratitude focuses us on what is right in the world – and there's a hell of a lot. Think of all of the things that, with a mere tap on our phone you can have turn up on our doorstep tomorrow. This was an utterly inconceivable luxury when I was young let alone for our 130,000 ancestors alive in 1600, almost all of whom (unless you are super-pukka) were dirt poor, could neither read nor write and were struggling just to survive and make ends meet. **The realpolitik is that we all inherit this cornucopia *solely* as a result of the labours of our ancestors – whether they are in our family tree or not.**

SECONDLY, ancestral-focus enables us to practise (as in aim to "get better at") *forgiveness* – another super-powerful attribute to cultivate that is diminishing fast in modern society. Our ancestors screwed up, but hey, so do we and we would wish to be forgiven for our trespasses in turn. We cannot forgive ourselves if we cannot forgive others. Forgiving ancestors makes one more conscious of one's own fallibility and the need to avoid trespassing today.

THIRDLY, in terms of "ancestral mistakes" we live with their consequences in the present *and therefore must understand the original mistakes if we are to fix them today* – and **we can only "fix the past" today.** Recent decades have seen increasing levels of hysteria about the past but the past is past. It would be infinitely more valuable to campaign against wars, slavery and injustice *today*.

FOURTHLY, **we need to understand what our ancestors were doing,** what challenges they were trying to solve, in order to properly understand how **to better solve our challenges today.** Whatever mistakes were made, whatever flaws (or experiments – "life is perpetual beta", discuss) were introduced in designing the Company V1, V2, and V3 are all "water under the bridge". However they are the causal roots of today's challenges. Most policymaking in history has probably been myopic – it's always easier to tinker, applying ad hoc solutions to the presenting challenges and not addressing the tap roots. This applies in spades to those officials who have no democratic mandate – they need to inch in their preferred direction to avoid drawing attention to their constitutional illegitimacy. But tinkering never tackles the roots. It is as if the person you bought your house from had been lax with the lawn. If you are conscientious but myopic you will focus on cutting off the heads of the dandelions before they turn to seed. This may be palliative but would not be getting to the roots (sic) of the problem as you fail to understand that the seeds of your problem were sown long ago. You cannot go back in time and prevent that seed from growing but you can root out its consequences today and replace those with a better seed.

FIFTHLY, rejection or defamation of one's ancestors is definitely not good although it is very common in the mainstream narrative today (which is not good too). At one level it makes no sense saying, for example, "in the 19thC *the British...*" as "The British" (all n million of them) never did anything en masse. Generally the phrase "the British" refers to decisions by a tiny few not the vast majority of Brits who didn't even have a vote let alone involve themselves in anything outside their village. In the tsunami of books launched upon the bookshops every time there is an anniversary of some imperial disaster or other we always read "the British". In the latest example of woke publishing with shouty covers the fault lay with the orders given by *one* officer not a whole nation. Besides, at an aggregate level, "the British Government and its armed forces" were responsible for far fewer deaths than those who the woke crowd lionise and maybe even fewer deaths than the modern wars we continue to participate in.

Jung developed the idea of the shadow side of one's personality:

> "Unfortunately there can be no doubt that man is, on the whole, less good than he imagines himself or wants to be. Everyone carries a shadow, and the less it is embodied in the individual's conscious life, the blacker and denser it is. If an inferiority is conscious, one always has a chance to correct it. Furthermore, it is constantly in contact with other interests, so that it is continually subjected to modifications. But if it is repressed and isolated from consciousness, it never gets corrected."[9]

Examples of this are passim. At the grandest scale I recall the not-entirely successful French President Macron talking about a "common destiny" that meant Europe "must" admit a vast number of Africans

---

[9] Jung "Psychology and Religion" 1938

(I have forgotten the number, 100 million, 500 million or 1 billion?). Curiously France never suggested anything like that when China had their population explosion challenge. We assume that Macron wouldn't like, or at least like to admit to liking, the 19thC concept of the "white man's burden" but surely this is the same paternalistic mentality? To me, the 21stC "it's our job to help these poor helpless people who can't help/govern themselves" sounds remarkably like the 19thC version which he has repressed into his shadow. Or as Euripedes put it:

"The gods visit the sins of the fathers upon the children."[10]

The Chinese, whose Confucian ethos both enchains their culture and yet protects it, inoculating it against infection, have a word for the current Western sanctimony and likes of Monsieur Macron – Baizuo.[11]

Macron is, however, not exactly Monsieur Sage and does come out with lots of words on lots of topics so let's take an actual example in the UK, where the woke narrative is all about how bad and rapacious we were *in the past*. The NHS is importing so many doctors and nurses that Nigeria has a shortage. Tell me how that is an improvement on the "plundering of natural resources" we were allegedly[12] responsible

---

[10] Euripides Phrixus Frag. 970

[11] Wiki: *"Baizuo (literally "white left") is a derogatory Chinese neologism and political epithet used to refer to Western liberal elites...the term is defined as referring to those who are hypocritically obsessed with peace and equality in order to satisfy their own feeling of moral superiority motivated from an ignorant and arrogant Western-centric worldview who pity the rest of the world and think they are saviours. A related term is shengmu (literally "holy mother"), a sarcastic reference to those whose political opinions are guided by emotions and a hypocritical show of selflessness and empathy, represented by celebrities."*

[12] I say allegedly as amazingly enough concrete data can be hard to come by. Richards was combing parliamentary papers to try amass real data re India before an untimely demise. The LSE's Tirthankar Roy has published Richards' raw spreadsheet data on the EIC Finances in India from 1766–1859. Two points leap out from the data. First opium, much beloved of narrative-spinners (though academic opinion has been shifting since the 90s), was insignificant at below 5% of revenues until as late as 1810. The second was an astonishing "profit" for "India" over the period 1794–1810 (when the EIC was an imperial agency) of minus £30.5 million which you sharp business folks will spot is actually a huge loss. The Moghuls had maintained themselves in opulence only by massive taxation of the natives they conquered. Interestingly, despite the "rip-off Britain" narratives, by 1914 taxation levels in India (as well as creating a huge infrastructure) were running at half of what the Moghuls had charged the populus. Thus, even though the EIC had unsurprisingly struggled in their complete phase change from merchants to administrative/imperial agency in the late 18thC, in the end the later EIC and the ICS it spawned eventually did create more cost-effective governance which also yielded superior benefits and one of the longest periods of peace in the history of the subcontinent.

for in the 19ᵗʰC? To me the 21ˢᵗC version is the same, if not arguably worse, just this time plundering trained people not resources. A recent plan to cut back on the importation of thousands of nurses *per month* from such countries was denounced as "racist" in the mad sections of the media who are less repressing their shadow side than not bothering to think (or actually projecting – another symptom of an unintegrated shadow). To me racism is plundering foreign countries of their trained doctors and nurses rather than training our own. We thus leave those countries and societies denuded of some of their most important human resources and picking up the tab for training doctors and nurses for *our* NHS. Another insidious form of racism is getting mobile phones made in countries and companies where the factories have suicide nets to stop workers jumping off balconies. Behind all the accounting terms ("unit cost of production") lies the harsh reality of exploiting workers overseas in a way you would not or could not in your own country.

SIXTHLY and finally, ancestor worship situates one not as an atom stripped of all context, importance and relevance (which undoubtedly contributes to our mental health crisis), but as a link in a chain stretching back to eternity. We are successors in an eternal firemen's chain of buckets – we have this precious, precious bucket right now, for a tiny, fleeting, moment in time so we should appreciate our good fortune. Situated as part of an eternal chain we have responsibilities to generations not yet born. We all create society for future generations. Whatever our role we all make a difference. I recently happened upon an example of this re "just a coffee van" which gets 5* from 28 reviews on Google maps, one of which says:

> "Charlie's is amazing, not only does she know all her customers coffees off by heart, she has a smile and warm words all year round. I would hazard that she single handedly increases both productivity and wellbeing for the city of St Albans having just celebrated 10 years of standing in a car park :) We love Charlie's and love her little coffee shop too which has a devilishly good tiger bread BLT."

There are real Angels in this world.

Summarising ancestor-veneration it seems to me that consideration of our ancestors leads us towards humility, gratitude, forgiveness, a greater focus on the needs of today, a greater chance of overcoming our challenges today by understanding their genesis, an appreciation of the opportunities that being alive offers and last but not least all of our responsibilities to generations not yet born.

Apart from those I can't see much benefit in respecting the ancestors :-D Well, apart from having a stable society I guess.

STORIES AS CODE, TECHNOLOGICAL ERAS AS ENVIRONMENT

"Most peasant farmers and herders, who constitute the great majority of the world's actual food producers, aren't necessarily better off than hunter-gatherers. Time budget studies show that they may spend more rather than fewer hours per day at work than hunter-gatherers do."[13]

We need to understand stories in order to do that least valued thing in our myopic societies: *learn from our ancestors*. How do we learn from the V1, V2, V3 Companies to start thinking of a better plan for V4? At the same time we need to *learn new stories* for our technological age.

Societies, of which European-descended cultures are becoming prime examples, whose stories don't respect, understand or even pay much attention to their ancestors, or something transcendent (even an idea such as The Greater Good of the society and its people) end up sick, fragmented and atomised.

You don't need to have a shrine in your house to relate to your ancestors. Stories are super-important in this regard. Stories bind or divide us and teach us who we are.[14] Healthy societies *need* an, on balance, healthy set of stories. *Poisoning stories poisons society.*

We live in a super-rare major change of era – there have only been three major transitions in the whole of human history (between hunter-gathering, farming and industry eras). No-one predicted the interwebbed phone in all our pockets when I started my career let alone how it would

---

[13] Diamond "Guns, Germs, and Steel: The Fates of Human Societies" 1997

[14] A prime example in my career was of the Icelandic Sagas. They aren't stories about "the past" they are, at some archetypal but tangible level, insights into Icelandic people today.

impact society which we are still discovering. In historical terms, it's still quite a shock which we haven't even started to get our heads around.

If we see culture and society as a kind of computer code written in stories then Palaeoliths (hunter gatherers) had some 50,000 years to work out the bugs in their culture's software to interface successfully their hardware to their environment. Neoliths (farmers) had 10,000 years to come up with a match – ie a set of stories that "worked". Industrialised societies have had 200 years. Many countries, but not all, have stopped, literally and metaphorically, sending children up chimneys and creating satanic mills (or been forbidden from doing so by society at large). But the Industrial Era is still a comparatively super-young era and an obvious bug in the software is that we are consuming the world's finite resources and polluting it by way of thanks.

In contrast, us "Data-oliths" with mobile phones in our pockets have only been around for twenty years. Forty years or so ago when I first got involved with computers there wasn't the slightest concept of having the world's information in one's pocket. People were talking about colonising other worlds or visiting the stars – that was in the realm of possibility, of what could be imagined, but Android and iPhones were not. We are only just discovering consequences such as the likes of Twitter in particular appearing to foster political polarisation and social division, and only just discovering "code"/"hacks" such as coming off Facebook being good for your mental/emotional well-being and reducing depression.

In about 10,000 years we should have cracked it. In the meantime though our environment of data overload is messing with the most fundamental hardware systems in the brain. The dopamine system was designed to produce big payoffs for big things but it turns out that looking at a zillion tweets with a zillion micro-rewards hacks the system. At a software level much social media has descended to the same place that the mainstream news has been at for some time – promoting the worst of society not the best. We should note that successful ancestral societies from around the world, be they Lakota, Ancient Greeks or Chinese, included in their stories stories of heroes, of people to emulate. Such stories in our society are few and far between, swamped by non-stop immersion in tales of consumerism (advertising) and narratives about what "bad" societies we are.

As "survival machines" we are automatically more focused on "threats" than on "opportunities" and creation. It's one thing that founders do brilliantly well and that I have learned from them as a class – focus on creating not getting bogged down with what's worst in the world. At least that way you make the world a tiny little bit better. Frustrating for sure but if billions make the world slightly better it adds up. And as we shall see later being angelic and putting goodness into the world is possible in one of the apparently most modest and lowly of jobs.

You have ten fingers and ten toes but only have one attention. Use it well and decide what *you* want to put it on no matter how, behind the scenes, others devote their lives in the Data-olithic age to trying to steal your attention and put it on what *they* want you to put it on. But you entrepreneurs know how powerful the mind is. All that you see around you in your company is there only because of your mind. Your mind has affected not just your reality but created a new one for many people. Which if you pause for a moment is an incredible thing – our thoughts feel so insubstantial yet create the world we live in.

OUR WORLDS ARE MADE OF STORIES

"The limits of my stories are the limits of my world."[15]

None of us build our own psychological homes and estates, rather we get our society's and family's pattern book to start off with. In software terms you get a whole bunch of code libraries to save you having to write everything from scratch. These pattern books, these overarching ideologies, are ways of defining appropriate behaviours and of trying to organise and understand the world in all its splendour, all its manifest chaos and all the background "WTF is all this anyway?"

Man is, I believe (ha!), a believing creature first and a thinking creature second. We use our beliefs – our most important stories – to construct foundations, floors, walls, ceilings and rooms within which we live, we use them as comfy old sofas we have got used to sprawling on, as guard dogs on a long gravel drive, as gates, as fields, as a pleasing

---

[15] Loy "The World Is Made Of Stories" 2010

copse of trees to espy from the drawing room, as padlocks on doors leading to the basement where we have banished things we'd prefer not to think about and as habits to ensure that most of our life is on auto-pilot, freeing up as much as possible of our tiny amount of real-time attentive bandwidth. Our estate is far more civilised than Plato's cave but equally entrapping and perhaps even less secure. The more property you have, and we have a lot these days, the more you can lose. Any bounders coming to take away our possessions will be resisted and resisted fiercely if they are after our treasured possessions. People can fight to the death, and have done in their millions, over foundational beliefs.

Our beliefs, our set of premises are vast. Human babies at birth are very under-developed compared to other mammals most of which can get on their feet pretty quickly or at least (as with our nearest cousins) cling to their mothers. Fairly soon though babies learn by imitation and as soon as language enters the equation the floodgates open and a deluge of stories and beliefs flood in. Most of the stories we have we don't even realise we have. Until researching it I would have never thought of my "understanding" of limited liability as a story or belief at all – it was simply "just what it is". As I have painfully found, even taking one apparently simple almost non-story and really digging into it and researching its veracity can take up a good chunk of one's life. And that's one story out of the zillion that I've absorbed.

When I asked various business folks why we had limited liability, they *all*, and I mean all, robotically (sic) answered as I would have before my trip down the rabbit hole: *"well it's necessary for risk taking isn't it?"* I can't convey how bizarre this repeated experience was. If you told me that: *"Ah, you see, Mike, that is because all babies in hospital are hypnotised with that belief just after birth"*, I would have considered that as not just a possible but likely explanation. Naturally not one said *"well, it's no longer limited liability at all but rather zero/transferred liability"*.

These folks were also highly resistant to being dissuaded of their beliefs, which was interesting – obviously this is quite a core/foundational belief in businessfolks' homes.

Another story that shows that babies must be being programmed in maternity wards is about the complexity of the modern world. I heard many times an always hypnotically-recited story when I probed in this area: *"the world is more complex therefore we need complex rules"*. It has *some* truth to it so some plausibility and it's reassuring to believe that no-one is pulling a fast-one on you. However to me it's mostly complete BS. Rules are super-complex for two reasons. First as, after the widespread usage of the computer and especially the interwebbed computer, the potential complexity of rules could mushroom. And it did. Do you really think one could do millions of paragraphs-long regulation with an "old-fashioned" (it wasn't that long ago, lol) type-writer? Second, to Tom Cruise's "show me the money" principle – who benefits most from complexity? To an extent BigCo as the rules dig ever-deeper moats around their castles, although BigCos aren't generally too concerned about SmallCos, they can always buy them. More perti-nently, the real beneficiaries are regulators, accountants and lawyers – they all become more necessary, more important and more central. Oh, and by the way, who creates the rules? Regulators, accountants and lawyers. Funny that.

Having spun you on "the world is made of stories", as a story itself it is only a story. This story is not actually complete, our world also contains *experiences* in that tiny slice of forever called "now". If you come up to me and kick me in the shins that is an experience. However that momentary experience soon becomes storyised, eg: *"this nutter came up and kicked me for no reason"* or *"I happened to be in the path of a psycho who kicks people"* or *"it's my fault, he read the epilogue and got so annoyed he couldn't stop himself"*. Whatever story I make about a fleeting experience will utterly colour and give meaning to the memory of that incident. It will both be derived from and add weight to my pre-existing stories about myself and the world. Thus respectively eg: *"danger can strike at any time, I have no security"*, *"only a few people are nuts, don't worry you were just unlucky"* or *"I am always messing my life up, everything is my fault"*.

This "real-time experiences" bit of reality is a very tiny bandwidth compared to our vast internal library of stories and how little we attend to the here and now (look at people on a tube escalator, or on their phones, most of them are "miles away" from here and now). So, having noted it, let's put it to one side and get back to lionising stories. Stories as the *foundations of our worlds* have emotive and cognitive conse-quences (in a three-factor model we would add in visceral/embodied, as per the "being kicked" example but let's keep it simple). You experience "thoughts" and you experience "feelings". By now you may well be *cognitively* experiencing the *thought* "WTF is he banging on about?" and *emotively* experiencing a *feeling* of frustration.

Emotively our stories are tied up with who we were, who we are, how we relate to experience and what we can be in the future. At the individual level there are clearly healthier and unhealthier sets of stories which producing happier, more fulfilled lives or unhappier, less fulfilled lives.

Many people programmed with the belief/story that they will never come to anything, that they are useless, and so forth will have a hard time rising above this. This is especially the case if they were programmed at an early age when stories settle in the core of one's house and are thus far harder to shift. However even then the human spirit is a curious thing and there are some who succeed, despite, or even almost because of, adverse circumstances; just as a lotus grows out of a dank muddy pond, beauty can arise out of the most unprepossessing of circumstances.

Folks programmed with a more positive set of stories, that they can do stuff, that obstacles can make you stronger (the more weight you lift the stronger you get) and so forth will have far more chance of succeeding. But even then there has to be some itch, some irritation, some drive to get you off the sofa and venturing out on a journey.

Cognitively your stories constitute a map of the experienced world. The more accurate your stories are as guides to the experienced world the better for you. If Realpolitik's stories are good stories then absorbing those that speak most to you right now will mean that you are more successful with your Board. If you are not on a Board and never will be then they just become stories you read, and store in your vast library in case you ever need them. Ideally as we grow from being a baby we learn more about how the world works – ie we continually update the countless stories in our library to be an ever more accurate and useful map of the world. Of course God has some sense of irony as just as you are getting *some* sense of how it all works your body has fallen apart and it's game over. *Si jeunesse savait, si vieillesse pouvait.*

Some of these stories, eg limited liability or around the concept of a V4 Company, you plant as seeds in your garden and share with friends who scatter them in their garden where they may await fertile conditions. My podcast with Lord Turner[16] was interesting in terms of the super-long cycle of policy idea creation, the dormancy of seeds and then eventual flourishing when a crisis presents an opportunity for radical change and a politician with sufficient drive comes along, needs some new approaches and nurtures those seeds. The example that Turner gave was seeds sown by academics in the 40s/50s (~"wouldn't it be nice if the State didn't run everything") which laid dormant for decades until the 80s (privatisation). These old seeds then flourish and create a new ecosystem with a new set of challenges which eventually leads to a new crisis and a new set of seeds get watered. It was a highly compelling thesis albeit with a rather dispiriting timescale. Trees are always planted more for the next generation than the current one.

Fortunately, even if man is a believing creature, he does have the ability to re-write his own code (well, some people some times...). Plenty of people realise that their "set of a million beliefs" are in large part a whole list of *tentative hypotheses* not "cast-iron facts". Whether you immediately open your door to a new story or bolt it shut and pour boiling oil upon the postman from an upstairs window depends on how easily it would or wouldn't integrate into your house. How young were you when you absorbed related stories? Is it peripheral or central? How well does it complement your existing stories, your identity?[17] How much does it threaten them?

Sometimes you will open the door, let the story in with a "yeh, whatever" and you will stick it on a shelf and move on. In other cases you aren't suddenly about to let some lunatic story into your house. Evidencing this is that when talking about limited liability to family members (especially younger ones) who have spent their lives nowhere near the topic, they all readily accepted what I said and took it on board without any resistance: *"ah interesting"*. Others, more emotionally-connected to the topic, who really didn't want to change their belief structure in an area very close to their heart, barred the door, peered at me sceptically from behind the curtain of an upstairs window, or, in extremis, went off to boil some oil as if I was trying to pull a fast one and introduce woodworm into their house.

---

[16] LFP065 "Creating Society – Policy, Regulation & FS with Lord Turner former Chairman of the FSA"

[17] Itself a set of stories but that's another book :-D

Another example of my rapidly-aborted career in being a door-to-door short-story salesman resulted in being splattered with boiling oil. I separately suggested to a couple of folks, who are quite sensible and otherwise well-educated, that the EIC is much misunderstood and that, judged by the standards of their times, they were on the whole good chaps. The responses were similar. I distinctly recall one verbatim which was "steady on, Mike, that's going too far" along with a look of horror as if I had announced that I had been out to buy the full Nazi uniform which I wore at weekends as I goose-stepped around my estate. It's an interesting phenomenon which leads nicely into considering how the State's national curriculum and mainstream media program us as children and of course how accurate their stories are along with whether they are wholesome for individuals, for business and for the country.

Conversely, when circulating early versions of chapters for review there was no negative feedback around the EIC. By definition almost every reader out there has a far lower-resolution jpeg/story in their heads and filling in pixels isn't threatening – especially when they are factual. Anyway all experienced salesmen know these matters. Selling something similar to what someone has bought before is relatively simple. Try and sell something radically different and you will encounter much resistance and the sales process will be much longer (but it's still possible).

Although when I started I knew next to nothing about the EIC, it must be something else we are programmed with in maternity units as, for some reason, and I really don't know why, my first tentative approach was of caution rather like a little boy peering through his fingers from behind the sofa at the Daleks on TV. I had clearly somehow absorbed some negativity about the EIC. It's not like I knew anything about the Empire either which was never mentioned once at school. Which is, with hindsight, odd – not so much "don't mention ze war" as "don't mention the Empire, old chap". Vice versa I never quite understood why there was such an emphasis on the Classics. Apparently this relative teaching priority goes back centuries and thus wasn't entirely an artefact of a time of post-imperial decline.[18]

---

[18] There is an excellent article on these matters at www.britishempire.co.uk "Teaching The Empire". I didn't realise that Empire Day was as late as a 1904 creation, to try and drum up interest in a rather more apathetic population than one might imagine.

Talking of Empire and stories heard at a young age, I also never understood why so many were about gallant British failures. Scott was an archetypal example but surely he was the loser and Amundsen the winner? With hindsight I guess we were being taught to lose gracefully which was definitely the zeitgeist.

THE STRANGE STORIES WE TELL OURSELVES

"But for an intellectual, transference has an important function.... It makes it possible for him to be much more nationalistic – more vulgar, more silly, more malignant, more dishonest – than he could ever be on behalf of his native country.... When one sees the slavish or boastful rubbish that is written about Stalin... by fairly intelligent and sensitive people, one realizes that this is only possible because some kind of dislocation has taken place. In societies such as ours, it is unusual for anyone describable as an intellectual to feel a very deep attachment to his own country ... He still feels the need for a Fatherland, and it is natural to look for one somewhere abroad. Having found it, he can wallow unrestrainedly in exactly those emotions from which he believes that he has emancipated himself. God, the King, the Empire, the Union Jack – all the overthrown idols can reappear under different names, and because they are not recognized for what they are they can be worshipped with a good conscience. Transferred nationalism, like the use of scapegoats, is a way of attaining salvation without altering one's conduct."[19]

Orwell was writing in 1945 and yet is accurate today. His words are doubly shocking as they were written after Britain's greatest two-fold triumph: first standing alone alone for two years against the most evil empire Europe has ever seen and secondly in committing vast resources (more pro rata than America) thereby bankrupting itself. Without *both* of these the Nazis would probably still be ruling Europe (and doubtless Russia) to this day.

---

[19] Orwell "Notes On Nationalism" 1945

More recently philosopher Sir Roger Scruton summed this phenomenon up in two words – *xenophilia*, "love of the foreign", and *oikophobia*. Curiously enough the latter is not the all-too-passim at present denigration of the working-classes but a psychiatric term for an aversion to home surroundings. Scruton adapted it to mean "*the repudiation of inheritance and home*"[20] arguing that it is a natural stage of development that adolescents pass through (they would never move out otherwise) but that it has morphed into a hatred of one's own kind (and love of the "other"):

> "Self-loathing permeates our culture to such an extent that we no longer even see it for what it is. For many of us, it has come to be the natural way of looking at the world. We have become used to living in a permanent state of cultural cringe, of apology, of guilt for real or imagined acts; where our opinion formers appear to agree that western culture is an indefensible horror."[21]

Interestingly *xenophilia* and *oikophobia* have recently been quantified by American National Election Studies, a collaboration of Stanford University and the University of Michigan. They measured "mean in-group bias" by race/ethnicity (all groupings theirs and very much a US view of the world). The results were that all groups, apart from one, showed in-group preference: "Black +15.6, Asian +13.9, Hispanic +12.8". Whites they subdivided politically: "Non-liberal Whites +11.6 *White Liberal -13.2*":

> "...on average, white liberals rated ethnic and racial minority groups 13 points (or half a standard deviation) warmer than whites ... this disparity in feelings of warmth towards ingroup vs. outgroup is even more pronounced among whites who consider themselves "very liberal" where it widens to just under 20 points. Notably, while white liberals have consistently evinced weaker pro-ingroup biases than conservatives across time, the emergence and growth of a pro-outgroup bias is actually a very recent, and unprecedented, phenomenon."[22]

---

[20] Scruton "England and the Need for Nations" 2004
[21] Whittle "A Sorry State: Self-Denigration in British Culture" 2010
[22] ANES 2018 Pilot Study. Mentioned in Real Time with Bill Maher "New Rule: White Shame" YouTube 28/9/19

Babies are born with no sense of social group - it is something they are taught. If they are subsequently taught negative stories about their own group it is little surprise that they end up with an out-group preference. There has been, in Starkey's phrase, a "systematic denigration" of British history. We've denigrated the French enough, and they us, over the centuries and to a lesser extent our other old cousins the Germans. The difference is that historically we stood our end and put our own case with conviction. Now the establishment are all too often paeans of the woke and take the Christian "turn the other cheek" to the max – they slap the other cheek themselves to save the other chap the trouble.

All of which helps explain the portrayal of the EIC. As always the EIC, being the tallest poppy on the business front is the best barometer of trends.

As recently as 2011 historian Professor Bowen and two curators of the National Maritime Museum produced a wonderfully illustrated book on the EIC[23] full of examples of the museum's period artworks and treasures and with a pretty straight narrative. It's highly recommended if you want to know more about the EIC with some feel of the visuals if you can't face ploughing through Keay's straight and full, if densely worded, account.[24]

Fast forward to 2018 and the EIC room is a disgrace, childish, near art-free, stooping to deliberate misrepresentation and a super-simple woke narrative whose errors, after a mere few weeks reading about the EIC, I could have corrected with a crayon. In their shop they sold only one book on the EIC – Robins[25] which is easily the worst book[26] that contains actual shareprice and some dividend data.[27] Sadly, given his narrative, he fails to appreciate that his own data shows that over its history the total capital return was a pathetic 0.3% per annum. Even if you bought the shares at their issuance in 1657 and *sold at the very frothy peak* in 1769, the year before the wheels came off (which in passing led

---

[23] Bowen, McAleer, Blyth "Monsoon Traders The Maritime World of the East India Company" 2011

[24] Keay "The Honourable Company: A History of the English East India Company" 1991

[25] 2006. Op. non cit.

[26] As per my amazon.co.uk review: "*Robins is to be congratulated for his research and enthusiasm for the topic. And this book will definitely appeal to you if you think the Guardian is a rallying point for the far-right...*"

[27] HT Pinker "the humanities need to use more data". Robins only presents dividend data as a few data points (all of which are in the 6–10% range which was not exceptional).

to the 1773 Tea Act which led to the Boston Tea Party – consequences eh?), you would only have got a capital return of 0.9% per annum.

Not quite as the FT recently called it *"the most rapacious company in the world"* with *"an excessive focus on maximising shareholder returns".*[28] Of course the FT provided no data to back up that statement – just another ignorant grievance narrative. It's been strange seeing even the business press going woke.

Interestingly, and Robins is a good example, there is a bias towards inflating the success of the EIC. If you present it as rapacious and as "private company that conquers India" then that attracts more attention, you sell more books and you can also get far more wound-up about it than if you tell it like it really is.

This trend continued in 2019 with the publishing of popular historian Dalrymple's latest tome. This is published in different countries[29] under two titles: "The Anarchy: The Relentless Rise of the East India Company" and "The Anarchy : The East India Company, Corporate Violence, and the Pillage of an Empire". Dalrymple (one of whose ancestors one assumes was Alexander Dalrymple who gets mentioned on 4% of the pages of Keay), lives on his farm[30] on the outskirts of Delhi (curiously he seems to begrudge the EIC owning land in India but not himself and finds it necessary to have a security guard, just like those he begrudged for the EIC in far more dangerous times) and married the sister of a former colleague of mine. He writes well, researches deeply and I enjoyed his earlier books albeit over time they have got rather more woke. Like all too many books, or even FT articles it is narrative-driven. This makes it a more interesting read of course, but the absence of data and the requisite cherry-picking of a tiny few anecdotes from nigh-on three centuries leads to the ability to take the reader where one wishes.

---

28 FT "Empires of Excess" 2015

29 I was in a bookshop in Kuala Lumpur (Kinokuniya, KLCC – highly recommended if you are in the area) and saw some chap pick it up and buy it – these well-promoted books have ripples around the world (none to our advantage). Ironically he was standing next to a really impressive work (but not promoted by the globalist publishers): Volume 1 of "Penang The Fourth Presidency Of India 1805–1830" Langdon. This must be the ne plus ultra of private research (I feel we live in an age for history akin to Newton's for physics, private individuals are very empowered). Langdon's four volume series covers 25 years of a not-that-important EIC location and is ~2,000pp and weighs 2kg (I imported Volume 1, it is heavy enough). Now that is heavyweight.

30 architecturaldigest.in "Writer in residence: William Dalrymple opens the doors to his Delhi farmhouse" 20/5/16

The title refers to "The Anarchy" which unsurprisingly given the rest of the title the innocent bystander would imagine refers to the EIC. "The Anarchy" is the phrase the Moghul empire used about itself when it was collapsing (as all empires do, or maybe not quite all[31]). This was a result of many factors, and once again to the systemic over-estimation of the EIC's importance, the EIC played a comparatively small role in this.

So the first two words of the title are already massively misleading. As to "relentless rise" I have told you of their century-long Startup travails (can you be a Startup for a century?!) and near bankruptcies. Far from "relentless rise" it was actually a "struggle to survive". We'll get back to corporate violence and pillage in the subcontinent later.

The *first sentence* of the book itself starts with English inheriting the word loot from the Hindustani for plunder. It goes on to say (you see how "history by spun anecdote" works):

"For Powis is simply awash with loot, room after room, of imperial plunder, extracted by the East India company in the eighteenth century."

Powis was not owned by the EIC but was Clive's home and unlike everything the Moghuls took from India these items were not plundered. Clive had cut himself so much of a good deal at Plassey that Parliament hauled him over the coals (although he was later sent back and set about reforming the administration from traders into the genesis of what would eventually become the Indian Civil Service). Let's quote Robins, rabidly anti-EIC:

"In one stroke, Clive had netted £2.5 million for the Company and £234,000 for himself. Today this would be equivalent to a £262 million corporate windfall and a cool £24.5 million success fee for Clive. Historical convention views Plassey as the first step in the

---

[31] With the curious exception of the British Empire. We pretty much packed-up and went home (eg Lee Kwan Yew even after gaining independence begged the Labour government to stay longer but they did not), apart from anything else, as we were bankrupted by WW2 [or rather the US unexpectedly withdrawing all financing on VJ Day. Keynes had no doubt, as he promised the incoming Labour Government (who were shocked, especially given their expensive manifesto program that we were bankrupt) that the US would write off the debts (we paid in cash for the first two years). They didn't.]

creation of the British Empire in India. It is perhaps better understood as the East India Company's most successful business deal."

So Clive took 10% of a business deal – and *he* chose the percentage. That
seems low by standards of commission and the absolute figures in the
historic context were tiny compared to the vast wealth of local rulers. As to
comparisons "in modern money", when I started my podcast four hedge
fund managers were being paid a billion dollars *per annum*. Furthermore,
far from Robins' epithet of the EIC's "most successful business deal" it led
to their bankruptcy (too many non-business-savvy authors quote revenue
forgetting that you have to subtract costs (I'm not joking)).

I couldn't even finish the first page of Dalrymple's introduction:
phrases like *"dangerously unregulated private company"* are (a) anach-
ronistic, the word/concept didn't exist at the time, (b) inaccurate – they
had a short lead to the King, and (c) speak to the deeper agenda of the
book, "dangerously unregulated MegaCos today" and the ignorance of
the woke chatterati that business is astronomically more regulated now
than at any time in history.

The EIC is spun as "using violence since 1602" when it boarded a
Portuguese vessel with no mention of the context – *strip the context and
you change the meaning*. England was utterly fearful of the Spanish/
Portuguese at sea, *all* European ships were always fracas-ing at sea
around the world for centuries and the Portuguese ran a vast protection racket and defended its century-long monopoly fiercely. The Dutch
VOC in order to avoid Portuguese aggression didn't even sail the safe
route up the east coast of Africa, but risked going straight to the Spice
Islands which no-one had ever dared to do before. No mention by
Dalrymple that the EIC renounced violence and *was* an honourable
trading company, by the standards of its time, literally exemplary.

Anyway, Dalrymple having flung dung soon skates over *150 years* as
they would entirely refute his narrative/title. He does pause the skating to
mention the single event of anti-Moghulness in the whole of the 17th C[32]
as if that were somehow typical as opposed to utterly atypical. Before
you know it we are onto the *"violent, utterly ruthless and intermittently
mentally unstable predator Clive"* – that'll be a balanced assessment then

---

[32] Child's ill-considered 1686 attempt to have a go at the Moghuls – an immediate failure.

lol. According to Google books, Dalrymple only mentions three times in nigh-on 600 pages the crucial Board of Control. The first mention, far into the book, rather undermines his introduction:

> "Between them, the two bills [1773, 1784] had done much to take control of political and military affairs of British India out of the hands of the Company directors in Leadenhall Street and into those of the Board of Control, the government body set up in 1784 to oversee the Company."

Ah, so not so "dangerously unregulated" after all and the stale canard about private company captures a subcontinent is also wrong then William?

History has always been a means of fighting the battles of today in the past. Dalrymple, like many, transfers in Orwell's sense, his patriotic allegiances elsewhere. That's fine by me, good for him.

The problem is not oikophobic authors like Dalrymple but the fact that those voices who work amazingly hard to research a balanced account (eg Langdon footnoted above) will not be amplified by the super-woke publishing industry.

Moving on to xenophilia, Dalrymple is super-Moghul-ophilic (an old British trait) having written a book about the "Last Moghul". A fascinating empire no doubt but phenomenally destructive and super-colonial (I thought that was supposed to be "bad" these days? Or isn't it bad if they are not "white"?). Unlike the British, who came and went (leaving infrastructure behind them: ICS, railways etc), the Moghuls *colonised for good* – Pakistan and Bangladesh would not exist without them and most Muslims in India are descendants of Hindus who were forcibly converted. A recent very much Church of the Woke book aims to rehabilitate the Moghul Emperor Aurangzeb. It's as mad as trying to rehabilitate Mao:

> "Aurangzeb's Deccan campaign saw one of the largest death tolls in South Asian history, with an estimated 4.6 million people killed during his reign."[33]

---

33 Wiki.

More broadly, the Moghuls – in trying to rid the lands they conquered of "pagans", of people "not of the book" – were responsible for the biggest genocide in human history:

"The Islamic conquest of India is probably the bloodiest story in history."[34]

"From the time Muslims started arriving, around 632 AD, the history of India becomes a long, monotonous series of murders, massacres, spoliations, and destructions. It is, as usual, in the name of 'a holy war' of their faith, of their sole God, that the barbarians have destroyed civilizations, wiped out entire races."[35]

"The massacres perpetuated by Muslims in India are unparalleled in history, bigger than the Holocaust of the Jews by the Nazis; or the massacre of the Armenians by the Turks; more extensive even than the slaughter of the South American native populations by the invading Spanish and Portuguese."[36]

The sources for much of this are Muslim chroniclers of the time:

"The magnitude of crimes credited to Muslim monarchs by the medieval Muslim historians, was beyond measure. With a few exceptions, Muslim kings and commanders were monsters who stopped at no crime when it came to their Hindu subjects. But what strikes as more significant is the broad pattern of those crimes. The pattern is that of a jihad in which the ghazis of Islam 1) invade infidel lands; 2) massacre as many infidel men, women, and children, particularly Brahmins, as they like after winning a victory; 3) capture the survivors to be sold as slaves; 4) plunder every place and person; 5) demolish idolatrous places of worship and build mosques in their places; and 6) defile idols which are flung into public squares or made into steps leading to mosque."[37]

---

34 Durant "Our Oriental Heritage: The Story of Our Civilization" 1997
35 Danielou "Histoire de l'Inde" 1971
36 Gautier "Rewriting Indian History" 1996
37 Goel "The story of Islamic imperialism in India" 2001

Estimates vary but figures of **tens of millions to eighty million** Indians killed are not uncommon.[38] The Moghuls destroyed all Hindu temples in the north of India. They obliterated Buddhism so much from the face of India where it was born and thrived[39] for well over 1,500 years that it wasn't until the British archaeologists found evidence that it was realised that similar but disparate religions around Asia had a common heritage in ancient India.[40] Under the Moghuls you either converted, were killed or became a *dhimmi* – non-Muslims had to pay the *jizya* – a special tax on non-Muslims – as well as submit to onerous restrictions.

I raise these points not to pass any judgement on the Moghuls or anyone in the past at all but rather simply to flag up the truly bizarre nature of the modern "Western" liberal intelligentsia's cultivated contempt for their own society and wilful blindness to the wrongs and ills of societies or peoples or even ideas to whom they transfer that allegiance.

In a more sane world perhaps historians would have a kind of Imperial Top Trumps.[41] If they did so then, if you had the British Empire card, you would of course live in fear of being called out on your score on "objective perception of own strengths and weaknesses". However you would be well advised to call out the other player on their score on governance.

TELLING BETTER STORIES – AMNESIA AND HISTORIA

"A society can't just pull up its civilisational roots and choose some other value system, nor can it invent from scratch a whole new set of values and habits. It's been tried with disastrous results – remember the attempt to create Soviet man. But you can weaken your civilisation by neglecting it and despising it and we've arguably gone too far along that road already. Then you risk being left not with some better system of values but with no shared values at all, no sense of common purpose, no basis for solidarity, no understanding of

---

[38] Eg Elst "Negationism in India: concealing the record of Islam" 2014
[39] Including the Buddhist University at Nalanda which was the largest in the world at that time.
[40] Allen "The Buddha and the Sahibs" 2002 a tale well told.
[41] I wonder whether they have had to rebrand their game due to the US presidential connection?

who and what we are. Instead you just have impatient assertions
of individual entitlement and corresponding claims to victimhood,
two sides of the same coin and two of the most annoying symptoms
of our present demoralisation."[42]

Gardening starts by removing the weeds. We need to move on from the
harmful stories and the distortions of current story-tellers:

"The conscious and intelligent manipulation of the organized habits
and opinions of the masses is an important element in democratic
society. Those who manipulate this unseen mechanism of society
constitute an invisible government which is the true ruling power
of our country. ...We are governed, our minds are moulded, our
tastes formed, our ideas suggested, largely by men we have never
heard of. This is a logical result of the way in which our democratic society is organized...In almost every act of our daily lives,
whether in the sphere of politics or business, in our social conduct
or our ethical thinking, we are dominated by the relatively small
number of persons...who understand the mental processes and
social patterns of the masses. It is they who pull the wires which
control the public mind."[43]

One poignant and memorable phrase I saw was by Professor Laurie
Johnson[44] comparing the stories the Ancient Greeks told themselves
with the stories we tell ourselves (or are told) today – "From Hero
to Consumer".

O tempora o mores!

We need to recover our stories from a collective amnesia, wilful
blindness and systemic misdirection.

"'The first step in liquidating a people,' said Hubl, 'is to erase
its memory. Destroy its books, its culture, its history. Then have
somebody write new books, manufacture a new culture, invent a

---

42 Institute of Public Affairs "Professor Robert Tombs: Why Western Civilisation is our
   Future" YouTube 28/3/19
43 Bernays "Propaganda" 1928
44 On her excellent YouTube channel "PoliticalPhilsophy".

new history. Before long the nation will begin to forget what it is and what it was. The world around it will forget even faster.'"[45]

"This is one of the ways in which the past influences the present; not what happened, but what we choose to believe."[46]

We need to get a much more accurate picture of our historia, about our ancestors' goals scored, goals let in, fouls committed and fouls received.

As to how fast we can achieve that balance – we appear to be like learner drivers stamping on the accelerator and brake alternately. Thus even before Reaganistic national positivity, President Carter could say in a speech in 1979,[47] and no-one would bat an eyelid:

"As a people we know our past and we are proud of it."

Which might be described as looking only at the goals scored and how America had overcome the fouls committed on them.[48] On the other hand a few decades later chants of "No Trump, no wall, no USA at all" might be said to come from those only looking at goals let in and fouls committed.

"Civilisation is an action-packed adventure story it seems to me not a philosophical treatise and that is how we should teach it. The obvious danger of not doing so is that generations grow-up, I'm afraid, have grown-up, not understanding that Western civilisation is an extraordinary achievement but not an inevitable or eternal one. It is dangerous to criticise the failings without recognising the successes and it's equally dangerous to take the successes for granted."[49]

Perhaps given the cultivated contempt of much of the intelligentsia and the new emergent ruling class we also need to start counting the own-goals.

---

[45] Kundera "The Book of Laughter and Forgetting" 1978
[46] Tombs "Time Warp" Spectator 17/8/19
[47] "Crisis of Confidence Speech"
[48] Am struggling to think of all that many :-D
[49] Institute of Public Affairs "Professor Robert Tombs: Why Western Civilisation is our Future" YouTube 28/3/19

Peter Thiel in his pre-Paypal days wrote of the early days of the US college campus culture wars.[50] He believes that the education sector is ripe for massive disruption, most students as he says pay a fortune and the data shows that, unless they went to a top school, they do not get a good RoI. Besides in the internet age why not listen to the best lecture in the world on relativity or Nietzsche rather than that of the lecturer in front of you? Why put up with blatant political bias when you could (in US terms) hear a convinced and authoritative democrat tell you of the wonders of the democrats, a convinced and authoritative conservative about the wonders of conservatism and a convinced and authoritative libertarian tell you of the wonders of libertarianism? Wouldn't that be a far more balanced education for the next generation?

Prior to such an educational reformation generations are not just forgetting their heritage but even the most basic elements of history are not being taught well. As a result some catastrophic ideas are coming back into fashion. A recent poll[51] showed that one in five US millennials are favourably disposed to communism! Boy has their education gone wrong.

In 2015 the New Culture Forum[52] commissioned UK pollsters to poll 16 to 24 year-olds. They found that 70% had not heard of Mao, 10% did not associate him with crimes against humanity, 20% did. Also 49% had not heard of Lenin, 20% did not associate him with crimes against humanity, 31% did. The only major genocidal maniac they (well, 92%) had heard of was Hitler. No wonder "Nazi" is the only political insult going, it's the only baddie that anyone has heard of these days. Even then:

> "Four in ten American millennials, and at least one in three Europeans, say they know "very little" about the Holocaust, and one in five young French respondents are not even aware it took place."[53]

---

50 Thiel "Diversity Myth: Multiculturalism and Political Intolerance on Campus" 1998. A key chant from a 1987 march of hundreds of students led by the Reverend Jesse Jackson at Stanford University to rally against the school's humanities program was: *"Hey hey, ho ho, Western Civ has got to go"*. This, as Thiel says, was deliberately ambiguous referring both to a curriculum class and to their sentiment about "western civilisation". Fast forward and how often have you heard the phrase "western civilisation" recently?

51 HooverInstitution "Thomas Sowell on the Origins of Economic Disparities" 17/5/19

52 Sewell "The Second Time as Farce: The crimes of communism, retro-Bolshevism and the centenary of the 1917 Russian Revolution" New Culture Forum 2016

53 Kotkin "Elites Against Western Civilization" 10/4/19

In 2003 the National Assessment of Adult Literacy reported[54] that 14% of Americans had "below basic" literacy and 29% "basic". 70% of the prison population only has fourth grade (9–10-year-old) levels of literacy.

Higher up the educational scale one study of American college students found that over 40% *"did not demonstrate any significant improvement in learning over four years of college".*[55]

As Academia is for the most part run by the State this is of course a catastrophic failure of State Governance.[56] Back to de Tocqueville's "soft despotism" you do not entirely avoid this challenge by taking one's children "out of the system" – you can only take them out of the schools but in the system they must remain (the National Curriculum and its mark scheme). You try writing an A level history answer that doesn't agree with what the "soft despots" will give you marks for.

Even with the challenges of the ever-more politically skewed 21[st]C academia, plenty manage to keep their heads down and do good work whatever the political climate on campus. However in academia the long-term trend has infamously been "to know more and more about less and less". This inevitably ends up in reductio ad absurdum – the average academic humanities paper is quoted zero times. Some academic work must be about building pictures out of all these ever-smaller pixels. Professor Robert Tombs, quoted earlier in this section, is a prime example of someone who spent most of his career on pixels but can also put them together to form a lucid, clear and *educational* picture.[57]

Not learning from history is an ancient human failing, or as that stand-up comedian Hegel put it:

"We learn from history that we do not learn from history."

---

[54] Naude "The Age of the University has Ended" 23/5/19

[55] Kotkin op. cit.

[56] Along with health (anyone with ageing relatives needing the NHS or who has had to go to A&E will have plenty of anecdotes). And there is money (a dollar a century ago is worth a cent now). And that's before we get to destroying countries (Iraq, Libya). If the State were a Company it would have failed or been taken over a long time ago – or (ha!) been beaten to a pulp at Select Committees.

[57] Tombs "The English and their History" 2015 (a mere 1,024 pages)

We can though. If we want to. If we know our history that is. Our new era and dramatically different technologies has reinforced subconscious feelings that the past doesn't have much to teach us:

> "I believe we are living in a world where the present looms so disconcertingly large it leaves us little time for reflection. It seems that our memory span is getting shorter and what fills our information matrices so often is meaningless trivia."[58]

"Those who don't know history are doomed to repeat it" especially springs to mind re banking's credit cycle. Every generation of bankers gets by by saying to themselves that "the prior generation didn't understand and we do" until once more this new generation cocks it up and the cycle repeats.

I am only aware of one example where the importance of understanding business history had an action attached to it. A joint House of Lords and House of Commons "Report of the Parliamentary Commission on Banking Standards" recommended this need to remember yesterday and use it to inform one's understanding of today and one's policy towards tomorrow:

> "Banking history is littered with examples of manipulative conduct driven by misaligned incentives, of bank failures born of reckless, hubristic expansion and of unsustainable asset price bubbles cheered on by a consensus of self-interest or self-delusion. An important lesson of history is that bankers, regulators and politicians alike repeatedly fail to learn the lessons of history: this time, they say, it is different... Had the warnings of past failures been heeded, this Commission may not have been necessary...
>
> ...The Commission recommends that an additional external member be appointed to the FPC [The Bank of England's Financial Policy Committee], with particular responsibility for taking a historical view of financial stability and systemic risk, and drawing the attention of FPC colleagues, and the wider public through speeches

---

[58] Mirza "Memory in the Age of Amnesia" 2018

and articles, to historical and international parallels to contemporary concerns."[59]

It's not clear from the Bank of England's website whether this was ever enacted.

Not only was not one of the dozens of UK Corporate Governance code writers an entrepreneur who knew how to create something from nothing, neither was one a historian either. Education is the State's second largest expenditure – some £90bn pa in the UK.[60] It beggars belief that those astronomical funds – times a decade or several – could not present Cadbury with *one book* on the historic governance of the Company. Not one book from all those universities. **How the hell can you fix today if you misunderstand** *or are not even informed about* **yesterday?**

I hope in laying out governance history you can see that current policy *has to be informed* by understanding prior policies. No-one can do any job without learning from previous intentions and mistakes and as Aristotle tells us the job of rule-maker for society is the most important one of all. Aristotle wouldn't have come up with unresearched proposals. Creating the rules of a game *for the wealth-creating sector* is super-important for the whole of society. Maybe, just maybe, there is one historian out there who understands the long-term history of the Company and, as per Parliament's recommendation to the FPC, should be involved in the formation of governance policy?

Failing that Corporate Governance "progress" will continue to be knee-jerk, ad hoc, addressing symptoms not root causes.

Talking of which, myopia applies big time to the "accounting industry and governance" issue. Today I saw a headline fingering the role of the auditors in the recently-failed Thomas Cook.

It's like bloody Groundhog Day, isn't it?

---

[59] www.parliament.uk "Changing banking for good" June 2013
[60] Nuffield Foundation "2018 Annual Report on Education Spending in England"

SO LONG AND THANKS FOR ALL THE FISH

"On the planet Earth, man had always assumed that he was more intelligent than dolphins because he had achieved so much – the wheel, New York, wars and so on – whilst all the dolphins had ever done was muck about in the water having a good time. But conversely, the dolphins had always believed that they were far more intelligent than man – for precisely the same reasons."[61]

Our journey is all but over. We've covered the essential aspects of SmallCos and their Boards. We've looked round the table at the roles on the Board and shared hundreds of quotes from nigh on a hundred entrepreneurs. We've looked at how companies were governed over the centuries since they were invented and seen the rise of State interference, especially from the unelected bureaucrat who is able to issue de facto laws (and police and judge them) outside of parliamentary process and traditional judicial restraint. We've looked at fixing broken Boards. We've looked at the huge travails of being a Startup in the 16th and 17th centuries and felt glad we are living now (even if somehow generations after us need to shake off the shackles of despotic micro-control).

All changes of era present huge challenges. Imagine the changes in culture and stories that were required when it sank in that in farming, unlike hunting, where if you missed today you could always try again tomorrow, if you missed this year (or the rains failed) you'd have to starve for another year until you could try again. We also saw story mismatch when farmers became industrialists. At first it was "this is cool" with no-one quite knowing what to do with it all, then they started to find practical applications of their new technology and then in a flash things went rather wrong and it was some time before they developed *stories* about not sending children up chimneys or people into dark satanic mills.

In our new Data-olithic age once again we face many challenges as a society *especially in the stories required to flourish rather than suffer*. This time the transition into the new era is super-rapid. The fact that this time the technology is in all of our pockets and is deliberately designed to be addictive compounds the problem: recent headlines

---

[61] Douglas Adams "The Hitchhiker's Guide to the Galaxy" 1979

– "Americans on average check their phones 80 times a day", "The average Brit checks their phone 10,000 times a year".

The mental health crisis[62] is as clear a barometer as one could need of stress and strain. In the UK one in four take *prescription* addictive psychoactive medications.[63] Another barometer of the *crise de confiance* is perhaps that the birth-rate in Europe is 1.6 per woman compared to a replacement rate of 2.1. The continent is literally dying out.[64]

These canaries in the coal mine are perhaps similar to excess deaths and industrial injuries in the 19thC and in neolithic times deaths from starvation. We have to face the era-change challenges at a time when, incredibly ironically given the outrage promoted in our societies, we have record prosperity and quantities of goods in our homes. We also have the only societies ever incorporating universal benefits for all. However oikophobic stories and a loss of confidence – when did you last hear about the glories of western art, culture and music? – along with a pressured economy (house prices, debt, competition levels) mean that it is not clear, to put it mildly, that people are happier than when everyone had less and life was simpler.

Bringing this down to the business level, stories have always been super-important to the formation of the next generation of business men and women:

"A nation becomes what its young people read [MB: /hear/see] in their youth. Its ideals are fashioned then, its goals strongly determined."[65]

The world is saturated with anti-business narratives served up for the young in all sorts of garbs. Whatever the challenges of some MegaCos practising the deeply concerning Ethicless/ethics-light Corporatism it is easily forgotten that, *by number*, only a tiny tiny percentage of all businesses fall into that category, and that overall unless there is a thriving wealth-creating sector there will be no money, no taxes to pay for all the State expenditure.

---

[62] A highly recommended free online resource in re is: Council for Evidence-based Psychiatry "Unrecognised Facts about Modern Psychiatric Practice" 2014

[63] NHS headline 10/9/19 covering a report by Public Health England (the NHS policy arm).

[64] Although not in Hungary whose pro-family policies have been successful in increasing the birth-rate. Interesting that conversely in much of Western Europe the general propaganda lionises non-reproductive modes of sexuality. Quite some difference.

[65] James A. Michener

You can make a difference. Tell your SmallCo stories at a local school or offer to conduct a tour of your offices to let kids see for themselves. Good businesses do not just make a profit, they give people a home and training and company and a mission in life to improve the world. Let the young know that there are good communities trying to improve the world out there that they one day might join. Even improving the world in a small way is a noble mission. You are noble. Share your nobility and enthuse others just like Hakluyt did in the 16[th]C.

While I am busy volunteering you on your behalf here are three other ideas for making a difference to the world.

FIRST: if you think this book is useful, helpful or interesting **do spread the word, Amazon five-star reviews are most welcome.** All founders and Boarders wish to do their best and it is no cushy number; unlike in the past, it can be a very pressured gig. But in particular, as per some founder conversations that I did not quote, first-timers don't have a clue (how would they?). So if you feel that there are useful ideas herein then spreading the word that this book exists will make future founders' journeys easier.

SECOND: you now know the history of governance. Amazingly, this would appear to make you quite unique individuals and you certainly know far more than any Corporate Governance code author. Any of you with high-level political connections try and persuade the buggers that Business Governance matters so much that it must be an item for super-bright super-smart folks like your political chum. Those with business establishment connections do volunteer for the next Corporate Governance code committee (or tear out chapters two and three of this book and send it to them). Prove Hegel wrong! We can learn from history! **If we are to succeed as a society in the 21[st]C we need once again to have the best Company Governance.**

THIRD: whilst academia is heavily siloed, politically-skewed and stuck in the drill-down mode of "knowing more and more about less and less", business schools need to be more "integrationist". Those of you connected to business schools might nudge them in the direction of including in their syllabuses a historical perspective that goes slightly further back than the day before yesterday. We will not solve society's business challenges by continuing "more of the same" approaches and attempted remedies. We need a deeper understanding.

Before wrapping-up with some thanks let's start with some apologies. I wholly subscribe to Chris Rock's "blame the game not the players". If I inadvertently gave the impression of dissing people not roles (eg bureaucrat, regulator, politicians and so forth) I apologise without reservation. In my direct experience of many areas of society most people get up in the morning and go out and try to do a good job of whatever it is that they do in order to pay the bills. I seek merely to suggest different ways of thinking about rules and "the games" in society for the benefit of all in society – directly in terms of making everyone's work more fulfilling and indirectly in terms of improving society as a whole.

This book has only been made possible by the kindness of many many founders and Boarders who generously donated their time. I, and we, owe immense thanks to these unnamed folk. I trust that in reading this they all benefited as this is a field that no-one can ever perfect. Indeed, as with most arts, it is those with most experience who are always learning something new.

Talking of which, my thanks to Brian, who is a prime example that involvement in creating businesses keeps you fresh and enthused. I ought to add that he was too modest to mention his super-impressive CV as an entrepreneur and it was only as a result of me suggesting that I would make something up on his behalf that he added a rather more accurate version. I have been on balance complementary about much of what has been achieved on this island but we, and "Western" society as a whole, do have many failings. One of the main failings is that, contrary to every traditional society, we listen far too little to our elders. I am fortunate in having Brian kindly share his long and broad view.

I'd like to thank the Muses for dropping so many ideas into my mind, where would we all be without their charm, grace and generosity? Talking of which finally thanks to Bridget, the girl espied from the oriel, for ensuring that my sanity never dipped too far below zero and for having to repeatedly hear about my latest off the beaten path rambles having been cast aside as those travellers' tales would take up too much space.

And finally advice to would-be founders out there. One in a thousand of you might be able to jump in the deep end and learn to swim when in the water. For the rest, do yourself a favour and apprentice yourself by working for a great entrepreneur first – time spent apprenticing will make your mastership[66] come that much sooner.

And as a final tale, a curious thing. You must notice these occasional synchronicities too. Although two years ago I knew nothing about the EIC it had always been quite near to me. I spent well over a decade working next to Philpot Lane (the EIC's first home for decades). Furthermore, having drunk rather too much wine in wine bars in Leadenhall market, I had not appreciated that it was also adjacent to what was later a much grander East India House, a fine print of which now hangs on my study wall.

Totally randomly, a decade or so ago, long after my merchant banking incarnation, I was invited to some meeting in the West End for my opinion on a fund-raising. I attended, gave my thoughts and then promptly forgot about this as it seemed nothing special at the time. It was however raising money for Indian businessman Sanjiv Mehta's new luxury products business. No big deal other than as I now recall he had acquired the rights to the EIC name and it was thus a fund-raising for a company called the East India Company.[67]

The final synchronicity was that the Christmas before I had the slightest idea of ever writing a book my younger daughter (who of course knew nothing of this irrelevant meeting I had forgotten I ever went to) bought me some "EIC" tea and an EIC-crested mug from the new "EIC":

"There are more things in heaven and earth, Horatio, than are dreamt of in your philosophy."[68]

Live long and prosper.

---

[66] Progress up a Guild was a strictly enforced scheme of apprenticeship (five to nine years), thence journeymen (who could work for any master and were paid wages) and, once the journeyman had shown evidence of his competence (his "masterpiece") he joined the select group of masters.

[67] Talking of over-hyping the EIC in looking up Mehta's name I read a BBC article announcing his new business which said "At its peak, the company employed a third of the British workforce"?! Say what?

[68] Shakespeare "Hamlet"

Appendix A – Regulation in 2000 BC and 1000 AD

"Many deep-seated aspects of ancient societies have proved to be remarkably enduring, changing their clothes as fashions have moved on so that they ever seem a natural part of the contemporary landscape."[1]

OVERVIEW

Regulation is a very fuzzy concept today. What is it there for? What is it? As a phenomenon in the UK it is a proliferation of over 700 peri-statal undemocratic bodies dictating to everyone what to do. Especially businessmen. In increasing amounts of footling intervention it ties Gulliver down with a million threads. **It is the most micro-controlling system of State governance in human history.**

At Citigroup 30,000 out of 200,000 employees work in compliance, risk and other control functions.[2] What a huge burden! **What a crazy way of trying to achieve whatever it was that was the end goal in the first place! I don't even know what that goal is – all too often control has become the goal.**

It's also something of an extortion racket. Let's take one example – banks alone *or more precisely their shareholders* have been "fined" astronomical sums *just in two narrow areas*:

"Regulators have fined financial firms at least $28.4bn for money-laundering and sanctions violations since 2008; BNP Paribas alone paid up $8.9bn for sanctions shenanigans. Aiding tax evaders has cost banks at least another $9.5bn."[3]

---

[1] Kemp "Ancient Egypt: Anatomy Of A Civilisation" 2007
[2] Economist "The past decade has brought a compliance boom in banking" 2/5/19
[3] Ibid.

We need to deconstruct the term "economic sanctions". They are rather the Imperial overlord's "warfare by economic means". List the countries that the US likes and you will find none on their "sanctions" list and vice versa. Standard Chartered Bank stood against the overlord some years back saying they had no right to prevent a UK Bank doing business with Iran. Nice idea and having coughed up $1.8bn for their lèse-majesté they are still suffering for their impudence. Has the world really changed from a thousand years ago when absolute rulers' wishes were inviolable?

More generally, but still politically, as Tucker says in his oeuvre, we shouldn't call regulators' output regulations as they are actually extra-parliamentary laws (along with, I might add, their extra-judicial courts and extra-police force investigators and extra-statal prosecutors). **It has become the invention of a parallel state and one more controlling than Stalin ever was and just as unaccountable to the people.**

A thousand years of English/British struggle for liberty from arbitrary and undemocratic tyranny junked in a couple of decades as far as citizens and businesses are concerned.

Regulators tell business folk what to do every day and micromanage our lives and environment. One recently banned an advert that showed a mother and her baby in a pram as "gender stereotyping". Good God! Motherhood is the fountainhead of all humanity not a bloody stereotype. As I recall that regulator had received less than one handful of complaints. In FS the FCA has started regulating people – no P2P can sell me more than a small percentage of my NAV to invest in P2P loans. Who are the FCA to tell me how to invest my money?[4] Examples are legion.

It was not always thus. It wasn't thus as recently as when I started work. Let's take a step back in time for some perspective. Historically the Law defined business structures, contracts and so forth. So what was regulation, regulators and regulating? Did they always exist?

REGULATION IN 2000 BC

Starting with our oldest records in Mesopotamian much of what we might call regulation is contained within Hammurabi's law code[5]. A simple

---

4   Their argument would be they are restricting the firms but this is transparent sophistry.
5   Source: en.wikisource.org

example of ancient regulation – in this context laws covering business – would be weights and measures. These developed in early Mesopotamia and spread when rulers imposed them on conquered territory.

One type of regulation is economic – **price controls:**

"221. If a physician set a broken bone for a man or cure his diseased bowels, the patient shall give five shekels of silver to the physician.

228. If a builder build a house for a man and complete it, (that man) shall give him two shekels of silver per SAR of house as his wage.

239. If a man hire a boatman, he shall give him 6 gur of grain per year."

Another type of regulation is **quality control** – standards and penalties. Note the **simplicity and clarity** of the regulations:

"108. If a wine-seller do not receive grain as the price of drink, but if she receive money by the great stone, or make the measure for drink smaller than the measure for corn, they shall call that wine-seller to account, and they shall throw her into the water.

233. If a builder build a house for a man and do not make its construction meet the requirements and a wall fall in, that builder shall strengthen that wall at his own expense.

229. If a builder build a house for a man and do not make its construction firm, and the house which he has built collapse and cause the death of the owner of the house, that builder shall be put to death."

Groups of businesses had "self-regulation" overseen by a State official. Over time the Old Assyrian merchant colony, the *karum*, came to have a **degree of self-government** led by an official known as *wakil tamkari*, the overseer of the merchants.[6] **This notion of "a community that retained a separate identity and had a degree of self-government"** continued

---

6   Larsen "Ancient Kanesh – A Merchant Colony In Bronze Age Anatolia" 2018

in one form or another, one country or another, eventually morphing into Medieval Guilds. Guilds were a community "with a degree of self-government" which oversaw (ie regulated) a trade or craft. Guilds morphed in turn into the V1 Company whose "self-government" (sic) led to our Boards today and was defined in their charter which in turn evolved into the V2's Articles of Association. V1 Companies, ChartCos, had a close tie to the State, if only because in their early days the Monarch was a Supreme Ruler and in later times Parliament. So we can say that from 1550–1844 (the creation of CoLawCo V2.0 and Companies House) ChartCos had "self-regulation" (their internal government had "Lawes" and governance procedures) overseen by the State qua Monarch or Parliament. Fast-forward to today and we see that whilst Companies still have parameters set by the State – in essence rules of the game – and a degree of self-government, the imposed rules are vast and there is not one *wakil tamkari* but 700 of them in this country alone before we start considering European and Global regulation.

REGULATION IN 1000 AD

How were Guilds overseen? As Guilds lasted for over a thousand years and covered much of Europe there is no single answer. However we do have a fantastic datapoint. Let's leap forwards 3,000 years from Old Assyria to an extraordinary document from the Byzantine Empire. In 1891 *"To Eparchikon Biblion"* – literally "The Book of the Eparch [Prefect]" but perhaps more helpfully "The City Governor's Manual" – was "discovered" in a library in Geneva. That must have been one sleepy library as the book itself was a 14[th]C copy of an original written in the 10[th]C. Its purpose was to help the local Governor manage trade via *collegia* – organised groups of merchants. This is the same **regulatory structure** as in Old Assyria – **overseen delegated governance** – with clear rules and responsibilities delegated down to *collegia*, Guilds, which oversaw/regulated traders operating on their own accounts.

The Book of the Eparch is a compilation of regulations covering some twenty-odd trades. The goals of the Governor and his regulations/rules were raising taxation, reducing black market activities and maintaining a constant flow of goods through the Guilds. In other words we can see this as being about microeconomic management – the Eparch's job was to ensure that his city had supplies of necessary goods (something which these days is left to "the market") and that people weren't ripped off.

Economic regulation was still a thing 3,000 years after the first surviving evidence of its Mesopotamian usage. This approach still exists today especially for formerly state-owned utilities. Let's look at one example of an economic regulation from the Book of the Eparch. Note how rule and punishment are contained in two sentences – effective regulation was, and is, concise:

> "Grocers §5. Grocers shall sell their wares and make a profit of two miliaresia per nomisma. If their measures show that they have exacted a greater profit they shall be flogged, shaved and cease to trade as grocers."[7]

Sticking with grocers we have the same **regulation of standards** that we saw in Old Assyria:

> "§2. Any grocer who has weights or measures which do not bear the seal of the eparch or who files the coinage (i.e. sweats), or refuses to take a tetarteron, bearing for authenticity the effigy of the sovereign, shall be flogged, shaved and exiled."

Structural regulation, which we might compare to creating watertight compartments in a ship such that the holing of one does not sink the whole vessel, has always been super-important:

> "1. Grocers may keep their shops throughout the city as well in the squares as in the streets, so that the necessaries of life may be easily procurable.
>
> They shall sell: meat, salt fish, meal, cheese, honey, olive oil, vegetables of all kinds, butter, dry and liquid resin, cedar oil, camphor, linseed oil, gypsum, bowls, vessels, etc. nails, bottles in fact every article which can be sold by steelyards and not by scales.

---

7   All Eparch rules are from Stephenson "The Book of the Eparch" 2012

They are forbidden to sell any article which comes within the trades of perfumers, soap-chandlers, linen-drapers, taverners or butchers. Any contravention is punished by flogging, shaving, and exile."

Printed in Great Britain
by Amazon

58223R00201